Censorship Moments

Textual Moments in the History of Political Thought

Series Editors
J. C. Davis, Emeritus Professor of History, University of East Anglia, UK
John Morrow, Professor of Political Studies, University of Auckland,
New Zealand

Textual Moments provides accessible, short readings of key texts in selected
fields of political thought, encouraging close reading informed by cutting-
edge scholarship. The unique short essay format of the series ensures that
volumes cover a range of texts in roughly chronological order. The essays in
each volume aim to open up a reading of the text and its significance in the
political discourse in question and in the history of political thought more
widely. Key moments in the textual history of a particular genre of political
discourse are made accessible, appealing and instructive to students, scholars
and general readers.

Available in the Series
Utopian Moments: Reading Utopian Texts, edited by Miguel Avilés and
J. C. Davis

Forthcoming
Feminist Moments: Reading Feminist Texts, edited by Katherine Smits and
Susan Bruce
Patriarchal Moments: Reading Texts on Patriarchalism, edited by Cesare
Cuttica and Gaby Mahlberg
Revolutionary Moments: Reading Revolutionary Texts, edited by Rachel
Hammersley

Censorship Moments

Reading Texts in the History of Censorship and Freedom of Expression

Edited by

Geoff Kemp

B L O O M S B U R Y
LONDON · NEW DELHI · NEW YORK · SYDNEY

Bloomsbury Academic

An imprint of Bloomsbury Publishing Plc

50 Bedford Square	1385 Broadway
London	New York
WC1B 3DP	NY 10018
UK	USA

www.bloomsbury.com

Bloomsbury is a registered trade mark of Bloomsbury Publishing Plc

First published 2015

British Library Cataloguing-in-Publication Data
A catalogue record for this book is available from the British Library.

ISBN: HB: 978-1-4725-0822-5
PB: 978-1-4725-1284-0
ePDF: 978-1-4725-1724-1
ePub: 978-1-4725-0543-9

Library of Congress Cataloging-in-Publication Data
A catalog record for this book is available from the Library of Congress.

Typeset by Integra Software Services Pvt. Ltd.
Printed and bound in India

Contents

List of Illustrations

Contributors

Federico Barbierato Lecturer in Early-Modern History at the University of Verona; author of *The Inquisitor in the Hat Shop: Inquisition, Forbidden Books and Unbelief in Early-Modern Venice.*

Gregory Claeys Professor of the History of Political Thought at Royal Holloway, University of London. His latest book is *Mill and Paternalism.*

Edwin Curley Professor of Philosophy Emeritus, University of Michigan; editor and translator of *The Collected Works of Spinoza* (volume 1, 1985; volume 2, forthcoming); editor of Hobbes's *Leviathan*; author of *Spinoza's Metaphysics* and *Behind the Geometrical Method.*

Bryan Garsten Professor of Political Science at Yale University; author of *Saving Persuasion: A Defense of Rhetoric and Judgment*; editor of *Rousseau, the Enlightenment, and Their Legacies*, a collection of essays by Robert Wokler.

Bruce Gordon Titus Street Professor of Ecclesiastical History at Yale University; author of *Calvin* and *The Swiss Reformation*; editor and translator of Hans Guggisberg's *Sebastian Castellio: 1515–1563*; editor (with Matthew McLean) of *Shaping the Bible in the Reformation.*

Miles Hollingworth Professor at the Patristic Institute, the Augustinianum, Rome; author of *Saint Augustine of Hippo: An Intellectual Biography* and *The Pilgrim City: Saint Augustine of Hippo and His Innovation in Political Thought.*

Stephen Ingle Emeritus Professor of Politics at the University of Stirling; author of *Narratives of British Socialism* (2002), *The Social and Political Thought of George Orwell: A Reassessment* (2006) and *The British Party System* (4th edn, 2008).

Sue Curry Jansen Professor of Media and Democratic Theory at Muhlenberg College, Pennsylvania; author of *Censorship: The Knot That Binds Power* *and Knowledge, Critical Communication Theory*, and *Walter Lippmann: An Introduction to Media and Communication*; co-editor of *Media and Social Justice*.

Daniel J. Kapust Associate Professor of Political Science, University of Wisconsin–Madison; author of *Republicanism, Rhetoric, and Roman Political Thought*, and articles on Tacitus, Cicero and Hobbes.

Geoff Kemp Senior Lecturer in Politics at the University of Auckland, New Zealand; editor of the four-volume *Censorship and the Press, 1580-1720* (with Jason McElligott, Cyndia Susan Clegg and Mark Goldie).

Melissa Lane Professor of Politics at Princeton University; author of *Eco-Republic* and *Plato's Progeny*; co-editor of *Politeia in Greek and Roman Philosophy* (with V. Harte) and *A Poet's Reich: Politics and Culture in the George Circle* (with M. A. Ruehl).

John Christian Laursen Professor of Political Science at the University of California, Riverside; author of *The Politics of Skepticism in the Ancients, Montaigne, Hume, and Kant*; co-editor (with María José Villaverde) of *Paradoxes of Religious Toleration in Early Modern Political Thought* and *Forjadores de la Tolerancia*.

Jason McElligott Keeper of Marsh's Library, Dublin; author of *Royalism, Print and Censorship in Revolutionary England*; editor (with Eve Patten) of *The Perils of Print Culture*; general editor (with Geoff Kemp) of *Censorship and the Press, 1580–1720*.

Robert W. T. Martin Professor of Government at Hamilton College, NY; author of *Government by Dissent: Protest and Radical Democratic Thought in the Early American Republic* and *The Free and Open Press: The Founding of American Democratic Press Liberty, 1640–1800*.

Thomas Meyer Privatdozent (Adjunct Professor) at Ludwig-Maximilians-Universität, Munich, and Visiting Professor at the Elie Wiesel Center for Judaic Studies at Boston University; author of *Was heißt und zu welchem Ende studiert man jüdisches Denken?* and a forthcoming intellectual biography of Leo Strauss.

Helen Pierce Lecturer in British Art at the University of Aberdeen, Scotland; author of the book *Unseemly Pictures: Graphic Satire and Politics in Early Modern England*.

David H. Price Professor of Religious Studies, History, and Jewish Studies at the University of Illinois, Urbana-Champaign; author of *Johannes Reuchlin and the Campaign to Destroy Jewish Books* and *Albrecht Dürer's Renaissance: Humanism, Reformation, and the Art of Faith*.

Arlene W. Saxonhouse Caroline Robbins Professor of Political Science at the University of Michigan; author of the books *Free Speech and Athenian Democracy*, *Athenian Democracy: Modern Mythmakers and Ancient Theorists* and *Fear of Diversity: The Birth of Political Science in Ancient Greek Thought*.

Takashi Shogimen Associate Professor in History and Associate Dean (Research) for Humanities at the University of Otago, New Zealand; author of *Ockham and Political Discourse in the Late Middle Ages*; co-editor (with Vicki A. Spencer) of *Visions of Peace: Asia and the West*.

Debora Shuger Distinguished Professor of English at UCLA; author of *Censorship and Cultural Sensibility* and *Political Theologies in Shakespeare's England: The Sacred and the State in 'Measure for Measure'*.

Katherine Smits Senior Lecturer and Head of Politics and International Relations at the University of Auckland; author of *Applying Political Theory* and *Reconstructing Post-Nationalist Liberal Pluralism: From Interest to Identity*.

Series Editors' Foreword

At the heart of the serious study of the history of political thought, as expressed through both canonical and non-canonical works of all kinds, has been the question (to which we all too readily assume an answer), 'How shall I read this text?' Answers have varied greatly over time. Once the political works of the past – especially those of Classical Greece and Rome – were read with an eye to their immediate application to the present. And, until comparatively recently, the canonical works of political philosophy were selected and read as expressions of perennial, abiding truths about politics, social morality and justice. The problem was that this made little or no concession to historically changing contexts, that the 'truths' we identified were all too often *our* truths. A marxisant sociology of knowledge endeavoured to break free from the 'eternal verities' of political thought by exploring the ways in which past societies shaped their own forms of political expression in distinctive yet commonly grounded conceptions of their own image. The problem remained that the perception of what shaped past societies was all too often driven by the demands of a current political agenda. In both cases, present concerns shaped the narrative history of political thought off which the reading of texts fed. The last half century has seen another powerful and influential attempt to break free from a present-centered history of political thought by locating texts as speech acts or moves within a contemporary context of linguistic usage. Here the frequently perceived problem has been a (by-no-means inevitable) narrowing of focus to canonical texts while the study of other forms of political expression in images, speech, performance and gesture – in all forms of political culture – has burgeoned independently.

We have, then, a variety of ways of approaching past texts and the interplay of text and context. The series 'Textual Moments in the History of Political Thought' (in which this present volume is the second to be published) is designed to encourage fresh readings of thematically selected texts. Each chapter identifies a key textual moment or passage and exposes it to a reading by an acknowledged expert. The aim is new insight, accessibility and the encouragement to read in a more informed way for oneself.

The history of censorship and debates about it has rarely been seen as central to the history of political thought. But, as we are shown in these essays, from its

beginnings in the attempt to maintain standards of political morality, the work
of the censor in controlling the expression, communication and dissemination
of ideas goes to the heart of issues of authority, obedience, subjection, civility
and the discrimination of the public and private spheres. Modern liberal,
secular, Western societies have tended to regard censorship as a historical
issue, a problem resolved. The flimsiness of that judgement is swiftly exposed
if we think of contemporary concerns with the control of speech, writing and
performance damaging or hurtful to others in terms of ethnicity, religion,
gender, sexual orientation and a range of other issues. In these respects, the state
may still feel obliged to limit freedom of expression and the good citizen may be
one who practises self-censorship. On the other hand, the hegemonic pressures
of patriarchy, ideology, ethnic superiority or subordination may silence or limit
the forms of expression of subordinate groups even of majorities. In these cases,
it may be that those who break the bonds of hegemonic self-censorship are both
seen as good citizens and may become our heroic models. In other respects,
we can still feel that there are reasons of state security which forbid the leaking
of state secrets or even the workings of state agencies. Control of what we may
know and what we should supposedly remain in ignorance of is still a disputed
issue. Such questions impact on our sense of the relationship between the many
and the few, the nature of and our trust in democratic institutions and what
may and may not be in the public domain. These are difficult, complex and
unresolved issues which will be a mainstream feature of political debate for the
foreseeable future.

  In the present collection of essays, Geoff Kemp has assembled an international
team of experts who explore the nature of debates over censorship from Socrates
and Cato to the later twentieth century. As we read them, we realize that the
history of censorship is not a straightforward narrative of the triumph of freedom
of speech and expression over repressive tyranny. There is much to be learned
from that history. One of the striking things which emerges from these essays is
not so much the immediate applicability of this past thinking but its resonances
for our own debates and its parallel complexity. Thinking and learning about
how to read these texts will enhance our sensitivity not only to the past but
to the issues which need to be grappled with in our own confrontation with
censorship.

John Morrow

J. C. Davis

Introduction

Geoff Kemp

Censorship has been a part of human experience for at least 2,500 years and in that period has been a recurring presence for political thought, whether as active repression, a shaping context for expression, or as itself an object of analysis and argument. From the conviction and death of Socrates to Milton's *Areopagitica* to twenty-first-century Chinese protesters echoing a mythologized Western past – 'I disagree with what you say but will defend to the death your right to say it!' – acts of silencing have provoked passionate and often penetrating responses that speak to the historical moment and to a longer-term agenda of political and personal ideas, aims and conflicts.[1] Thinking and writing about the regulation of thinking, speaking and writing is a thread running through past political discourse, and the questions raised and problems addressed remain a relevant and important part of our political present. *Censorship Moments* provides a ready point of access to a range of contributions to that thread, offering new essays on past 'censorship texts' in the innovative format of the series in which the book appears.

The importance of thinking more about censorship's past arises not least because, in the Western self-image, censorship *is* the past, an idea left behind, and free expression is the present and future. The familiar narrative is that of censorship by state and church being subordinated to freedom of expression, politically and intellectually, over the last few centuries, as part of a shift to modernity marked by the ascendency of liberty and rights, toleration and secularism, popular sovereignty and state neutrality, and a capitalist industrial order whose powers included making media central to all our lives. As a result, free speech and a free press became enthroned at the right hand of modern democracy, attended by the First Amendment and Fourth Estate, and cloaked in memorable phrases. Opposition to censorship is central to our political creed, its past stirred in public memory as a struggle by word and deed against the forces of repression. It may be complained that a commitment to freedom of expression is today proclaimed more than practised by governments and others (along with not being proclaimed universally enough), though this has an air of paradox. If espousing ideas is 'only words', of no consequence, there would seem no need to regulate words in practice, or indeed protect them, inviting instead a kind of 'liberalism by default'. Censorship is the homage paid to the power of words and images.

The advance of freedom of expression over censorship is, by common agreement, one of the most notable of human advances. While no pre-modern European state had the practical and conceptual tools to aspire to be truly 'totalitarian', it was equally the case that no state countenanced immunity from the threat of punishment for subjects uttering words it hated, particularly those judged to be seditious or impious. The threat was present for all persons, high and low, literate and illiterate, but loomed more immediately for writers on politics and religion, a condition of insecurity that discouraged arts and letters though was never a complete deterrent. John Aubrey's report that the Anglican bishops wanted Thomas Hobbes burned as a heretic in the 1660s was hyperbole, though mainly because burning for heresy was seen as the Roman Inquisition's style, whereas the English way was burning books, mutilating religious dissenters on charges of seditious libel and executing printers for treason. Yet by the close of the century, England had forsaken pre-publication licensing and acquired a Toleration Act; a century later, the United States codified freedom of thought and expression in the First Amendment. The exchange of a dangerously uncertain world for one of relative security is a gain that no one who studies the history of ideas will fail to appreciate, or indeed anyone living in modern constitutional democracy.

The question can be asked, however, whether free expression displaced censorship as 'master narrative' at the cost of partly suppressing how it did so, discouraging attention to the diverse dimensions of the subject. In ending up on the right side of the argument, so to speak, freedom of expression encouraged a Manichean assumption that there were plainly two sides in dispute from the beginning, in the process condemning the other side to the dark ages before enlightenment. The story of censorship becomes one told from its ostensible end, at the threshold of defeat by free expression, prior to which its character can be assumed because censorship has 'the same characteristics in every era'.[2] Arguments in the present readily become struggles to label an intervention 'censorship' and delegitimize it by definition, since every right-thinking person is against censorship.

An example might be the mainstream debate in and around the recent Leveson Inquiry into the British press. Leveson's report declares that press freedom was 'hard won' as 'one of the cornerstones of our democracy', invoking Thomas Jefferson and drawing subsequently on John Stuart Mill, Oliver Wendell Holmes, John Wilkes, George Orwell and Milton's 'immortal' *Areopagitica*. Having traced historical opposition to government licensing and censorship, the report observes that a primary argument currently advanced against action on press abuses relies on a 'mistaken conflation' of state censorship with the ordinary democratic processes of statute law. Leveson's view that there is no necessary connection is taken to be confirmed by his resort to history, conveying ideas of press freedom serving the public interest.[3] The concerted response of the majority of British national newspapers was to continue to run the story of possible intervention as '300 years of freedom under threat' and 'CENSORED', shrinking an already limited historical horizon to headline slogans.[4]

Leveson's inquiry and academic inquiry alike have limits but an aim of this book is to contribute to widening the horizon, historically and intellectually, by scrutinizing a range of 'moments' over the past two millennia when thinkers addressed the theme of censorship, conveying the variability of ideas about censorship and free expression without precluding the tracing of conceptual patterns and historical trajectories. In doing so, the book's aim chimes with recent scholarship emphasizing 'moments of censorship' rather than timeless repression, and with the broader movement towards contextual understanding in the study of the history of political thought.[5]

The relationship between censorship and political thought is aptly conceived in terms of 'moments'. The introduction to *Utopian Moments*, the first volume in this series, remarked that attention to censorship 'rarely tells anything like the full story' about a work, criticizing a tendency to view utopian writing merely as a device to evade the censor (p. xvi). The comment carries another resonance, however, because censorship has indeed rarely, if ever, been the 'full story' of any extended political or theoretical work in the past. This claim may sit oddly with the idea of free expression rising to be a cornerstone of democracy, though partly this is because the ascent itself fostered expectations of expansive, clear-cut and free-standing denunciations of censorship. Yet when we look back, the literary-political 'cornerstones' of the tradition in English have been a forty-page pamphlet (*Areopagitica*), a sixty-eight-page chapter (in Mill's *On Liberty*), and scattered utterances of writers, politicians and judges, amplified by an expanding consciousness of the freedom through beneficiaries such as the press, along with the scholarly systemization of the tradition and concept.

In *not* constituting the 'full story' of a work, however, censorship may be no less important to the study of the history of ideas. One reason is that moments of active repression, or the concern to avoid them, shape the text and can inform its interpretation. Political thought itself is not solely 'thought' but expression and communication too, susceptible to intervention by authority. But another consideration is the way in which reflection or comment within the text about the control or freedom of thinking, expressing and communicating is itself a moment of political thought, as a rule. The concerns and concepts which writers articulate in relation to censorship typically connect to the central themes of the history of political thought. They engage, or touch on, questions of authority, law, sovereignty, liberty, rights, toleration, deliberation, legitimacy, the public and private, equality and others. The concerns of censorship and free expression flow alongside the mainstream of past political discourse, sometimes submerged under pressing political and philosophical matters but surfacing at moments such as those forming the basis of this book.

Censorship Moments provides fresh readings of a range of well-known works and thinkers, as well as novel interpretations of less well-known texts, and of two printed images, viewing all these works through the prism of censorship and free expression. The essays begin by presenting a 'textual moment' – a quotation or image – which serves as a springboard to engage with the subject in various ways: a closer reading of the work as a whole, a clearer view of the author's purposes, an awareness of relevant contexts, enhanced grasp of concepts and connections with wider thinking. An international team of experts has been gathered, with each asked to provide a short and accessible account, keeping scholarly apparatus to a minimum but intellectual insight to the fore. The hope is that the essays will stimulate thought and lead to further critical reading of the featured texts and others.

The choice of texts and authors is necessarily highly selective in covering a long time span and a diverse range of historical and political texts and agendas. As a book about past political thought, the main focus is official and overt censorship, by state and church, applied to political and religious expression, though the boundaries are porous. Prior restraint and subsequent punishment both feature. There is a place for famous 'moments', such as the death of Socrates and burning of Michel Servetus, and attention to celebrated names in the Anglo-American free speech tradition, including Milton, Mill, Holmes and James Madison. They are joined by major writers and thinkers from the wider realm studied by historians of ideas, extending geographical and chronological borders, without pretending to universal coverage, and incorporating defenders of censorship. There is consideration of Plutarch, Tacitus, Augustine, Aquinas, Ockham, Spinoza, Rousseau, Kant, Constant and Lenin, as well as the less canonical figures of Johannes Reuchlin, Castellio, Paolo Sarpi, Henry Parker and, more indirectly, Calvin, Hume, Tocqueville and others. The bias is towards published writing, the mainstay of political thought, but the role of speech is prominent and two chapters of the book examine images: William Marshall's frontispiece to *Eikon Basilike* and the satirical print *The Royal Shambles*, by William Hone and George Cruikshank. The penultimate chapter addresses the relation of censorship to interpretation, through Leo Strauss, and the final chapter considers the silencing of women, with Catharine MacKinnon's *Only Words* as the starting point.

The final part of this introduction draws brief attention to a number of themes with which chapters engage, while recognizing the variability of ideas relating to censorship across time, place and circumstances. Perhaps the readiest way to confirm the variability of a notion of 'censorship' over time is to point out that for most of the past two millennia the word has not been taken to mean what we generally take it to mean, and did not have today's negative connotations. Until well into the nineteenth century, the term 'censorship' mainly recalled, usually positively, the ancient Roman office of Censor, whose duties embraced public accounting (via the census), alongside oversight of *mores* in society and integrity in the senate. An idiosyncratic survival is the title of a college fellow at Christ Church, Oxford, where John Locke's memorial tablet informs visitors that he too was once 'Censor of Moral Philosophy', thirty years before helping end pre-publication censorship in England. The most famous of Roman Censors, Cato, is the subject of the first chapter, with ancient and modern senses of censorship also linked in the essays on Tacitus and Rousseau.

It is worth pausing to consider the history of how the words 'censor' and 'censorship' acquired their modern English meaning, which tracks the emergence of representative government as a principle and practice centred on authorization tied to accountability. Milton's isolated reference to the 'censor's hand' in *Areopagitica* preceded the linking of the classical meaning to print from the early eighteenth century, though not as state-imposed press control but by periodical writers proclaiming themselves censors of society's virtue, in the Roman manner but bringing nascent public opinion to bear on transgressions. From this moral and literary beginning emerged the claim that the press could bring the power of the public to bear on politicians' virtue or vice, encapsulated towards the end of the century in Jefferson's contention (echoed by Madison) that 'the people are the only censors of their governors', and newspapers the vehicle of censorial public opinion. Later in the next century, Mill's famous fear was public opinion's 'hostile and dreaded censorship' of individual belief and behaviour, guiding a government 'identified with the people'. In the decades around *On Liberty*, 'censorship' consolidated its passage to the term and evaluation recognizable today, describing official, primarily state regulation of expression, decried in liberal circles. The accountability function of censorship was meanwhile assumed by the 'Fourth Estate', censuring and correcting government in the public's name and claiming freedom from state censorship to do so. Writers were now the anti-censors, not the censors.

Viewing the past through the lens of censorship in its modern sense allows the examination of a range of concerns broached by past writers, who generally lacked our usage of the term. 'State' censorship itself is seen in various forms, being more and less identified with the people: the liberty and constraint implied in the public free speech of the citizen body of democratic Athens; censorship by the political executive from Roman emperors to the European monarchies; the challenge to monarchical censorship by proponents of representative government; and in turn the resistance to censorship at the hand of elected government. Of course, this is too summary and linear to convey the complexity of the accounts given, and a similar caveat applies in noting the prominence of ecclesiastical censorship, from the archetypal censorship of the Roman church and its *Index Expurgatorius*, detailed here via *Areopagitica's* major source, 'Padre Paolo' Sarpi, to the restraints and punishments imposed by Protestant authorities. Most frequently, however, censorship marked a joint effort of spiritual and political authority, an often unstable combination.

State and church censorship of political and religious expression does not exhaust the categories addressed. A broader concern with societal censoriousness is explored in Mill, and its positive potential in Rousseau, a reading emphasizing the non-coercive reinforcement of virtue. The potential for politics itself to censor, forcing the quest for truth into a compromise with peaceable popular acceptance, is broached in Augustine and Strauss. Several essays consider, in different ways, forms of 'market censorship': Kant's descent from philosophy to the prosaic problem of book piracy; the coincidence of Holmes and Lenin advancing views on the 'market of ideas' in 1919; and Orwell's protest at a left-leaning literary and publishing establishment obstructing criticism of the Soviet Union. In the final chapter, the (non-) censorship of pornography is at issue.

Extending the book's timescale back beyond the modern free speech narrative brings to the fore disputes over religious belief and defences of censorship, while belying simple divisions of religious and secular, pro- and anti-censorship. Religious censorship appears archetypal to modern eyes because of the propensity to target opinions alone, literally beliefs of no earthly use, and not clearly harmful. However, what can be called the heresy model is complicated in several ways when interpreting thinkers who believed heresy carried the ultimate cost. Augustine's 'compelle intrare' directed towards the Donatists is linked here to Machiavellian *realpolitik* in a context where no higher *political* morality is mandated. Ockham confronts the dilemma of how to respond to a putatively infallible papal authority that confirms its own heresy in censoring his allegedly heretical writings. Aquinas is shown to have approached transgression by words not as a matter for heresy law, a later model whose opposite is individual liberty rights, but by drawing on Roman law concepts of injurious words and 'sins of the tongue', emphasizing the dignity rights of those harmed and the motivations of the harmers. The connection to debates about hate speech is striking.

Two broader themes suggested in the foregoing discussion are worth amplifying. They might be loosely categorized as the relations between opinions and actions, and between opinions and public opinion. The first category can be divided further, into questions concerning what actions are taken against opinions, whether opinions constitute actions, and what actions stem from opinions, including the familiar issue of harm.

Discussion of the type, focus and degree of action taken against expression shows considerable variety. Castellio 'hated heretics' but hated their destruction more, in the tradition of the spiritual weapon being the word, not the sword; Reuchlin opposed banning Jewish texts (and the Qur'an) on a blanket supposition of heresy; Madison extended opposition from pre-publication to post-publication measures because of their 'chilling effect'; Hume's own punishment was 'censorship' by university (non-)appointment.

Whether thought in words constitutes deeds, forms of outward action prone to punishment, is a question raised by numerous writers, notably Spinoza, overlapping with the question of whether and when words cause harms that authority might legitimately seek to control. If Mill is an obvious source here, so too is Cato's stunning accusation that Socrates sought a tyranny of words, inviting acts of questioning that undermined the virtuous deeds on which republics depended. As suggested earlier, the very idea of censorship seems to concede much power to words, images, ideas, speech and writing. It is because they are powerful that they need to be controlled. A number of essays play around the notion that there may be forms of society in which ideas are rendered less powerful (by bread and circuses, consumerism, the corruption of language and even the self-assurance of rulers) and thereby censorship becomes redundant, producing 'liberalism by default', in effect: if ideas do not matter, their circulation does not need to be regulated.

The question of harms also raises that of intention, with Aquinas's notion of verbal 'sins' giving priority to intent over propositional content, while the problem of assessing intent in turn raises issues of interpretation: Tacitus depicts Cremutius Cordus being censored for insufficient praise, not overt criticism; Kant is found to use disingenuous flattery in deflecting censorship; Spinoza and Hume make ironic use of Tacitus's praise of the rare good fortune of the writer living in a time of freedom.

The second of our larger categories, the relation of opinions and public opinion, returns us to the question of whether censorship most offends against individual belief and expression (the heresy model) or against collective self-determination, forged through open deliberation and accountable government, as well as whether the latter may invite regulation in the public interest. Constant rejects as the basis for press freedom the possibilities of public opinion forged in tandem with the state (the early view of Guizot) or by associations outside the state (the later view of Tocqueville), emphasising defence of individuality as its foundation, the key notion for others such as Mill and Orwell. At the same time, individual opinion is not seen only as self-expression, with a recurring theme being dialogue or deliberation, a relevant one for contemporary thought, though like censorship appearing in varied guises. Ockham's 'heresy' is a matter of conscience but securing religious truth is also a matter of allowing 'dissenting voices', at appropriate levels; Milton's similar thinking runs counter to Parker's support for censorship, but both are committed to a process of deliberation oriented to non-arbitrary political outcomes, the political 'truth'. Kant emphasizes the freedom to think in common; Calvin rejects dialogue as a source of true knowledge, since this places knowledge before faith.

The world evoked in these essays and the ideas of censorship and free expression they convey are by turns alien and familiar. Those who fear for the fragility of the free speech tradition may prefer to find comfort in simple certainties, but arguably they underestimate the complexity of their subject in the present as much as in the past. An example which runs through the book is the complex relationship between official, public, overt censorship and self-censorship or hegemonic/social censorship. Censorship's past is not all burning books, though books were burned; it is also the books that were never written. The history of political thought rests on the more hopeful fact that books are survivors. It is hoped that this book will provoke thought, extend knowledge of past thinkers and encourage further inquiry.

Cato the Censor and Socrates the Tyrant

Arlene W. Saxonhouse

When he was now well on in years, there came as ambassadors from Athens to Rome, Carneades the Academic, and Diogenes the Stoic philosopher.... Upon the arrival of these philosophers, the most studious of the city's youth became their devoted and admiring listeners. ... But Cato, at the very outset, when this zeal for discussion came pouring into the city, was distressed, fearing lest the young men, by giving this direction to their ambition, should come to love a reputation based on mere words more than one achieved by martial deeds. And when the fame of the visiting philosophers rose yet higher in the city... Cato determined... to rid and purge the city of them all. So he rose in the Senate and censured the magistrates for keeping in such long suspense an embassy composed of men who could easily secure anything they wished, so persuasive were they. 'We ought', he said, 'to make up our minds... and vote on what the embassy proposes, in order that these men may return to their schools and lecture to the sons of Greece, while the youth of Rome give ear to their laws and magistrates, as heretofore.' This he did, not, as some think, out of personal hostility to Carneades, but because he was wholly averse to philosophy, and made mock of all Greek culture and training, out of patriotic zeal. He says, for instance, that Socrates was a mighty prattler, who attempted, as best he could, to be his country's tyrant, by abolishing its customs, and by enticing his fellow citizens into opinions contrary to the laws. ... And seeking to prejudice his son against Greek culture, he... declar[es], in the tone of a prophet or a seer, that Rome would lose her empire when she had become infected with Greek letters.[1]

Thus writes Plutarch about Cato the Censor. Plutarch, often described as a 'Platonist' because of his many writings exploring Platonic themes, nevertheless is mostly known for his *Parallel Lives* telling of notable historical or semi-historical Greeks and Romans. As Plutarch follows his characters from birth to death, questions of character, virtue and vice provide cohesion for his studies. In the preface to his life of Alexander, Plutarch emphasizes that he is writing 'lives' and not histories. To write a life, for him, means to capture his subject's moral character. He explains: 'In the most illustrious deeds there is not always a manifestation of virtue or vice. A slight thing like a phrase or a jest often makes a greater revelation of character than battles where thousands fall.' He compares himself to a painter who finds 'character' in 'the face and the expression of the eyes' rather than in the 'other parts of the body'. Thus, he asks to be allowed to devote himself to 'the signs of the souls of men' and let others deal with great battles and 'more weighty matters'.[2]

The quotation at the head of this chapter is just such an anecdote, intended to illuminate the character, the virtues and the vices, of Marcus Cato, active in Rome during the first half of the second century BCE. We learn early on from Plutarch's 'Life' that Cato led a frugal and temperate life, working in the fields alongside his slaves, scorning profligacy and ostentation. Plutarch reports that Cato 'tells us that he never wore clothing worth more than a hundred drachmas; that he drank … the same wine as his slaves' (4.3). Stories about his ascetic ways were legion and his pithy aphorisms about the deformity of vice point to Cato's impatience with those who had abandoned the virtues and moral rectitude of early Rome. The enmity between himself and the great Roman general Scipio, the protector of Rome against Hannibal, for instance, arose from Cato's criticism of Scipio's financial generosity to his soldiers. Such generosity, Cato claimed, would corrupt 'the native simplicity of his soldiers, who resorted to wanton pleasures when their pay exceeded their actual needs' (3.5). Cato openly denounced Scipio in the Senate as one 'whose boyish addiction to palaestras and theatres' suggested a 'Master of a festival' and not a 'commander of an army' (3.7).

At the same time as Plutarch records such 'signs of [Cato's] soul', he also traces Cato's rise from obscurity to political power, such that he is first elected Consul and, most importantly, ten years later Censor. The Censorship was a position that (in Plutarch's words) 'towered … above every other civic honour, and was, in a way, the culmination of a political career' (16.1). Plutarch explains the position and functions of the Roman Censor, two of whom were elected each year:

> The variety of its powers was great, including that of examining into the lives and manners of the citizens. Its creators thought that no one should be left to his own devices and desires, without inspection and review, either in his marriage, or in the begetting of his children, or in the ordering of his daily life, or in the entertainment of his friends.

In language recalling his own practice of assessing human character, Plutarch adds that the Romans, 'thinking that these things revealed a man's real character more than did his public and political career, they set men in office to watch, admonish, and chastise, that no one should turn aside to wantonness and forsake his native and customary mode of life'. These Censors 'had authority to degrade a knight, or to expel a senator who led an unbridled and disorderly life' (16.1–16.2).[3] Plutarch's account underscores the differences, while anticipating the connection, between the Roman Censorship and later understandings of censorship as the control of expression.

Ancient Roman historians such as Sallust and Livy attribute Rome's spectacular development to the virtue of her citizens, whether the private virtue of chastity exemplified by Lucretia, whose suicide after being raped led to the overthrow of the kings, or Horatio's courage defending the bridge against the invading Etruscans. The decline of Rome, as imagined by Sallust in particular, followed the abandonment of those virtues and the purpose of writing history was to offer *exempla* of such deeds for the Roman youth to emulate. Like their ancestors, they were to devote themselves to the glory of the Republic, irrespective of the cost to themselves. Censorship, therefore, in its initial formulation, was to prevent the loss of those virtues that were judged the source and foundation of Rome's greatness. The Censor intervened in the lives of citizens insofar as such interventions might preserve that ancient morality essential to the stability and success of the polity. Through the office of the Censor the Romans institutionalized efforts to maintain that citizen virtue. It would, they hoped, ensure that the profligacy that might arise from the riches flowing into Rome as the result of her imperial expansion did not undermine the moral fibre of just those citizens who would serve as soldiers and as models for the young. Profligacy was not simply a personal vice; it undermined the entire political body.

Cato, as a practitioner of the modest hard-working life with little time for private pleasures, was the perfect candidate for an office devoted to protecting Rome from the incursion of what were feared as alien and threatening mores and practices. And just as threatening to the ancient Roman virtues as the wealth and customs of the nations that Rome was conquering was Greek philosophy, bound up as it was with questioning all things and with its emphasis on the power of speech rather than deeds. Thus, Rome needed to be rid of those representatives of Greek philosophy, Carneades the Academic Sceptic (who could argue for justice one day and make the opposite argument the next) and Diogenes the Stoic, before their practices of philosophic questioning could infect Rome's youth. The danger that Cato perceives from the visiting Greeks leads Plutarch to report Cato's infamous remark about Socrates' tyrannical ambitions. Earlier in the 'Life', when Plutarch was noting Cato's excellence as a father, he quotes Cato's remark: 'There was nothing else to admire in Socrates of old except that he was always kind and gentle in his intercourse with a shrewish wife and stupid sons' (20.2) – a backhanded compliment if ever there was one.

Cato's attitude towards Socrates sits uneasily next to the sort of praise that Socrates has earned from others, both ancient and modern. Plato ends the *Phaedo*, his dialogue recounting the death of Socrates, calling Socrates the 'best and wisest and most just' of all men who lived in their time.[4] According to Xenophon's *Memorabilia*, Socrates, 'by letting his own light shine, … led his disciples to hope that they through imitation of him would attain to such excellence'.[5] John Stuart Mill in *On Liberty* writes, 'Mankind can hardly be too often reminded, that there was once a man named Socrates' who was 'the head and prototype of all subsequent teachers of virtue'. Cato, however, was not so easily drawn into this chorus of admirers. And while Plato, Xenophon and Mill all express their dismay or even horror at the execution of the man who (in Mill's language) 'probably of all then born had deserved best of mankind', Cato ascribes to Socrates the most hated name, for Romans, of 'tyrant'.[6] Concerned as Cato was with maintaining the greatness of the Republic, he portrays Socrates as a threat to the city and its young.

Though the lives of both Cato and Socrates were marked by moderation and abstinence, Cato sensed in Socratic philosophy a threat to the traditional virtues of the city – one based on Socrates' claim that his wisdom lay in knowing that he did not know. Cato saw in his own life of hard work and devotion to Rome, in his refusal to drink the best wines, eat the finest delicacies or wear jewel-encrusted robes, a commitment to carrying on the founding principles of those who had built and guided Rome in its early years. As Censor he was entrusted with preserving what was now threatened by the new sources of honour. Scipio, indulging his soldiers with wealth and land, fostered a focus on sensual satisfactions, thereby weakening the bodies with which they might fight for Rome. Philosophy's crime was to make men find power and success in speech rather than in the deeds, the austere practices and values of republican Rome. Socrates had urged his followers to question the ancient mores, not to venerate them, and to see inherent contradictions in their assumed certainties. The speech of such a man could dismantle the laws and tradition that preserved and protected the polity about which Cato cared so deeply.

In a peculiar section of Plato's *Apology*, Socrates allies himself with Achilles, the great Homeric hero, who willingly faced death, fearing more to live as a coward than not avenge the death of his comrade Patroclus. Like Achilles, Socrates also willingly faces death, but the absurdity of this assimilation of the glorious demigod and noble warrior to the stooped, bug-eyed, snub-nosed old man would have been apparent to all. The analogy between himself and Achilles mocks the traditional hero who performed great deeds on the battlefield. Socrates offends Cato's principles even more when he explains his decision to remove himself from traditional forms of political engagement: 'A man who really fights for the right, if he is to preserve his life for even a little while, must be a private citizen, not a public man' (32a). As a private man he talks to all, young and old, citizen and foreigner (30a). His conversations serve the city not by supporting its ancient traditions, but by unsettling the city. Outrageously calling himself a gift from the gods, he explains (in what he calls a laughable image) that he is a gadfly biting the large sleepy horse that is Athens, reproaching her citizens for not caring truly about justice and the other virtues, for being too complacent to allow philosophic inquiry to distract them from their daily lives (29e). But just like the horse with the gadfly that is biting it, he predicts that Athens is likely to slap at him and easily kill him – and so they do.

Scholars have suggested multiple reasons for Socrates' execution by the Athenian democracy in 399 BCE,[7] but none has given much credence to Cato's suggestion that Socrates longed for tyranny. Should they? Xenophon, as he tries to defend Socrates against accusations of corrupting the youth, explores the sources of those accusations. He cites one accuser who said that Socrates taught his companions to 'despise the established laws by insisting on the folly of appointing public officials by lot', something that would not be done when choosing the pilot of a ship. This, the accuser argued, 'led the young to despise the established constitution and made them violent' (I.2.9). Xenophon also describes Socrates' relationship with Critias (who later became one of the Thirty Tyrants installed by the Spartans at Athens after they defeated Athens in the Peloponnesian War) and Alcibiades, the flamboyant and 'insolent' (according to Xenophon) Athenian general who eventually defected first to the Spartans and then to the Persians. Xenophon explains that these two came to Socrates as ambitious young men who admired his independence and especially his ability to control others through speech. They hoped that by associating with Socrates they would 'attain the utmost facility in speech and action'. Once they acquired that facility, however, they no longer needed Socrates and pursued political power on their own. Socrates' philosophic explorations gave them tools for acquiring power, Xenophon argues, but they themselves were responsible for using that power as they did (I.2.12–I.2.16). And yet, without a Socrates, they would have lacked the verbal skills to achieve their political goals.

In Plato's version of the *Apology*, Socrates credits the prejudices against himself in part to Aristophanes' comedy *The Clouds*. The story told there matches just what Xenophon tries to discount. Socrates, the teacher of the art of speech that can make the worse cause appear the better, enables one practising that art to become powerful. The principles behind this art of speaking surface in *The Clouds* in a speech offered in Socrates' supposed school, the Thinkery. A figure cast as 'Unjust Speech' articulates Socrates' new education, one that mocks virtues like moderation.[8] A heavily indebted Athenian whom Aristophanes calls Strepsiades has sent his son to Socrates' school to learn this art of speech so that he might help his father weasel out of his debts. The problem set by the comedy, though, is that the son learns the lessons too well and justifies through argument beating his father and then also his mother. Strepsiades comes to realize the consequences of urging his son to study with Socrates. If a son can beat his mother, what else is open to him? Not only is the economic foundation of the city threatened, but, in Aristophanes' portrayal, the family itself disappears with Socrates' new education. Realizing this, Strepsiades is beside himself; his response is to burn down Socrates' school, to destroy those who mock the old and introduce those new arts that undermine the traditional forms of self-discipline and grant power to those who know how to manipulate words rather than perform well.

Power in this tale derives from speech, not moral virtue. An education that develops such mental agility threatens the security of the political body; it questions the old, unsettles the givens according to which the young have been raised, mocks the ancient heroes and opens the door for new sources of power, especially tyrannical power. Strepsiades uses the only resource he has to fight the threat: fire. The Athenians had grander resources than fire, namely a legal system that allowed those threatened by Socrates to indict him on the charges of corrupting the young and introducing new gods into the city. While we may find Socrates honourable in his efforts to unsettle the Athenians, the Athenians themselves (and Cato) saw the dangers that Socrates posed to the fabric of Athenian society by practising such 'corrosive' citizenship.[9] For Cato, Socrates – and by association philosophy – corrupts the young; those later representatives of philosophy, Carneades and Diogenes, likewise threaten to corrupt Roman youth as Socrates corrupted the young of Athens.

Socrates' execution troubles modern readers. Democratic Athens created no such office as the Censor. Indeed, they prided themselves on their practice of free/frank speech (*parrhêsia*), naming one of the city's ships *Parrhêsia*, and Socrates in several Platonic dialogues prided himself on practising *parrhêsia*. Yet, the Athenians also discovered the challenges of allowing for unbridled *parrhêsia*. The term itself entails more than the modern language of 'free speech'; it emphasizes daring, a willingness to question authority, a freedom to speak what one truly believes, without dissimulation or flattery. *Parrhêsia* (and *isegoria*, equal freedom to speak) lay at the heart of a democratic Athens that depended on the open discussion of issues confronting the city: war, peace, expansion, taxes. But the city nevertheless found itself threatened by this practice. The boldness to speak openly can also – as in Socrates's case – trigger a lack of reverence for the foundational principles of the society in which such unlimited speech is enjoyed. The challenges that Socrates posed to the accepted definitions of moral terms – 'courage', 'virtue', 'piety', 'moderation', 'justice' – and the way he flustered his interlocutors when he interrogated them about the meaning of such words may have fully expressed this democratic *parrhêsia*, but it also captured the fundamental tension in a democracy that relies on openness but also suffers from the instability created by philosophic questioning.

The universal adoration of Socrates over time makes Cato's description of Socrates shocking. A prattling old man talking with the young could hardly be a tyrannical threat to the city – and yet, precisely by daring to urge the youth to question the givens of their moral lives, he was. Strepsiades recognized it, though the solution to the threat he posed was crude. Socrates' accusers in Athens recognized it and executed him. Cato recognized it and as Censor, the defender of moderation, asceticism and the ancient virtues, thus demanded the banishment of philosophy from Rome. It was all part of his effort to protect the young from the 'corrosive' practice that would undermine a devotion to the Republic and introduce into the city a dangerous new source of political power, the facility with words.

The Case of Cremutius Cordus: Tacitus on Censorship and Writing under Despotic Rulers

Daniel J. Kapust

'*It is my words, conscript fathers, that are criticized, so completely am I innocent of deeds; but not even they were directed at the princeps or the princeps's parent, whom the law of treason embraces. I am said to have praised Brutus and Cassius, whose achievements, though many have compiled them, no one has recalled without honour…. Posterity pays to every man his due repute; and if condemnation is closing in on me, there will be no lack of those who remember not merely Cassius and Brutus but also myself.' Then, leaving the senate, he [Cremutius Cordus] ended his life by fasting. The cremation of his books by the aediles was proposed by the fathers; but they survived, having been concealed and published. Wherefore it is pleasant to deride all the more the insensibility of those who, by virtue of their present powerfulness, believe that the memory even of a subsequent age too can be extinguished. On the contrary, the influence of punished talents swells, nor have foreign kings, or those who have resorted to the same savagery, accomplished anything except disrepute for themselves and for their victims glory.*[1]

The passage with which this chapter begins serves to conclude what is arguably the most famous description of censorship in Roman historiography: Tacitus' description of the historian Cremutius Cordus' trial and death (25 CE) during the reign of Tiberius (ruled 14–37 CE). Tacitus' account of the trial of Cremutius Cordus is remarkable for a number of reasons, not the least of which – and the most pertinent to the present volume – is its status as 'perhaps the fullest and most explicit assertion of the alleged suppression of free speech by the Empire'.[2]

Cordus, as we shall see, was prosecuted not for overt criticism of Tiberius, but instead for offering excessive praise of Brutus and Cassius. Cordus' fate captures not just the constraints that might be placed on written expression as a result of offending the emperor, but it also occurs in the context of an atmosphere of informants and prosecutors: Cordus is tried through the machinations of those surrounding the emperor. But the account is noteworthy for other reasons. Tacitus' portrayal of Cordus is the only depiction of a historian giving a speech or taking so central a place in a historical narrative in ancient historiography. And then there is the fascinating relationship between Tacitus the historian – who 'gives very little away', in the words of Ronald Syme – and the historian Cordus, who gives too much away.[3] Each is writing in the context of a monarchical regime, and each is confronting the tensions and potential dangers that attended artistic expression under such a regime. There is, to be sure, some irony in the story of Cremutius Cordus: in spite of the fame of Tacitus' account of him, Cordus himself has 'little historical significance' beyond the story of his prosecution in the *Annals*, and almost nothing remains of his work, apart from a fragment preserved by Seneca.[4] Were it not for Tacitus' account, Cordus would be little known to posterity. Cordus' fate – both his death and his obscurity – seems to represent the danger that someone like Tacitus might have faced himself in seeking to engage in written expression in the Imperial context.

The use of the term 'censorship' in the Roman context is strange in certain ways: as the previous essay indicated, the term 'censor' existed in Latin, though differed from the modern usage. A *Censor* was a public official, two of whom comprised an institution created during the Republic. The *Censores* were originally charged with compiling the Roman citizen list, and possessed the power of censuring those who they found to be disgraceful in their morals or behaviour. One of the chief functions of the office, then, was to help ensure that standards of virtuous behaviour were upheld. The Censors' office even allowed them to remove individuals from the senate or the equestrian class through censure. Yet even if a *Censor* wasn't a censor in our sense, the office did seek to regulate behaviour. And it is also true that what we describe as censorship – the suppression of speech at the hands of public officials – was certainly present in the Imperial period of Roman history, most particularly in what Rosalind Thomas terms 'that Roman peculiarity': the burning of books.[5]

Cordus' case, as mentioned, is noteworthy in part because it so clearly illustrates the constraints that monarchy might place on speech in Imperial Rome, constraints which Cordus himself contrasts to the liberty with which Roman Republican and Greek writers wrote. Cordus is not engaged in exaggeration: while the Romans certainly might describe certain forms of speech as *licentia*, or licence, the value of free speech was important enough 'that the word *liber* can be used *tout court* to mean "speaking one's mind".[6] There were, to be sure, legal restrictions on speech during the Republic; thus Brunt notes a provision of the Twelve Tables that allowed for the death penalty for one defaming 'a man with opprobrious songs', but he doubts that it would have been used often, while also emphasizing that it was highly restricted in scope.[7]

That was the Republic. When we move to the Imperial period, 'defamation was more strictly repressed, and if directed against the emperor or leading men, assimilated to treason' – that is, *maiestas*.[8] Cordus is an example of just such a change, and insofar as Cordus' writings were burned, his speech was censored. Other writers' books were burned, too, during the Julio-Claudian period: Titus Labienus and Titus Cassius Severus under Augustus, and Mamercus Aemilius Scaurus under Tiberius. Labienus overtly critiqued Augustus' monarchy, while Cassius Severus praised Labienus and criticized members of Rome's elite. Aemilius Scaurus wrote a play, the *Atreus*, which featured a line that Tiberius took to be veiled criticism, while Cremutius Cordus, as noted above, simply praised Brutus and Cassius while not praising Tiberius or Augustus.[9]

Insufficient praise, not overt criticism, was the alleged crime for which Cordus had been charged with violating Tiberius' *maiestas*. *Maiestas* is a fraught term. It originally – and exclusively – applied to the Roman people as a whole in the Republican period. During the period of the later Republic, *maiestas* referred both to the superlative status of the Roman people as compared to other peoples, and to the Roman people's supremacy within the Republic itself. Originally, then, one who committed crimes of *maiestas* committed crimes against the Roman people, and could be tried for such crimes by a court created by Saturninus in 103 BCE. What constituted crimes of *maiestas* in the Republic was a slippery issue, and alleged crimes could extend beyond treason. The term *maiestas* shifted in usage over the course of the first century BCE, and it would eventually 'inhere most importantly in the emperor himself'.[10] By the end of the first century BCE, those deemed to have committed offences against *maiestas* had committed offences against particular people, Augustus and his family, but also other prominent Romans.[11] With this came a transformation in notions of who was a criminal and what constituted criminal behaviour. Cassius Severus was twice charged for targeting particular powerful persons with criticism, and one might even be charged with *maiestas* for having adulterous relations with Augustus' daughter. Moreover, the Republican *quaestiones maiestatis* were no longer the sole venue for trials by the time of the rule of Tiberius; Cremutius Cordus was tried before Tiberius. What might count as violations of the *lex maiestatis*, while initially vague, became even murkier during the Imperial period, and for good reason: as Domitian (in)famously remarked, 'the lot of princes was most unhappy, since when they discovered a conspiracy, no one believed them unless they had been killed'.[12]

Against the backdrop of the *maiestas* law, Cordus' case was remarkable in part because it was a new sort of prosecution, with Tacitus himself remarking *in propria persona* that Cordus was 'arraigned on a charge which was new and heard only then for the first time'; his prosecutors were 'clients of Sejanus' – the corrupt and corrupting manipulator of Tiberius (34.2). The offence in question was not overt criticism of either Augustus or Tiberius, as it had been with, say, Titus Labienus, but rather Cordus' praise for Brutus and description of Cassius as 'last of the Romans' in annals he had published (4.34). Being prosecuted for praise – rather than blame – was new, as was his being targeted exclusively for what he had written rather than what he had said, or rather what he had said and written. Moreover, as Martin and Woodman note, the applicability of the *lex maiestatis* to the alleged crime was unclear: the law 'did not extend beyond' Tiberius, Augustus and their respective households.[13] For the law to be readily applicable, Cordus' praise of Brutus and Cassius would need to be construed as blame of Augustus or Tiberius, and Cordus denies this, as he also denies that his praise of those who were dead has practical effects.

In defending himself against the charges, Cordus makes a number of arguments. He is 'innocent of deeds', and targeted for his words – words that were not directly aimed at Tiberius or Augustus, whose persons were protected by the crime of *maiestas*. Earlier writers had overtly criticized Julius and Augustus Caesar, and their writings still existed, borne or 'ignored' by Tiberius' predecessors. Nor was Cordus' praise of monarchy's opponents unprecedented: he notes that Livy had praised Pompey and yet remained in Augustus' favour, for example, while Cicero's praise of Cato was answered by Caesar in a speech, not by suppressing Cicero's expression. Moreover, ignoring speech that displeases is an effective strategy on the part of the powerful: as he remarks, 'if you become angry, you appear to have made an admission' (4.34). This provides an in-built defence against accusations of veiled criticisms, suggesting that the one who views himself as the target confirms the very veiled charges that he would deny, making him – and not just the ostensibly innocent writer – complicit in the criticism. Cordus adds that those who are dead, such as Cassius and Brutus, are no longer the subject of 'hatred or favour', and his praise of Cassius and Brutus was not done in public with the aim of stirring up sedition, and – one infers – does not constitute blame of either Augustus or Tiberius.

Thus ran Cordus' defence; it would prove futile. The trial itself seems to have had a foregone conclusion, with Tacitus remarking that the prosecutors' status as Sejanus' clients, along with 'the callous look with which [Tiberius] Caesar received his defence', sealed Cordus' fate (4.34). Cordus himself 'ended his life by fasting' (4.35).

On its face, Tacitus' account seems to be a straightforward defence of free expression in the context of political constraint. Those who engage in censorship come out looking badly, while those who risk life and limb to express themselves, like Cordus, are vindicated by history. The very sensitivity of Tiberius to the *potential* criticism lurking behind Cordus' praise of Cassius and Brutus indicates that Tiberius was no good ruler – as does the destruction of Cordus' writings, destruction that proved incomplete, and hence futile. That a ruler like Tiberius might serve as a contrast – or a warning – to other rulers is evident in Tacitus' *Histories*, where he describes (with reference to Nerva and Trajan), 'the rare good fortune of an age in which we may feel what we wish and may say what we feel' (1.1) (see also Chapter 11, this volume). Theirs was not the age of Tiberius.

Matters become murkier, though, when we turn our attention to the digression that precedes the trial narrative in the *Annals*. In the digression, Tacitus – like Cordus – contrasts the 'freedom' of prior historians with his own context, writing, 'My work, on the other hand, is confined and inglorious: peace was immovable or only modestly challenged, affairs in the City were sorrowful, and the princeps indifferent to extending the empire' (4.32). In spite of his work being 'confined and inglorious' due to his context and subject, it may still be of use in the context of the Principate, where 'there is no salvation for affairs other than if one man is in command' (4.33). In such a context, Tacitus' history helps to teach 'the honourable from the baser, or the useful from the harmful' (4.33). Tacitus' subjects are themselves not pleasurable: 'savage orders, constant accusations, deceitful friendship, the ruin of innocents and always the same reasons for their extermination' (4.33). Writers like Tacitus face a further problem: when writing about, say, the reign of Tiberius, 'you will discover persons who, owing to a similarity of behaviour, think that the misdeeds of others are being imputed to themselves' (4.33). As a result, 'Even glory and courage receive a ferocious response, as being critical of their opposites from too close at hand' (4.33). His dilemma is identical to that with which he describes Cordus. Tacitus is describing here a situation calling for 'figured speech': that is, the ways of expressing 'oneself safely, tactfully, and effectively in almost every imaginable situation' such that 'the critical links in thought must be established by his reader or listener'.[14]

Read with the narrative of Cordus' trial, the digression is striking, as Cordus falls victim to precisely the danger Tacitus describes: his depiction and praise of Brutus and Cassius' virtues brought about a ferocious response; he was an innocent ruined. He may have defended himself in speech – for crimes allegedly committed in writing – but he failed, and the trial seemed to be a foregone conclusion. Cordus was too direct: to praise Brutus and Cassius – and to call Cassius the 'last of the Romans' – was to suggest 'the most radical of political claims, namely that the Republic *was* Rome and that with the fall of the Republic Rome is spiritually and politically dead'.[15] Moreover, even if Brutus and Cassius were long dead, Cordus' praise of them might have politically subversive consequences; Domitian may have been paranoid, but he was not wrong to worry. If Cordus had intended to engage in veiled criticism of Tiberius, he did not do a very good job of veiling; if he had not intended to engage in veiled criticism, he did not seem to understand his situation very well.

Yet Cordus' fate makes his implied criticism that much more pointed: some of his readers, it seems, were able to put the pieces together to read his praise of Cassius and Brutus as a criticism of Tiberius and others. Or perhaps the response of Tiberius and Sejanus' clients made the connection – even if unintended – that much more real. Tacitus' readers, in turn, are able to connect Cordus' fate with the savagery of Tiberius, bringing him into disrepute.

If this is a vindication of the writing of history in the face of censorship, on one level, it succeeds: those who engage in such prosecutions do not look particularly good to posterity. (One might note, though, that they will only look bad if history finds out.) On another level, however, it is a fairly weak defence: almost nothing of Cordus' work survives, little is known of him and he is not particularly apt at writing under the constraints of despotism. If Tacitus outlines the constraints of writing under an emperor – and points to the technique appropriate to doing so – Cordus fails. In this regard, he is like the poet Maternus in Tacitus' *Dialogue on Orators*, who also finds himself in a dire situation because his play, *Cato*, was too strong for 'court circles' (2.1). Maternus, unlike Cordus, does not deny that he had done anything wrong; instead, he ups the ante, stating that he will soon be reading out his work *Thyestes*. Cordus may be naïve; Maternus, by contrast, is truculent.

All the same, Tacitus' narrative of the prosecution and fate of Cordus, even if it undermines itself, highlights the constraints of despotism. If one was fortunate enough to live – and write – under a *good* ruler, one might come close to fulfilling Tacitus' hope of being able to say what one thought. But if one lived under a bad ruler, or if one was not entirely sure of how to read a ruler, it was necessary to tread lightly, and to write in such a way that criticism would be hard to detect. Yet even if it were possible to write in such a way (a point that cannot be addressed here in full), the need to engage in such a form of writing – and the harms that come to those who do not succeed in concealment – highlights just how tenuous the situation is for a writer active under a ruler who, in Tacitus' words, embodies 'savagery' and did not accomplish 'anything except disrepute for themselves and for their victims glory'. The personality of the ruler trumps the impersonality of institutions in such a situation. The uncertainty of what could and could not be said, the possibility that even praise might be read as blame and criticism – these are the sorts of dilemmas that constrain expression, and that constitute the effects of a regime of censorship.

The Peace of Babylon (and What it Censors): St Augustine of Hippo's *City of God*

Miles Hollingworth

After the city or town comes the world, which the philosophers identify as the third level of human society. They begin with the household, progress to the city, and come finally to the world. And the world, like a gathering of waters, is all the more full of perils by reason of its greater size. First of all, the diversity of tongues now divides man from man. For if two men, each ignorant of the other's language, meet, and are compelled by some necessity not to pass on but to remain with one another, it is easier for dumb animals, even of different kinds, to associate together than these men, even though both are human beings. For when men cannot communicate their thoughts to each another, they are completely unable to associate with one another despite the similarity of their natures; and this is simply because of the diversity of tongues. So true is this that a man would more readily hold conversation with his dog than with another man who is a foreigner. It is true that the Imperial City has imposed on subject nations not only her yoke [iugum] but also her language, as a bond of peace and society, so that there should be no lack of interpreters but a great abundance of them. But how many great wars, what slaughter of men, what outpourings of human blood have been necessary to bring this about.[1]

In this essay I want to talk about the iconic 'censorship moment' involving Augustine and the late Christian Empire: namely, the well-known part he played in enlisting and combining the powers of Church and state in order to quell the Donatist schism in North Africa. Then I want to counterbalance some of its apparent features with my passage, above, from *City of God*, XIX, 7.

When Augustine succeeded Valerius to become Bishop of Hippo Regius, in 395 CE, the Roman North African Church was not as secure in its domains as one might have thought. It faced a formidable challenge from the schismatic

Donatist Church. In fact, the Donatist Church was the better represented, and certainly the more entrenched, in the rural dioceses that made up the largest part of the province of Africa Proconsularis. It considered itself to be the only Christian church worth that name, and employed radical means to keep itself apart from mainstream church life. Hippo was typical of the situation the Donatists inclined against, being a relatively prosperous harbour city, with a self-consciously Romanized outlook and a clergy which, as Peter Brown has shown, could constitute a 'new style of urban leadership'. In towns like Hippo, he notes,

> Bishops and clergy received immunities from taxes and from compulsory public services. In each city, the Christian clergy became the only group which expanded rapidly, at a time when the strain of empire had brought other civic institutions to a standstill. Bound by oath to 'their' bishop, a whole hierarchy of priests, deacons, and minor clergy formed an *ordo* in miniature, as subtly graded as any town council, and as tenaciously attached to its privileges.[2]

Donatism took its name from its de facto founder, Bishop Donatus (d. ca 365). As a theology, it wished to walk alone, believing itself to be the right side of a historical wrong that had invalidated the saving graces of the traditional African Church. The origins of what conspired to put Donatus and his movement outside the mainstream African Church went back to the Diocletianic persecutions of 303 and 304. These were among the last official persecutions of Christians in the Roman Empire; the practice ending altogether with the issuing of the Edict of Milan in 313. In Africa, the decree 'non licet esse Christianos' (it is not lawful to be a Christian) was enforced with particular severity by Imperial agents against a Christian community already well-adjusted to martyrdom. Augustine's own writings provide ample commentary on what he saw as the African propensity to veer from the universal solaces of Christianity into the age-old cabalisms of bloodline and magic, purity and reproach. Essentially, Augustine would accuse Donatism of portraying its bishops as ancestral figures – historically clean of stain, and on that basis, fit to be the appointed intercessors between their communities and God. So his point of view can be likened to the difference that a contemporary anthropologist might mark between a traditional religion and modern Christianity, which cannot support witchdoctors or theurgists because it operates at the level of the universal brotherhood of man – preaching the innovation of Christ as the one true intercessor for humanity-at-large, and abhorring the cultic elevation of any merely human priest.

Donatum donatistae pro Christo habent, 'The Donatists have it that Donatus is placed ahead of Christ.' This is how Augustine would sum up their schism in one of his sermons.[3] Under the Diocletianic persecutions, as under the earlier Valerianic persecutions, Christians had been required on pain of torture and death to sacrifice publicly to the old gods of the civic religion. Priests and bishops had been required to go the further step of handing over the Christian Scriptures. The conditions of North African Christianity seem to have allowed the latter act of 'handing over' (*traditio*) to gain a special infamy. By 347, there was a bishop – Donatus – claiming to be the legitimate primate of Carthage, and commanding a church led by clergy proclaimed to be untainted by any relationship, direct or indirect, to the *traditores*. The central tenet of Donatism was simple, as well as proudly Cyprianic. The only true, valid and efficacious Church in Africa was the Donatist Church, because only it could say that it had taken stringent enough measures to ensure the purity of the Christian sacraments. The key here was rebaptism and reconsecration: the Donatists insisted on the rebaptism of those Christians wishing to enter their ranks from the Roman Church as well as the reconsecration of churches and altars associated with the act of *traditio*. Such codes soon allowed them to imagine the rest of the Church outside them as weak and inconsistent – in fact, as spiritually ruined by the *traditores*, and no better than an institution co-opted into the secular world-at-large.

Donatus was succeeded by Parmenian as Donatist primate of Carthage, with Donatism thriving on its emotional energy to become far and away the dominant Church in North Africa. Indeed, it was only around the time of Augustine actually becoming Bishop of Hippo that the situation started to show signs of turning back in the Roman Church's favour. Parmenian had died sometime in 391 or 392, and this would allow Augustine to start zeroing in on the serious fault of Donatist theology that could 'place Donatus ahead of Christ'.

The apostles had taught that the germ of human sinfulness is the heart: fallen, and deceitful to itself. And furthermore, they had taught that it was in order to strive to correspond to this information that the Church on earth should make no claim to be anything other than the appointed destination of Divine aid. Priests should honour the pre-eminence of Christian truth by observing the proper *decorum* in their customs, spirituality and words, while Church buildings, and the worship within them, should follow the same *decorum* by being as beautifully and as mysteriously adorned as possible. In everything there should be this effort, so that future evangelization would be able to utilize the achievements and models of historical Christianity. But because of human pride (or the havoc that evil wreaks with self-love), these structural and symbolical features must not be allowed to assume any life of their own, lest they be abused. God works through them in Christ: and it is this through-working, impervious to nefarious meddling, which honours the good faith of believers, and guarantees the integrity of the sacraments they receive. Augustine would become particularly skilled at showing how it is the fact of predestination which gifts believers their final emancipation from the alternative, merely human contrivances for salvation, and their webs of envy and praise, suspicion and partiality.

St Peter put this instruction to the Church in his famous words: 'If any man speak, *let him speak* as the oracles of God; if any man minister, *let him do it* as of the ability which God giveth: that God in all things may be glorified through Jesus Christ'.[4] Nearly 400 years after him, it would be Augustine's turn to issue the same instruction and warning – but this time in language adapted to a Church about to win the ascendancy in Western Europe:

> The Church would never pray to persevere in the faith of Christ (not deceived nor overcome by the temptations of the world) unless it completely believed that the Lord has our heart in His power. And in His power in the sense that, whatever of good we are able to bring about, we bring about only because He has somehow worked in us the very will to do so. For if the Church were to ask these things from Him, but thinking that the same things are given to itself by itself, it would be praying prayers that were perfunctory rather than true – which be far from us![5]

The serious fault of Donatism, to Augustine, was its cruel insistence on pitching the Christian back from this wide open assurance into the merely human 'webs'. One of the Donatist bishops, Petilian of Constantine (d. ca. 419), was unambiguous in mocking the value of the heartfelt petition, supplanting it wholesale with the caste of the thoroughbred Donatist priest:

> If you pray to God, or utter supplication, it profits you absolutely nothing whatsoever. For while you have a blood-stained conscience, your feeble prayers are of no effect; because the Lord God regards purity of conscience more than the words of supplication, according to the saying of the Lord Christ, 'Not every one that says to me, Lord, Lord, shall enter into the kingdom of heaven; but he that does the will of my Father who is in heaven'.[Matt. 7.21].[6]

The question of *censorship* in relation to Augustine, Donatism and the history of political thought arises because the schism became something of a paradigm case for the recently Christianized empire. Emperor Constantine quickly took a dim view of it: and long after him, when Catholicism had won the whole of North Africa, the 'Donatist' label would live on as a byword for disunity and dissent from the Holy Roman Church, and a target for censorship and repression. The letters of Pope Gregory the Great (c. 540–604) contain many examples of him applying the label in this way, and indiscriminately, to continuing tensions in the African Church. The same would apply to the general Italian view of African clergymen. The papal *Liber diurnus* even preserves a point-blank note to bishops that they should be wary of welcoming Africans into ecclesiastical orders: '… as they frequently turn out to be Manichaeans or *rebaptizati* [Donatists]'.[7]

Augustine's historical-political role was to be the active force and personality in appealing to the Roman see *and* the Roman state against the Donatists. The exclusionary theology of the Donatists was clearly in defiance of the Roman Church's magisterium, while the preference of certain Donatists to violently harass Catholics in Augustine's district and elsewhere raised the problem to a question of political and social order. The Donatist clergy could boast many intellectuals to whom Augustine was happy to pay the highest respect, but its martyr-logic could also be a wild and simple creed, perfectly suited to the type of man looking for an excuse to hit back against the Roman state, its taxes and its highbrow city culture.

A desperate problem for Augustine became the bands of *Circumcelliones*, as they were called, who roamed the countryside, attacking and murdering Catholics and pursuing hit-and-run tactics against representative targets of the Imperial authorities. By Augustine's time, they were being especially malicious towards Donatist converts to the state religion – bishops and clergy as well as lay people. One plan to murder Augustine backfired only because his travelling party happened to take a wrong turn, avoiding an ambush. The *Circumcelliones* lived like outlaws, lurking around the shrines of Donatist martyrs and fanatically intent on the same glory for themselves. Their precise relationship to Church Donatism was as loose and opportunistic as one might expect. What they did was in its name, certainly; but modern scholarship is increasingly inclined to read their activities as a kind of culture war – a militant attempt to reassert African ethnicity against overwhelming processes of Latin colonialism.[8]

In other words, Augustine and Donatism have become a tantalizing early prototype of how the project of the Christian West tends to be written about by historians. Augustine, after initially recommending rational and diplomatic methods against the Donatists (because you should not force belief), felt constrained by the *Circumcelliones* in particular to call in the full force of the Imperial laws against heretics. This was from about 416 onwards. His reasoning for this became his controversial *Compelle intrare* argument.[9] The niceties of toleration are one thing, he wrote, but in a situation as partisan as the African Church, the Christian state apparatus becomes morally obliged to enforce unity and save souls:

> No one could deny that it is better for men to be led to the worship of God by teaching, rather than being driven to Him by fear of punishment or pain. But it is not automatic that because the former course produces the better men, those who cannot yield to it should be neglected. For many have been saved (as we have proven, and are daily proving by experience) by being first compelled by fear or pain: so that afterwards they have their chance to be influenced by teaching: and then at last to follow by action what they have learned through these words.[10]

So there is something of the knight crusader in Augustine's part, and something of Frantz Fanon in the Donatists' role. And I suspect that scholars will increasingly want to exploit this difference.

What I want to do here is no more than to turn to my quotation from *City of God*, XIX, 7, and suggest one or two ways in which it might give a worthwhile pause for thought. Augustine begins, as Aristotle does in the *Politics*, with a pathology of the polis – taken right down to the household, the 'first circle of human society'. This allows him to end, as Bernard Crick did in his classic work *In Defence of Politics* (also following Aristotle), with a justified politics of action. Crick said that it was differences between citizens within a sovereign territory, and a technologically advanced society, that produces politics as the response to those differences; in other words, to him, politics was ethical bargaining writ large. And freedom, the Western ideal of freedom, was its special discovery. He meant that politics should always be self-referencing the conditions which bring it into being. To forget these is to leave it vulnerable to the vanity that it can be about *ideas*: that is, ideas that hint of one true way of thinking and acting, or the modern menaces of ideology and dictatorship. A 'politics of action' always faces off against a politics of monism.[11]

Augustine gets to this same place by using the rather more radical example of wars and bloodshed to denote the concept of difference in human affairs. Nations – if I may use an anachronism for late antiquity – wage wars; and if hostile foreigners cannot be found, then social and civil wars are soon cooked up. Such is the way with human nature and the *libido dominandi*. Political theorists have often been delighted to discover this modern, almost postmodern, Augustine, whose vision of political justice can be so secular.

So what, then, of the Augustine of Donatism, and his Christian statesman who censors in the name of God and truth? Where do the two interact?

The answer comes in the middle bit of my quotation: that delightful image of the man more able to converse with his dog than with a stranger from another land, speaking a foreign tongue. Augustine is not being facetious with this; he is using all his rhetor's flair to say that the whole business of politics really can be so simple! We tend to think of the Christian Roman Empire, and Augustinianism, as representing one, theocratic version of truth in society – and then democracy and moral pluralism as a competing, more enlightened version. This explains why we can attribute such high virtue to the 'peace of Babylon', and the rational basis for securing temporal peace in the science and history of human behaviour; and then turn around and be appalled when its method produces a Machiavelli. Or when – as happens earlier in the *City of God* – Augustine uses the same science and history to make his notorious comparison between an empire and a robber band.[12]

Augustine appears to be freer than us. He is prepared to lampoon politics all the way to its ignoble beginnings in the fall of man, and pride. He doesn't need to take a side, or produce a theory of politics that is morally superior to all other such theories on all points. Politics is always *realpolitik* for him. Its only reasonable justification is peace. A Christian statesman is a bonus situation, and a free ball and a free hit. So the Church should make the most of it, and seize an opportunity to save more souls. This is what Augustine did in the end with the Donatists: *compelle intrare*.

As for the peace of Babylon, we should not be overly beguiled by it. For it is itself a form of censorship, though hardly noticed, as its proscriptions are the very conditions of life itself, from language on up. It is a yoke [*iugum*], beneath which we must all pass.[13] All political theories worth their salt prove in some way to be true to this fact. Derived from this fact, also, is Augustine's conclusion that there is no superior political truth, to rule all the others. The most secular and scientific and peaceful politics possible will prove what the first three books of Genesis were saying all along. The truest and most just and happy politics possible will not really be politics at all but the City of God in Heaven – which of course is what a close reading of the *City of God* shows Augustine to have been arguing all along.

The Regulation of Language in Medieval Theology: The *Summa Theologica* of St Thomas Aquinas

Debora Shuger

Let us next discuss verbal injuries [iniuria verborum] occurring outside a judicial context. ... Words, if considered with respect to their essence – that is, as audible sounds – injure no one, except perhaps by jarring of the ear, as when a person speaks too loudly. But, considered as signs conveying something to the knowledge of others, they may do many kinds of harm – one such being the harm done to the detriment of a person's honour or the respect due to him from others. ... As stated above, words are not injurious to others as sounds but as signs, and their signification depends on the speaker's inward intention. ... If by his words the speaker intends to dishonour another person ... this is no less a mortal sin than theft or robbery, since a person does not love his honour any less than his possessions.[1]

The above passage from the *Summa Theologica* of Thomas Aquinas (1225–1274) comes from the opening of the *Summa*'s quite lengthy discussion of wrongful language, or what St Thomas terms *iniuria verborum*. The term points to the source and conceptual underpinning for Aquinas' theological ethics of discourse: namely, the Roman law *de iniuriis et famosis libellis*, which treats wrongful language as battery, no less harmful – and therefore no less impermissible – than hurling sticks or stones.[2] Aquinas may or may not have consulted Justinian's *Digest*; the *Summa* draws principally on the corpus of Christian moral theology, but this corpus had itself long borne the impress of Roman law. As early as the eighth century, one finds the sins of the tongue (*peccati linguae*) regularly construed as *iniuria* or verbal battery: as, that is, attacks on persons, wounding their honour, good name and communal standing, rather than as challenges to beliefs, values, truths or regimes. Medieval theologians were not, of course, indifferent to these, but they did not treat such offences as sins of the tongue *per se*.

This *iniuria* model of verbal transgression, moreover, shaped not only the Christian ethics of language, but also, to varying degrees, its legal regulation. The canon law chapter on *iniuria* begins, 'He who has composed material attacking another's good name [*fama*] either in writing or by verbal insult and cannot substantiate the allegations, let him be whipped.'[3] In England, from the accession of Elizabeth in 1558 to the Interregnum, *iniuria* provided the model and matrix for the legal regulation of language – including, but not confined to, the censorship of print. Francis Bacon's overview of England's legal system groups verbal transgression together with beating, wounding and maiming; and for Bacon the protection of people's 'good names' from such attacks constitutes one of the three principal ends of the common law.[4] Sir Edward Coke's report *De libellis famosis* (1607), the foundational text for the common-law criminal action of scandalous libel (the sole common-law language crime[5]), echoes the *Codex* both in its title and in its construal of the offence as violence against persons, analogous, if signed – to use Coke's own comparisons – to killing a man in a duel; or, if anonymous, to poisoning him in secret.[6]

Some territories of the Holy Roman Empire likewise construed verbal transgression according to the same *iniuria* model that St Thomas and Elizabethan England alike inherited from Roman jurisprudence. However, canon law and the legal systems of most continental states, Catholic and Protestant (including England prior to 1558), adopt a different sector of Roman law as the dominant framework for the regulation of language – spoken, manuscript and print: namely, the heresy legislation that opens the *Codex*. Heresy law provided the basis for most continental systems of press censorship, which principally targeted misliked ideas: mostly, but not exclusively, religious ones. The best-known and most important of such systems was, of course, the Roman Church's *Index* of forbidden books, first promulgated in 1559, and regularly updated thereafter. Over 90 per cent of its hundreds of banned volumes are Latin theological tomes, although the *Index* also prohibited occultist and magical texts, scientific or philosophical works that contravened Church teachings, and writings deemed likely to promote immorality.[7] Protestant states did not, as a rule, draw up lists of banned books, but those disallowed in Calvin's Geneva fall into much the same categories, and were sometimes the same books (e.g., Rabelais' *Pantagruel*). This heresy-based model, in turn, stands behind the First Amendment's linking of freedom of speech and the press with the free exercise of religion, as it likewise stands behind the still-current view of censorship as an instrument of institutional power for suppressing critique and dissent, as also behind the still-current association of a free press with the liberty of individuals to doubt, question, argue and believe according to their own best lights. Censorship based on heresy law disallows such liberties; censorship based on *iniuria* law simply ignores them, since its concern lies not with the liberty-rights of speakers but with the dignity-rights of those spoken about.

Yet, although the principles that inform Aquinas' discussion of the *peccati linguae* also underwrite censorship law in England and elsewhere, the *Summa* itself deals with the morality of language, not its legislation. The *quaestiones* on wrongful language, from which the passage quoted above has been taken, identify four principal sins: affront (*contumelia*), defamation (*detractio*), tale-bearing (*susurratio*) and taunting (*derisio*).[8] These Aquinas distinguishes according to a double set of interlaced criteria. The first concerns the specific good that is threatened with harm by another's words, for 'a sin against one's neighbour is the more grave according to the gravity of the harm it inflicts, and the harm is so much the greater according to the greatness of the good which it takes away' (2.2.74.2). The goods targeted by the several modes of verbal *iniuria* are, respectively, honour, reputation or good name (*fama*), friendship and what Aquinas terms the 'glory of a good conscience', by which he means something close to what we would call a sense of inner self-worth.

The second criterion concerns the nature of the speech act *qua* social performance, with the central distinction being between overt and covert modes (the same distinction Coke makes in *De libellis famosis*). Affronts and taunts are, Aquinas observes, overt attacks, their in-your-face mode being inseparable from their power to hurt, since the very fact of the attack's overtness marks its object as weak, contemptible, not to be feared. Affronts, which Aquinas thinks are usually motivated by anger and thirst for revenge, seek to dishonour their target by the verbal equivalent of a slap in the face. Taunting, by contrast, is more like pinching someone's bottom, the point being to undermine the repose of conscience that comes from a sense of one's own worth and dignity. Aquinas judges such mockery in many cases a worse sin than affront since to deride someone implies a more utter contempt than the angry hurling of an insult.

Hate speech – that is, offensive reference to another's race, ethnicity or sexual orientation – is probably the most familiar modern species of Thomistic *contumelia*. Thomas, however, offers no paradigmatic examples of affront, nor for any of the other *peccati linguae*, a vagueness consistent with his double focus on the intention of the speaker and the harm done to the victim, rather than on the content of the words themselves. Indeed, he explicitly notes the irrelevance of semantic content to what he considers the gravest verbal wrong: namely, tale-bearing, or passing along information, whether true or false, to a person's friends for the purpose of destroying that friendship. The information, he points out, can be of itself innocuous – as, for example, the fact that B hosted a lovely dinner party last night – and yet, if told to a friend whom B did not invite, capable of doing grave mischief; and if told with malicious intent, a grave sin. And since friendships are, in Aquinas' view, of more value than honour, tale-bearing is a greater sin than affront.

Although he never spells out the relationship between intent and harm, Aquinas seems generally to regard them as two sides of the same coin: so the harm done by hate speech results as much, if not more, from the hate motivating the words as from their propositional content. Yet if he regards the harm caused by words as generally inseparable from the intent of the speaker, his *iniuria* framework ends up producing a more complicated picture, one that recognizes the possibility of culpable harm even in the absence of malicious intent, since a thoughtless sneer or jibe, although not meant cruelly, remains sinful in the same way and to the same degree as if one were 'carelessly to injure grievously another by striking him in fun' (2.2.72.2). One is responsible for the damage resulting from one's own careless indifference to the likely effect of one's conduct on others.

Tale-bearing and defamation are both, for Aquinas, covert modes of *iniuria*. As such, they tend to target superiors – those whose power one fears – usually out of envy, but whereas the former seeks to harm another by destroying the bonds of friendship, the latter attacks another's good name, typically by spreading malicious gossip that impugns the other's moral character. These reports may in point of fact, Aquinas adds, be lies, although it is not their untruth that makes them defamatory, but rather the intentional infliction of harm: one can, he thus comments, defame a person not only by outright lies, but also by making his faults seem greater than they are, by ascribing his good actions to discreditable motives, or by revealing something unknown (*occultum*) about him.

In current US law, by contrast, and in the historic common law, a claim that can be proven true is, *eo ipso*, not defamatory. Yet Aquinas' subtypes of true (or at least 'truthy') defamation do bear a family resemblance to the modern US dignitary torts of 'false light' and public disclosure of private facts. American jurisprudence usually ascribes both to Louis Brandeis and Samuel Warren's seminal 1890 article, 'The Right to Privacy'.[9] However, the article itself makes clear its own debt to the Roman law of *iniuria*. The overlap with Aquinas is not, that is to say, fortuitous.

The portion of the *Summa* dealing specifically with the *peccati linguae*, the sins of the tongue, gives the public disclosure of private facts only the single brief mention noted above, perhaps because the issue had already been treated in an earlier *quaestio* asking what a private individual (as opposed to, for example, an on-duty police officer) should do if he somehow learns of another's otherwise-secret trespass. If the offence poses a danger to third parties, Aquinas concludes, one must report the matter to the relevant authorities; but if it does not, one's principal concern should be for 'the amendment of the transgressor', and this concern 'pertains to charity', not justice. As a private person, that is, one has a charitable obligation to seek the transgressor's good but no legal or moral duty to enforce public justice (2.2.33.1). Moreover, he adds, if one is truly acting for the sake of the transgressor, one must try to deal with the matter in private, allowing the other to save face, given that spoiling someone's reputation by exposing his shameful secret is more likely to breed hate than repentance (2.2.33.7). In what follows, this construal of privacy as a dictate of charity slips towards something close to a privacy right: a right, that is, not to have one's hidden failings revealed even to the relevant authorities until after quiet warnings and counsel have been attempted and rebuffed. Thus if, during the visitation of a cathedral chapter or monastic community, a superior asks what you know concerning the secret wrongdoings of the other members of the community, the query should be ignored, since 'a prelate is not to be obeyed contrary to a divine precept'. But for a prelate to order a member of the community 'to say what he knows about things needing correction [*quod quis sciverit corrigendum*]' would violate Christ's rule that private admonition must precede public denunciation. Hence such an order 'should not be obeyed; for a prelate is not the judge of secret things [*occulta*], but only God alone, wherefore he has no power to command anything respecting secret matters', unless some evidence of them has already come to light, so that they are no longer, properly speaking, secret (2.2.33.7).

As with virtually every aspect of St Thomas' ethics of utterance, his grounding of privacy rights in the precepts of charity and his treating as defamation the public disclosure of another's private information remained axioms of both Protestant and Catholic moral teaching through the early modern period. So in a sermon against defamation (*Sermo contra vitium detractionis*) Luther observes that Moses forbids revealing another's 'sin or weakness'; that is to say, 'the truth [of the allegation] does not excuse it', but rather 'making public something true but previously hidden' is no less defamation than 'putting out something false', for how can 'you love your neighbour as yourself' if 'you think his failings … should be exposed, and yours kept quiet?'[10] A century later, the redoubtable puritan, William Ames, similarly argues that whoever, 'without just cause … revealeth a true sin of another man's, which otherwise would have been concealed … is a detractor', since such publication 'is nothing else but a spoiling the man's reputation to the intent to hurt him'.[11]

The medieval ethical principles regarding permissible and impermissible utterance, themselves adopted from Roman *iniuria* law, shaped the customary and, particularly in early modern England, the legal regulation of language. They also inform current civility norms (malicious gossip and taunting are still frowned upon), even retaining some legal bite: the dignitary torts and libel law being obvious US examples. Yet at least in America the moral and legal force-field of the *iniuria* model has shrunk to a very small potato. What laws there are do not, in any meaningful sense, extend to public persons, so that anyone considered newsworthy loses most privacy and dignitary rights. Moreover, even for private persons, laws regulating speech (except, sometimes, hate speech) tend to get trumped by the pervasive cultural assumption that all regulation of language is to be understood as the endeavour of those in power to suppress dangerous truths.

That US law, like the laws of most modern democracies, gives almost no protection to honour, *fama*, friendship, or the glory of a good conscience may in truth be a good thing. However, as the recent episodes of fatal cyber-shaming drive home, the erosion of traditional civility norms is not. Yet our own cultural and legal framework, with its heavy weighting of speakers' liberty-rights and the public's right to know, makes it hard for us to defend, or even conceive of, an ethical duty to tell something other than the whole truth, or even just other than the truth. St Thomas' treatment of the *peccati linguae* helps make intelligible an earlier framework, one not structured in opposition to modern freedoms of expression and information but by a different set of *positive* considerations, and grounded on the moral foundations of Roman law and Christian theology: that is to say, on the moral foundations of Western civilization.

William of Ockham on Ecclesiastical Censorship

Takashi Shogimen

Disciple *What if someone were to defend a heresy before the pope and were to say that he thinks that it is consistent with catholic faith?*

Master *They say that if he were to defend unknowingly a heresy a thousand times, even before the pope, with an explicit or tacit declaration that he is ready to be corrected when he learns that his opinion conflicts with catholic faith, he should not be judged a heretic unless he were proved to be a heretic by other legitimate proofs because, just as it is licit for him to defend an erroneous opinion unknowingly in this way the first time, so it is licit a second time and a third, and always until it has been clearly proved to him that his opinion should be reckoned among the heresies.[1]*

William of Ockham (c.1285–1347), a Franciscan theologian and philosopher, is widely known as one of the giants of late medieval scholasticism. His academic career at Oxford was aborted in 1324 when he was summoned by the papacy in Avignon, southern France. He was to be subjected to an investigation into the alleged heresy of his academic writings. The Roman Church's theological investigation into academics was nothing new. Since Stephen Tempier, the bishop of Paris, condemned 219 propositions in philosophy and theology on 7 March 1277, the Church's suppression of false teachings in the universities had been widespread in Paris and Oxford. After four years of investigation, Ockham escaped from condemnation. During his sojourn in Avignon, Ockham was requested by Michael of Cesena, the Minister General of the Franciscan Order, to examine Pope John XXII's bulls, which denounced the Franciscan ideals of evangelical poverty. After scrutinizing the bulls, Ockham came to a realization that in rejecting the orthodoxy of Franciscan poverty, the Pope had fallen into heresy. The Franciscan doctrine of evangelical poverty had been officially declared to be orthodox by Pope Nicholas III in 1279; therefore, Pope John XXII effectively revoked his predecessor's doctrinal decision, which was to Ockham nothing but a heretical error. In 1328 Ockham departed from Avignon along with a few Franciscan comrades in order to seek protection from Ludwig of Bavaria, the claimant of the imperial throne who was in a political conflict with the papacy. Based in Munich in the following two decades until his death in 1347, Ockham abandoned his academic career and devoted himself to writing a number of anti-papal polemical writings, in which students of medieval intellectual history find his political thought.

Ockham's polemical activities after 1328 were therefore motivated by the question of papal heresy. What if the pope falls into heresy? What action can – and indeed should – a Christian believer who knows that the pope is a heretic take? What if a heretical pope demands that Christians who are convinced of their orthodoxy renounce their faith and subscribe to a heretical belief? Is it justifiable for an orthodox believer to dissent from a heretical pope and if so how? Papal heresy had previously been a hypothetical problem for medieval theologians and canonists. Such an ecclesiastical nightmare, however, was Ockham's reality. In response to this question Ockham wrote *The Dialogue (Dialogus)*, a gigantic polemical work on the problems of heresy with special reference to papal heresy.

The work, which was left unfinished by the author, takes the form of a hypothetical conversation between the 'Master' and his 'Disciple'. One of its characteristics is that the 'Master', in response to the questions posed by the 'Disciple', presents a wide range of views without identifying their sources or showing which view should be the final word on the issue in question; thus, Ockham deliberately concealed the authors of all the views, including his own, because he wished the readers to derive their own conclusion without being influenced by knowledge of the authorship of each opinion.

This preference for 'blind refereeing' has echoes in Ockham's theory of heresy itself. For him, heresy was the deliberate contradiction of the correct definition of Catholic truth. This notion may appear a truism; however, Ockham maintained that the act of defining Catholic truths is twofold. One way could be labelled authoritative definition, which is the assertion concerning Catholic truths made by the official authority of popes and councils. The other may be described as cognitive definition, which is an assertion made through academic deliberation. Ockham did not think that an assertion concerning Catholic truth was true simply because it was so declared by official authority; its truth must be established 'cognitively' by means of theological scrutiny. Likewise, heresy is for Ockham not what ecclesiastical authority declares to be heretical. A proposition should be judged heretical only insofar as it is so defined cognitively through theological investigation and deliberation. Ockham defined heresy not in terms of who declared it to be heresy but in terms of what it is (I, i, 1; I, ii, 5).

This reconceptualization of heresy also led to a redefinition of heretics. In the medieval theological and canonist tradition, the hallmark of heretics had long been considered to be pertinacity: heretics were not those who simply made a doctrinal error but rather those who erred against Catholic truths pertinaciously. How was one judged pertinacious? It was by repeated refusal to submit oneself to ecclesiastical correction. Hence, heretics had traditionally been defined as those who repeatedly refused to accept the official teaching of ecclesiastical authority.[2] Effectively, then, pertinacity was persistent disobedience to ecclesiastical authority.

Ockham questioned the tacit assumption that doctrinal correction by ecclesiastical authority was theologically correct; if ecclesiastical correction was cognitively wrong, disobedience to such correction may be grounded in orthodox faith. Ockham therefore redefined heretics as those who failed deliberately or knowingly to assent to a theologically correct understanding of doctrinal texts.[3] The idea of cognitive, not authoritative, definition replaced, as the central characteristic of heretics, disobedience from ecclesiastical authority with the idea of deliberate dissent from theologically true propositions concerning Catholic truths.

The quotation in the opening of this chapter should be understood in light of Ockham's reconceptualization of heresy. In the quotation he vindicates the legitimacy of resistance to papal correction on the grounds of the corrected individual's conviction that he or she is faithful to the orthodox faith. Such a position would have been impossible without rejecting the 'mere' official authority of doctrinal definitions, which may not be theologically informed. However, Ockham's justification of radical dissent has often invited the objection of modern commentators: the conviction that an individual's position is orthodox does not necessarily warrant that he or she is *really* orthodox theologically. How is it possible to ascertain that a believer's conviction is actually anchored in orthodox faith rather than mere confusion, ignorance or self-deception? Is it not that Ockham has simply fallen into 'a morass of total subjectivity'?[4] Ockham's cognitive perspective to orthodoxy and heresy raises an epistemological question about the certitude of doctrinal knowledge. In order to shed light on this conundrum, the above quotation requires further explication from three perspectives: (1) the legitimacy of doctrinal demonstration; (2) Ockham's idea of explicit faith; and (3) the authority of individual conscience.

In the situation where a Christian believer is subject to doctrinal correction by a superior such as a pope, the legitimacy of the correction was conventionally not questioned as long as it came from the holder of an ecclesiastical office. This traditional view was predicated on the tacit assumption that doctrinal correction by an ecclesiastical authority is always theologically correct. Ockham by contrast started from the assumption that doctrinal correction by an ecclesiastical official is not always correctly informed. Thus Ockham attributed the legitimacy of correction not to the corrector's authority but to the correct knowledge that informs the act of correction (I, iv, 13). An important implication of this is that the relationship between the corrector and the corrected is reconfigured. According to the traditional view which assumes the cognitive correctness of official correction, the discourse on doctrinal correction was essentially about the duty of the corrected to obey ecclesiastical authority. Ockham's cognitive perspective by contrast attributed to the corrector the duty of demonstrating that his correction is correctly informed theologically. Thus doctrinal censorship cannot claim to be binding simply because it is official; it must be based on an evident demonstration that it is theologically correct. Hence Ockham insisted that the corrected is not obliged to submit to correction unless it is manifestly demonstrated that he or she is in error.

This argument, however, was not so anarchic as to allow ordinary believers to believe whatever they wanted to believe. Ockham's other important assumption is that the members of the Christian community share a cognitive commonality in the understanding of Catholic truths, which constitutes orthodox faith. Hence, every believer, regardless of educational or social background, must believe some propositions that are manifestly true for each and every Christian. One cannot, for example, deny the proposition that 'Christ was crucified' without becoming a heretic because everyone knows the proposition and its correct meaning. Ockham called the Catholic truths which a Christian believer must know 'explicit faith'. The content of Ockham's 'explicit faith' is not the same for every member of the Christian community, however. The number of the propositions that constitute 'explicit faith' is commensurate with the status one occupies within the ecclesiastical order. Hence, the higher the position one occupies in the hierarchy, the greater number of catholic truths one must know. So ordinary believers are only obliged to know a few basic facts, whereas popes and bishops must know minute details included in the Bible (I, vii, 18).[5]

This idea of 'explicit faith' is crucial for understanding Ockham's theory of heresy. I explained earlier that Ockham defined heresy as deliberate failure to assent to the true understanding of doctrinal texts. The criterion by which to ascertain heresy is for Ockham the deliberateness of rejecting a true proposition of Christian faith. The content of 'explicit faith' determines the amount of knowledge one is required and therefore assumed to have, and rejecting a proposition that is included in the explicit faith for the individual concerned would be judged deliberate because the rejected proposition is presumed to be known to him or her. The pope, who is assumed to have a full knowledge of doctrinal sources, therefore can hardly reject true doctrinal propositions without being deliberate, while ordinary believers, who only need to know a few things about Christian faith, may be likely to do so unknowingly. This argument replaces the traditional hierarchy of authority with a new hierarchy of duty of knowing explicit faith. Ockham was thereby cautioning high ecclesiastics against pronouncing doctrinal decisions hastily without careful theological deliberation.

The idea of 'explicit faith' helps Ockham to vindicate a believer who insists on an error without realizing it is an error if that error does not concern 'explicit faith'; thus he or she is insisting on the error unknowingly. Then, are Christian believers bound to know errors that are condemned explicitly as heresies? For example, if Christian believers commit an error that is condemned explicitly as heresy, are they bound to withdraw the error immediately regardless of the legitimacy of the correction they are subject to? Ockham's response to this question is unequivocal: even heretical errors that are condemned explicitly do not need to be withdrawn immediately until it is manifestly shown to the holder of the errors that they are explicitly condemned (I, iv, 15). In response to this issue, Ockham also appealed to the idea of conscience: as long as individuals do not know that they are committing an error they do not have to revoke the error lest they should tell a lie contrary to their conscience.[6] Here Ockham did not claim that following the dictate of conscience was always right. Rather he maintained that acting contrary to conscience was always wrong. This idea of the negative authority of conscience can be found in the work of Thomas Aquinas; however, Aquinas did not extrapolate it to the ecclesiological discourse on an inferior's dissent from a superior. Ockham's application of that ethical principle to ecclesiology meant that the decision to obey the command of a superior must not bypass conscience; that is, obedience contrary to conscience is never virtuous. But Ockham did not say that dissent dictated by conscience was always right. So what is the moral justification of dissent?

Once again Ockham addressed the issue of deliberateness in ignorance. He did not expect that ordinary believers have a full knowledge of heresies condemned explicitly by the Roman Church. That is why Ockham's account of ignorance about condemned heresies revolves around the cases where a believer refuses to revoke his or her (real) heresy *unknowingly*. When Ockham vindicated the dissent of an erroneously informed believer, he had in mind specifically the case of 'invincibly' erroneous conscience: conscience the dictate of which was erroneous in the matters that are beyond the presumed capacity of the person in question. Precisely because the heretical proposition in question was not included in what that person was obliged – and therefore presumed – to know, he or she is merely following the dictate of conscience, without realizing it is in error. Coupled with Ockham's idea of the legitimacy of doctrinal correction, which asserts that the burden of proof lies with the corrector, therefore, he could conclude that it was morally justifiable for a Christian 'to defend unknowingly a heresy a thousand times' (I, iv, 20).

In writing about ecclesiastical censorship Ockham was seriously concerned about the preservation of orthodox faith, which was the common good of medieval Latin Christendom, especially in relation to the potential danger that high ecclesiastics such as popes and bishops might fall into heresy. Ockham's theory of heresy entails a number of ideas that safeguard individual orthodox believers from the official imposition of heretical beliefs. But he did not reject the possibility that Christendom might be dominated by heretics under the sway of a heretical pope. The 'true' Church as the congregation of orthodox believers, Ockham famously said, might reduce to a few or even to one individual, possibly a woman or an infant (I, v, 1–3, 7, 11, 25, 32, 34). In stating this, presumably Ockham was writing about himself and his fellow Franciscans who disobeyed the pope. Admittedly the defenders of true faith (as the Franciscans considered themselves to be) were isolated and marginalized.

Ockham problematized this situation by addressing the issue of the duties of other Christians who witnessed the dispute between ecclesiastical authority and dissident individuals. One such duty, Ockham wrote, is entailed by the fact that those who knew that some Christians of orthodox faith were attacked by a heretical pope and said nothing would be the pope's 'accomplice in crime':

> he who does not defend, when he can, those who oppose the pope for his heretical wickedness, provides an opportunity for persecution or disturbance or harm, because if he offered defence, as he could, persecution or disturbance or harm done or to be done would be excluded. Therefore this person in failing to defend

papal opponents appears or is known to have inflicted the damage described. But no one must inflict persecution or disturbance or harm on opponents of the pope who impute heretical wickedness to the latter before it shall have been established that they acted with malice. Therefore everyone who can is obligated to defend them. (I, vi, 50)

Ockham argued thus in light of the Ciceronian idea of negative injustice: 'The man who does not defend someone, or obstruct the injustice when he can, is at fault just as if he had abandoned his parents or his friends or his country'.[7] Ockham and his fellow Franciscans in Munich hardly found any Christians who stood against the pope in their defence.

In the lamentable dearth of support from other Christians, Ockham discerned another theoretical point: dissenting voices must be heard. Ockham wrote in later years to his Christian audience:

The anguish I feel is the greater because you do not take the trouble to inquire with careful attention how much such tyranny wickedly usurped over you is contrary to God's honour, dangerous to the Catholic faith, and opposed to the rights and liberties given to you by God and nature; *and worse, you reject, hinder, and condemn those who wish to inform you of the truth.*[8]

In the *Dialogue* he had already contended that one of the duties of other Christians who witnessed believers dissenting from papal authority was to listen to the dissenting believers, especially if they were prudent and reputable individuals and their claims concerned the common good such as the preservation of orthodox faith (I, vii, 9). Thus Christian believers bear the duty not only to profess their correctly understood faith publicly but also to listen to dissenting voices.

In arguing so, Ockham conceptualized the Christian community as a public forum in which individuals write, speak, read and listen to one another, thus sharing the common correct understanding of Christian faith and discussing and scrutinizing the ambiguous meaning of doctrinal sources. Does this vision of the Christian community entail any defence of freedom of speech? The freedom Ockham envisaged was enshrined in an environment where individuals are able to subscribe to and defend true Christian faith voluntarily, thereby realizing a virtuous life. Volitional freedom was the *sine qua non* for an individual's pursuit of the moral life. Meanwhile, Ockham also assumed a cognitive commonality of understanding for basic elements of the Christian faith: any rational individuals with the capability of understanding doctrinal sources should be able to grasp the correct meaning of plain biblical propositions such as 'Christ was crucified'.

To be sure, an ordinary believer's duty of knowing 'explicit faith' is minimal; however, the fact remains that a believer must know some things about the Christian faith in a way that everyone else in the Christian community does; otherwise, he or she will be judged heretical. Hence if anything may deserve to be categorized as 'freedom of speech' in Ockham's theory of heresy, it is his vindication of free deliberation concerning Catholic truths which do *not* belong to 'explicit faith'. The papal declaration of an understanding of ambiguous doctrinal texts without solid theological foundations would, despite the 'official' nature of such a doctrinal pronouncement, force Christians to accept that understanding blindly, thereby depriving them of freedom that enables them to pursue a moral life. Ockham's vindication of freedom of speech was thus anchored in his desire to defend every Christian's possibility of realizing a virtuous life.

'Whether to Confiscate, Burn and Destroy All Jewish Books': Johannes Reuchlin and the Jewish Book Controversy

David H. Price

In matters pertaining to their faith, Jews are subject only to themselves and to no other judges. A Christian should not pass judgment on their faith … For they are not members of the Christian church and, therefore, their faith is of no concern to us. St Paul tells us this, when he writes: 'For what concern is it of mine to judge people who are outside the church?'… And, therefore, let this be our conclusion concerning the Talmud: it should be neither suppressed nor burned.[1]

In 1510, these words – and others like them in defence of preserving all types of Jewish literature – were stunning. Their author, Johannes Reuchlin, had been appointed to a special imperial commission in the confident expectation that he would condemn Jewish writings, thereby creating a theological and legal foundation for a cultural genocide: a campaign to confiscate and destroy all Jewish books in the Holy Roman Empire with the sole exception of the Bible in Hebrew. Instead of a potted endorsement of the Jewish book ban, the commission received a substantial work, grounded in sophisticated Hebrew scholarship and expert jurisprudence, which defended the legal rights of Jews to own and use their books.[2]

Reuchlin's *Recommendation* sent a powerful anti-Jewish campaign in the Holy Roman Empire into a tailspin just when complete suppression of Judaism in the empire appeared for the first time to be within reach. Moreover, the defence sent shock waves around much of Europe after Reuchlin published it in response to the anti-Jewish campaign's very public efforts to discredit him. Jacob Hoogstraeten, a man of several powerful offices (papal inquisitor, Dominican prior and professor of theology at Cologne), spoke for many when he contended that Reuchlin's portrayal of Judaism was without precedent, that he was the first and only Christian scholar to acknowledge integrity in the degenerate religion, and, even worse, that he was empowering Jews to blaspheme Jesus and the Christian faith.

The sweeping campaign against Jewish writing was also without precedent. On 19 August 1509, Emperor Maximilian I had handed down a death sentence for Jewish books in a document called the Padua Mandate. After it was vigorously contested by the Jewish community of Frankfurt and the city council of Frankfurt, the mandate was revised on 10 November 1509 (Roveredo Mandate) to place confiscation and destruction of Jewish books under the control of the Elector Archbishop of Mainz. He, in turn, delegated implementation of the Jewish book ban to Johannes Pfefferkorn, a convert from Judaism (and author of rabidly anti-Semitic pamphlets), and Hermann Ortlieb, professor of theology at the University of Mainz. Immediately, major confiscations ensued in Frankfurt am Main, Worms and five other Rhineland communities. The seizures in Frankfurt alone netted around 1,500 Hebrew books.

Then, in May 1510, Maximilian temporarily suspended the book pogrom in return for major fiscal concessions from a group of Frankfurt Jews. On 6 July 1510 (Füssen Mandate), the emperor initiated the new strategy that the book confiscations would be implemented if deemed theologically and legally warranted by four theology faculties (at Cologne, Erfurt, Heidelberg and Mainz) and by three individual scholars (Victor of Carben, Jacob Hochstraeten and Reuchlin). All were asked 'whether destroying the books that the Jews use … would please God and benefit Christianity' (20), and the answers were enthusiastically affirmative with the exception of Reuchlin's *Recommendation*.

Reuchlin's defence carried enormous weight for several reasons. Reuchlin was one of the most respected scholars in Northern Europe, arguably the only northern humanist before Erasmus to have an impact on more advanced Italian scholarship. He is widely credited as having been the first to introduce Greek studies to Germany and he is still celebrated as the founder of Christian Hebrew studies, author of the first Hebrew grammar and lexicon for Christians (1506). He was the only Christian scholar capable of commenting comprehensively on the entire corpus of Jewish writing, a feat he accomplished with masterful concision in the *Recommendation*. Hebrew scholarship was a powerful credential, but equally significant was Reuchlin's status as a legal authority. A renowned lawyer, with a doctorate in jurisprudence from the University of Tübingen, in 1510 he was serving as judge on one of the most significant constitutional benches in the Holy Roman Empire, the Court for the Swabian League. Ironically, Reuchlin had an additional credential that is now typically overlooked. In 1505, he published an anti-Jewish pamphlet, and the anti-Jewish campaign had no reason to suspect that his views had undergone such a dramatic shift.

In the *Recommendation*, Reuchlin acknowledged that book censorship was required by ecclesiastical and imperial law codes under certain conditions. Even so, he objected in principle to the destruction of Jewish books because study of Jewish scholarship and theology would bear fundamental benefits to Christianity. This applied to the Talmud, Bible commentaries, Kabbalistic works and, above all, the Masoretic text of the Tanakh. In passing, Reuchlin even asserted the desirability of preserving the Qur'an for scholarly and political purposes. He also charged that the intent of the censorship mandate was insidious, as is so often the case with book banning. Going beyond enforcement of blasphemy laws, the real goal was eradication of Judaism.

Loss of cultural knowledge and destroying Judaism were large issues, but Reuchlin also argued the case more narrowly from the perspective of specific Jewish legal rights. He contended, quite controversially, that as 'fellow citizens' ('concives' or 'Mitbürger') Jews enjoyed protection under imperial and ecclesiastical law from unwarranted seizure of property, in this case, from confiscation of books. Though vilified for it, Reuchlin would never retreat from this position as the foundation of his defence. In 1513, he published the following statement: 'I understand that my opponents are vexed because I said that Jews are our fellow citizens. Now I want their anger to rage even hotter, so that their guts burst, when I say that the Jews are our brothers.'[3]

Yet, even if Jews enjoyed the right to own such things as religious books, those books would still be subject to state censorship if they were libellous, blasphemous, or heretical. This was the crux of the matter and this meant that the analysis of the evidence – the entire corpus of Jewish writing – would be decisive. The sweeping charge that all of rabbinic Judaism was heretical was exceedingly perilous because, if sustained, it would outlaw the entire Jewish tradition as it then existed. Consequently, Reuchlin refuted the allegation of heresy on the basis of the history of legal toleration of Judaism, specifically on recognized precedents in imperial and ecclesiastical law that Jews, being outside the Christian faith, 'are not heretics' (33, Reuchlin quoting Gratian's *Decretum*). The firmness of this stance is notable because numerous anti-Semitic agitators, beginning with the burning of the Talmud in Paris in 1240, had formulated convoluted accusations that rabbinic Judaism was a perversion of biblical Judaism and should therefore be subject to heresy prosecution under Christian law.[4]

Allegations of libel and blasphemy, couched in viciously anti-Jewish rhetoric, were designed to inflame Christian hatred of Jews. Claims that Jews denied the veracity of the Christian faith and, moreover, cursed Jesus and Mary in their liturgies and prayed for the general demise of Christianity had been depicted in lurid detail by such figures as Petrus Nigri and Johannes Pfefferkorn in order to consolidate broad support for an end to legal toleration of Judaism.

Taking the bull by the horns, Reuchlin directly contested the specific allegations of Jews cursing Christianity. In an impressive display of philology, he parsed the Hebrew formulations in the suspect Jewish texts – above all, in the *Birkat ha-Minim* and the *Aleinu* prayer – and concluded that the imprecations in these important prayers could not reasonably be construed as assaults against Christianity.[5] More generally, Reuchlin emphasized that Jews always had the legal right to reject Christian teachings about Jesus as the messiah, something they did, according to his portrayal, largely without animosity. Reuchlin contended even more emphatically that canon law, specifically the papal bull *Sicut Judeis*, guaranteed Jews not only property rights but also the right to practise their religion in Christendom without molestation.

To the astonishment of his contemporaries, in the context of defending Jewish prayers Reuchlin delivered a scalding polemic against the Christian Good Friday liturgy with its notorious prayer 'for the perfidious Jews'. For Reuchlin, it was not that Jews libelled Christians, but the other way around, 'for as long as we publicly call them during our Good Friday services, year after year, "perfidious Jews"… they may respond among themselves and in accord with the law: "they are lying about us; we have never broken our faith" ' (53). As Reuchlin explained, devout Jews were anything but 'perfidious', for they had stood the test of their faith countless times. This is not to say that Reuchlin ever wavered in his belief that Jews should convert to Christianity, yet that should occur without compulsion, he insisted. Overall, Reuchlin's *Recommendation* created a detailed counter-narrative to the hegemonic portrayals of Jews as embittered enemies of Christianity and as practitioners of a godless heresy. As Reuchlin said, putting the Jews and their books beyond censure, 'The Jew belongs to our Lord God as much as I do. If he stands, he stands before the Lord; if he falls, he falls before the Lord. Each person will have to give a reckoning' (59).

This portrayal of Judaism and Jewish scholarship, while it helped end the campaign to destroy Jewish books,[6] nonetheless resulted in a second major censorship moment, an effort to ban Reuchlin's book and brand his perspectives heretical. At first, Reuchlin's unpublished *Recommendation* was furiously attacked from many quarters in an effort to restart the book pogrom. In response to a published attack, Reuchlin decided in 1511 to publish and defend his *Recommendation* in a book titled *Eyeglasses* (*Augenspiegel*). *Eyeglasses* was immediately banned by many authorities, including the emperor, archbishop of Mainz, the university of Cologne and the city of Frankfurt (specifically outlawing further distribution at the Frankfurt Book Fair). Spurred on by the French king's intervention, the University of Paris also censured it as outrageous heresy.

Arnold von Tongern, professor at the University of Cologne, drew up the first formal heresy charges against Reuchlin's book in 1512, some forty-three counts under the general charge of supporting positions that were 'excessively favourable to Judaism'. Soon, Papal Inquisitor Jacob Hoogstraeten initiated prosecution of the case but encountered stiff opposition. Indeed, the inveterate attacks on Reuchlin may well have been a strategic miscalculation for the anti-Jewish campaign because they provoked a tremendous outpouring of support from humanist scholars from all over the empire and beyond, including from Pope Leo X. Even Maximilian I would change sides and, by 1514, begin supporting Reuchlin. Reuchlin became an international *cause célèbre* not because scholars supported Jewish causes but because they feared that successful prosecution of their champion Reuchlin would undermine the advance of humanist studies. A patron of humanism, Leo X quickly intervened on Reuchlin's behalf, mandating a change of trial venue from Hoogstraeten's inquisitional tribunal to an episcopal court in Speyer. The bishop of Speyer ruled on 24 April 1514 that Reuchlin's book 'does not contain … any heresy … nor is it favourable to the Jews beyond what is appropriate or the law permits, nor is it harmful or disrespectful to the church of God'.[7] In an unprecedented move, the episcopal court saddled the papal inquisitor with the defendant's court costs.

Stung by this rebuke but still supported by many powerful forces in the empire and across Europe, Hoogstraeten appealed against the verdict to the Roman Curia, where the case was heard, intermittently, from 1514 until 1520. The protracted review created a supercharged environment for a fierce pamphlet war that pitted pro-Reuchlin humanists against the inquisition and the dominance of scholastic theology. In 1516, a tribunal of the church's highest prelates ruled in Reuchlin's favour despite being pressured by the king of France, the future Emperor Charles V, the future Pope Hadrian VI and many leaders in the Dominican and Franciscan orders. Cardinal Giles of Viterbo, an enthusiastic patron of the new discipline of Hebrew studies, poignantly wrote of the verdict that saved the 'Talmud from the fires': 'We have defended not you but rather the law; not the Talmud but the church. It is not that Reuchlin has been saved by us but that we have been saved by Reuchlin'.[8]

Nonetheless, on 23 June 1520, just eight days after signing the first thundering condemnation of Martin Luther, Leo X issued a final verdict, this time against Reuchlin. In the aftermath of Luther's *Ninety-five Theses* (1517), the Vatican was suddenly no longer in a position to allow challenges against inquisitional forces in Germany to go forward. Indeed, in April 1521, at the beginning of the Diet of Worms (where Luther would be condemned by the estates of the empire), Pfefferkorn wrote: 'Yes, Reuchlin, if the pope had condemned you eight years ago, Martin Luther and your followers ... would not have dared to ... contemplate what they are now publicly undertaking to the detriment of the Christian faith. Of all this, you alone are the spark and the enabler, to drive the holy church into error and superstition.'[9] It should be noted that Reuchlin never endorsed Luther's movement and remained a Catholic until his death on 30 June 1522.

Despite the papal condemnation, Christian Hebrew studies continued to flourish. In fact, in the very year of Reuchlin's condemnation as a defender of Jewish books, the Christian publisher Daniel Bomberg would begin printing the first edition of the entire Talmud and do so with a papal imprimatur. Moreover, while political circumstances caused Leo to condemn Reuchlin, the pope continued to sponsor Sante Pagnini's translation of the Jewish Bible into Latin, the first new Latin version of the Hebrew since the time of St Jerome.

Although it did not end Hebrew studies in Rome, the verdict against Reuchlin's *Eyeglasses* did prefigure the harsh paradigm of the Catholic-Protestant-Jewish dynamic that would soon emerge. As counter-reformation policies were implemented, tolerance of Judaism plummeted in the papal states. As of 1550, Jews in the papal states were subject to the inquisition; some were burned at the stake; strict ghettoization was first imposed in 1555; and in 1569, Jews were expelled from papal territories except for Rome, Ancona and the Comtat Venaissin. An emblematic figure for crushing all types of heresy, Paul IV issued the punitive *Cum nimis absurdum* (1555), a repudiation of *Sicut Judeis*, the legal foundation for Christian toleration of Judaism in the Middle Ages.[10] On 4 September 1553, the future Paul IV burned the Talmud in Rome, beginning a series of papal bans on the Talmud.[11] Legislation at the Council of Trent, which created the *Index of Prohibited Books*, also enshrined papal censorship of Jewish publications. Nonetheless, printing the Talmud remained legal in many other parts of Europe, albeit often in an expurgated form.

Reuchlin was not the only Christian of his generation who admired Jewish books and Jewish scholars but he was the first to represent Jewish theology and scholarship so favourably in public discourse. When it came to a few Jewish thinkers, his opponents' accusations that he valued Jewish authorities more than the doctors of the church were not entirely specious, though bitterly formulated. Major Jewish scholars such as Rashi, Maimonides and David Kimhi impressed him at a very deep level. It is not astonishing that he acknowledged the importance of Talmudic and medieval Jewish scholarship – in the aftermath of Reuchlin even Luther consulted Jewish scholarship for his Old Testament exegesis – but it is striking that Reuchlin so openly conveyed respect for the wisdom and piety of the Jewish authors he studied.

Reuchlin would also not be the only Christian Hebrew scholar to defend Jews and Judaism against injustice. One of his students, Andreas Osiander, the leading reformer of Nuremberg, diligently continued his studies of Hebrew and Jewish writings as part of his ministry and, in 1529, emulated his teacher by composing a scholarly refutation of blood libel (the accusation that Jews murdered Christian children to use their blood in rituals). But Osiander's theological rejection of the blood libel innuendo, grounded in knowledge of Jewish practices, provoked an unusually strident objection from another of Reuchlin's students, the Catholic theologian Johannes Eck. In this clash between two Reuchlin followers, we can plainly see that Christian Hebraists in the aftermath of Reuchlin would not by any means develop a uniformly favourable attitude toward Judaism. Reuchlin's most famous supporter who later opposed Judaism was, of course, Martin Luther, author of some of the most hateful and violent anti-Semitic tracts in the history of Christianity. After reading a 1543 book by Luther that called for the extirpation of Judaism in Germany, Heinrich Bullinger, the leader of the Reformation in Zürich, wrote, 'If today that famous hero Reuchlin were to come back to life, he would declare that Tongern, Hoogstraeten and Pfefferkorn had returned to life in the one person, Martin Luther'.[12]

To Kill a Heretic: Sebastian Castellio against John Calvin

Bruce Gordon

Calvin: *The fact that the sword has been used for persecution does not prevent the pious magistrate from using his rod to defend the afflicted Church, nor do the crosses of the martyrs impede the just aid of the laws that the faithful may worship God in tranquillity.*

Vaticanus: *If Servetus had attacked you by arms, you had rightly been defended by the magistrate; but since he opposed you in writings, why did you oppose them with iron and flame? Do you call this the defence of the pious magistrate? … To kill a man is not to defend a doctrine, but to kill a man. When the Genevans killed Servetus they did not defend a doctrine; they killed a man. The defence of doctrine is not the affair of the magistrate but of the doctor. What has the sword to do with doctrine?*[1]

John Calvin did not lose much sleep worrying about his enemies, who were legion, but one in particular haunted him for the last twenty years of his life: the humanist Sebastian Castellio (1515–1563), who was an almost exact contemporary.[2] Castellio is best remembered as an early proponent of toleration, a concept frequently misunderstood when applied to the early modern period either as a modern sense of openness to difference or as scepticism. Castellio's position on religion was neither, and he once declared 'I hate heretics'.[3] What he also hated, as indicated by the quotation above from *Contra Libellum Calvini* ('Against Calvin's Book', 1562), was any sense that a person should be put to death for his or her beliefs. Heretics were wrong, and profoundly damaging to the church, but they were deluded rather than malevolent. Their correction should be by persuasion, not fire, the fate of Michel Servetus, burned for heresy at Geneva in 1553.

Calvin violently detested Castellio for several reasons. In part, his dislike was personal. When Calvin returned to Geneva in 1541 (he had been forced out in 1537 by opposition), Castellio had been supportive, eager to bring a fellow humanist to reform the city and its environs. Initially the two men were friends, and Calvin found Castellio both a teaching position and financial assistance. However, relations quickly soured, forcing Castellio and his family to flee Geneva to settle in Basel, where he became professor of Greek. Calvin ridiculed Castellio's work on the Bible, both his translations and interpretations, with the Song of Songs proving especially controversial. Calvin held to the traditional interpretation of the biblical book as describing Christ and the Church, while for Castellio it was an erotic love poem.

There were, however, other reasons for Calvin's persecution of Castellio. In Calvin's eyes, Geneva was not big enough for the two humanists, particularly as Castellio was every bit as talented, if not more talented, as a linguist and scholar. Calvin felt threatened by Castellio, a feeling that never left him. Their disagreement over the Bible was a harbinger of what was to come, and the debate over the Servetus affair cannot be separated from their opposing attitudes towards the Word of God as well as their personal animosity.

Only a few copies of Castellio's *Against Calvin's Book* survive. It was not printed until fifty years after it had been written, in the original Latin in the Netherlands. The work followed Castellio's well-known text *Concerning Heretics* (*De haereticis*, 1554), in which he had developed, under a pseudonym, his initial arguments on toleration.[4] In *Concerning Heretics*, which proved highly controversial, Castellio had assembled quotations from many authors, including Erasmus and Luther, to demonstrate that executing a heretic was wrong. Indeed he even used a couple of quotations from Calvin's 1536 edition of the *Institutes of the Christian Religion*, in which the reformer had argued in favour of clemency for the Turks.[5]

Against Calvin's Book thus was not published during Castellio's lifetime, being first printed in 1612, although the exact reasons for the hesitation to issue the work are not known. Certainly the situation in Basel was uncertain, and the wisdom of publishing an anti-Calvin tract was questionable. The Genevan reformer had many influential supporters in the city and they kept close watch on both Castellio and his friend Celio Secundo Curione, whose theological work had been suppressed by censors. Although Basel had long harboured concerns about Calvin and Geneva, those who held senior offices in both the church and ruling Council were cautious about allowing the city to be torn apart by open debate and unbridled criticism. Castellio knew that he could easily antagonize the city's censors and he chose to have *Against Calvin's Book* circulate among friends in manuscript.

In *Against Calvin's Book*, Castellio prosecuted the same line of argument about toleration as he had in *Concerning Heretics*, but was more passionate and wrote with greater venom against Calvin. Although Castellio did not name himself as author, neither his readers nor the reformers in Geneva were in any doubt from whom the text sprang. The principal question of the book is found in the quotation heading this essay: should a heretic be put to death? As the passage reveals, Castellio was opposed to the execution of those who denied the faith not because he was sceptical of biblical truth, but because doctrine and capital punishment did not belong together. It is not given to men, he argued, to presume the judgement of God. Executions for matters of belief were against God's will.[6]

Castellio never understood the correction of error in terms of punishment. Correction was about persuasion, reflecting his belief in the essential reasonableness of humanity and doctrinal discourse. He belonged to the stream of reformation thought uncomfortable with the role of the magistrates in upholding theology and in having control over the church.

Castellio's *Against Calvin's Book* was a response to a particular text, the Genevan reformer's *Defence of the Orthodox Faith*, in which Castellio had been savaged for his supposed defence of Servetus as a notorious heretic. In response, Castellio was adamant that his arguments against executions were not to be conflated with condoning heresy, which he resolutely refused to do. 'I shall not defend the doctrine of Servetus', he wrote, 'but condemn the doctrine of Calvin.'[7] Indeed, to make matters deeply personal, Castellio wrote *Against Calvin's Book* as a dialogue in which the defender of the execution of Michel Servetus was the eponymous reformer, whose words were taken directly from his *Defence*. Nothing could have been better calculated to enrage Geneva than to have its arguments tossed back laced with irony. To make matters worse, the opponent in the dialogue of dispatching heretics was given the name 'Vaticanus', making Rome more reasonable than Geneva.

The personal nature of Castellio's accusations course through *Against Calvin's Book*, notably in his description of Calvin as having written his *Defence* with hands covered in blood. The incendiary language of gore and blood thirst was common among Calvin's opponents in the Servetus case, but Castellio's graphic image of brutality in Geneva circulated widely among readers and served to spread the 'black legend' that would damage Calvin's reputation for centuries.[8] By reputation moderate and self-effacing, Castellio unleashed the hounds in *Against Calvin's Book*, cataloguing in detail his opponent's character flaws: Calvin was harsh and unforgiving, lusting both to hate and to kill. Such traits were evident in his loveless theology, which emphasized a spiteful God of double predestination; a God who was the author of sin and nothing less than a tyrant. Indeed, that God was more the image of Calvin himself than any loving deity. Castellio had abandoned hope of reconciliation with Geneva; there was no moderation, only venom as he sought to discredit Calvin through a humiliating dialogue in which the Genevan reformer offered nothing but self-righteous condemnation.

To a certain degree, Castellio flattered Calvin by making him wholly responsible for the suffering of the miserable Servetus, who had been roughly handled in France, falsely tried and burnt in Champel in October 1553, just outside the walls of Geneva. At every stage, according to Castellio, Calvin was the chief force for evil. Castellio would have known full well that Calvin did not possess the authority to have Servetus executed, but it served his purposes to make the Genevan reformer the face of persecution. Servetus, for his part, was also turned into a literary figure, attributed all the misery of Christian martyrs and made into an innocent victim of the church's accumulated cruelty.

Although Castellio was careful not to defend Servetus' heretical views, such as his denial of the Trinity and of the divinity of Christ, in *Against Calvin's Book* he attributed error to the unimaginably harsh physical and psychological treatment to which the Spaniard had been subjected. Castellio turned the tables by making Calvin the author of error through his calumny. Indeed, Geneva's protestations that Servetus had been treated according to the law were, Castellio wrote, nothing more than the lies of the fork-tongued devil. 'Had Calvin ever languished in a Spanish prison', Castellio scoffed, 'then he would know how reasonable are the admonitions of the enemy.'[9]

In *Against Calvin's Book*, Castellio viewed Servetus in a light entirely different from that perceived by the Genevans. The Spaniard had not sought to destroy the Christian religion, he argued; indeed his works proposed nothing of the sort. Castellio made a crucial distinction also found in his earlier work: heretics were to be distinguished from blasphemers and deniers of God, who could be legitimately punished by magistrates. Heretics were mistaken, and were genuinely concerned with the renewal of the faith. Their doubts may have been misplaced, but they did not amount to a capital offence. Calvin, by contrast, read Castellio's *Concerning Heretics* as a serious threat to the Reformation and church. The body of Christ was stained by the presence of heretics who denied the very nature of God; it was, therefore, as an instrument of divine will that he acted to remove the mark of denial of the truth.

The cited passage takes us to the heart of Castellio's argument, if we set aside the polemic. The Savoyard, in contrast to Calvin, saw the Servetus issue as a question of deeds, not belief. His criticism of both the Frenchman and the Genevans focused on how they had responded to Servetus, not on the Spaniard's supposed doctrinal errors. In an Erasmian vein, Castellio saw one's actions as revealing one's attitude towards truth and charity.[10] The Servetus case, therefore, was not primarily about heresy, but about how the Genevan magistrates had dealt with a man.

The opening disagreement in the quotation demonstrates two entirely different lines of argument, consistent in their internal principles, which were impossible to reconcile. 'Calvin', who, as we have seen, speaks in the words of his *Defence*, argues on the level of actions by distinguishing between persecution and defence of the faith in terms of the use of force. The church, Calvin argues, has long suffered violent persecution, but this fact does not permit Christians to inflict harm on others. However, despite the persecution suffered by Christians at the hands of worldly authorities, it could not be denied that faithful rulers possess by divine warrant the authority to put criminals to death. For Calvin, therefore, persecution and the legitimate duties of Christian magistrates were not to be confused. The role of the church as interpreter of the Gospel was to ensure that the magistrates' decisions were in accordance with the Word of God. However, temporal authority also had a responsibility to follow the legitimate laws of the state, and as denial of the Trinity was a legal offence and not only doctrinal error, the magistrates were compelled to act. Castellio could not accept the logic of this position that collapsed the distinction between force and faith. Violence could only be a legitimate response to violence, and 'Vaticanus' counters Calvin's claims by pointing out that Servetus did not physically attack Geneva.

Castellio's arguments help us to understand part of the reason why his work could not be printed in Basel and would have been censored. Not only had the religious leaders of the city supported the execution of Servetus in 1573, but the implications of Castellio's arguments were wholly unacceptable to any early modern government, which would not have wanted to limit its rights to execute those who denied the faith of the state. This was the principle the Swiss cities of Basel, Zurich and Bern had supported. Castellio's distinction between action and belief was not widely shared beyond a small group of humanists and sceptics, and he would have enjoyed little support among the

Basel rulers. Their hostility was a key component in making *Against Calvin's Book* unacceptable for the public.

For us to understand the gulf between Castellio and Calvin illustrated in the quotation, we can usefully return to the Erasmus/Luther dispute over free will in the early 1520s. Erasmus and Luther opposed each other not only with different arguments, but with two entirely different methods of debate. While Luther took a direct approach, seeing the crux of the matter in terms of the acceptance or denial of human free will in salvation, Erasmus addressed the subject as conversation. In other words, Luther sought precision of argument in a debate over a matter of great importance, while Erasmus wanted a dialogue in which the truth would emerge from discussion.[11]

Like Luther, Calvin never wrote dialogues. That literary form was for him an inadequate means of communicating theological truth. He worked towards absolute answers, while Castellio was prepared to explore matters of doubt as open questions. For Castellio, as for Erasmus, written texts were the place for discussion, and should not be confused with the black and white moral issues of physical confrontation. To draw writing, where thought might be explored more expansively, into the physical realm of warfare and punishment was in itself error. That position was unacceptable to Calvin, who held a writer directly responsible for what his text said. For the Genevan, what Servetus wrote in his offensive works reflected his offensive views and posed a danger to the community. Castellio, in contrast, saw Servetus' books as loci for discussion and debate. The debate between Calvin and Castellio focused on certainty. Calvin, at the beginning of his *Institutes*, argued that faith is knowledge, that because we know that God has saved us, we are able to have faith in him. Castellio, in turn, believed that knowledge only pertained to empirical things, outward actions that could be understood. Faith, therefore, was akin to belief, which was received from God and did not belong to the senses, so was not knowledge. This fundamental distinction divided the two men. Both believed that the other had faith and knowledge in the wrong order.

Although loath to say so directly, Castellio's assumption was that scripture is not always clear, and thus there is room for doubt on certain matters. Such lack of clarity creates room for disagreement among theologians and makes decisions to execute heretics all the more lamentable. Castellio's distinction between an act of aggression by Servetus and his doubts about doctrinal matters was based on his beliefs about human knowledge, which did not possess certainty concerning outward human actions. Concerning external acts, agreement on whether something is right or wrong is possible; thus, if Servetus had used physical force against Calvin or the Genevans, his actions would have been punishable. On issues such as the Trinity and infant baptism, however, scripture does not provide unambiguous guidance, and their truth is therefore not evident to the mind or senses. Castellio prized above elusive doctrinal certainty those outward actions that could be judged with certainty – piety and moral action. Calvin and the magistrates were to be judged on their responses, and Calvin was amongst those in error, for he had behaved with intolerance and viciousness on matters on which there could be legitimate disagreement.

On the other side, Calvin, and later Theodor Beza, his successor in Geneva, suspected that Castellio denied revelation and held that Christianity was little more than ethical code about moral improvement. Indeed, what Castellio wrote in his early works on toleration could easily lead to such a conclusion, and he was eager to make refinements in light of the harsh criticism from Geneva. He did not wish to undermine the authority of scripture, nor did he want to say that reason had no place in revelation. He was also sensitive to accusations that in making the Christian faith an ethical code, he left no distinction from Islam or Judaism. To do so would deny the special role of Jesus Christ.

We return to the quotation. For Castellio, or 'Vaticanus', temporal authority could have nothing to do with the faith per se; its role was constrained to protecting the church from threat, but doctrinal difference was not such a threat. As Hans Guggisberg has written, 'For the humanist Castellio, each individual as a divinely created being endowed with reason was worth much more than any unifying ecclesiastical doctrine'.[12] Because Christians are sinful and therefore prone to immorality, the state needs to intervene to punish. This authority, however, did not extend to matters of belief. Magistrates were to protect the community, often from itself.

Paolo Sarpi, the Papal Index and Censorship

Federico Barbierato

Besides (said Becatelli) there is no need of bookes, the world hath too many already, especially since printing was invented: and it is better to forbid a 1000 bookes without cause, then permit one that deserveth prohibition. ... Fryar Gregorie, Generall of the Heremite, said, he did not think it necessary to observe so many subtleties. For the prohibition of a Book, is as the prohibition of a meate, which is not a sentence against it, nor against him that hath prepared it, but a precept to him that is to use it, made by him who hath the charge of his health; therefore the credit of the Victualer is not in question, but the benefit of the sicke, who is forbid to eate of a meat that is hurtfull to him, though in it selfe, it may be good. So the Synod, as a Physitian, ought to forbid that which is hurtfull, or dangerous to the faithfull; wherein none will receive wrong. For howsoever the booke may bee good in it selfe, yet peradventure it may not agree to the infirmitie of the minds of this age.[1]

These are the words, in translation, of Paolo Sarpi (1552–1623), the Servite friar who was a legal and theological consultant to the Republic of Venice.[2] They are taken from Sarpi's prohibited book *The History of the Council of Trent*, first printed in Italian in London in 1619 and translated into English a year later. The manuscript of the work had been transcribed in Venice and arrived in London in a complicated way via cooperation between merchants, the Archbishop of Canterbury, George Abbot, and the English Ambassador in Venice, Sir Henry Wotton.[3]

Sarpi's *History* had an explosive impact in Reformed Europe. His role extended beyond that of an analyst – he was depicted holding a pen like a knife and was dubbed 'the disemboweller of the Council of Trent'.[4] After publication in May 1619, the book was unsurprisingly placed in the *Index of Prohibited Books* on 22 November. Published under the pseudonym of

Pietro Soave Polano, an anagram of Paolo Sarpi Veneto, it was arguably the
most important, clearest and most devastating critique of papal power that
had ever been produced in the Catholic sphere, an effective weapon against
Roman pretensions that provided a fundamental critical basis in the Gallican
Church. However, Sarpi's writing met with most success in England, where it
had been hoped that Venice would sensationally break away from the Church
of Rome to create an independent structure similar to the Anglican Church.
The concept of the civil function of religion later played a role, for example,
in the Erastian approach and Hobbes's *Leviathan*. But it was on Milton that
Sarpi probably exerted most influence on English shores, notably in terms of
the role of censorship, discussed in book VI of *History*, though his *History
of the Inquisition* provided equally important inspiration for *Areopagitica*.
Although written confidentially for the government of the Republic, *History
of the Inquisition* was distributed quite widely and translated into English by
Robert Gentilis in 1639.[5]

While this led to an image of Sarpi as a champion of freedom of the press,
his position was actually less clearly defined, sometimes ambiguous and always
tied up in the historical context.[6] The background setting was the split dividing
Europe caused by the Reformation and the attempt to react through the Council
of Trent. When Sarpi wrote the passage quoted above, he was implicitly referring
not only to the Trent debate, but also to at least fifty years of discussions about
censorship, how to apply it and which texts to ban. His basic assumption reflected
the view that the Council had distanced the Church from its original mission
and definitively sanctioned its wrongful interference in the field of civil power;
the Council fathers had mixed up the cities of God and man in their thinking
with devastating effects for Catholicism.

The main long-term directives of Catholic censorship had been drawn up
during the sixteenth century. The first official Roman *Index* was promulgated
in 1559, the result of ten years of work by the Roman Inquisition and the strong
repressive will of Pope Paul IV, a former Grand Inquisitor. The condemnations
– a thousand in total – were extremely harsh and the application of the
Index was wholly entrusted to the network of inquisitorial courts in Italian
states. Confessors played an important role, since they could not absolve the
owners of prohibited books or those who simply knew somebody that read
them. As penitents had to clear themselves by reporting the offender to the
Sant'Uffizio, confessors became a kind of offshoot of the latter, engaged in
the struggle against prohibited books in their 'internal court'. The Pauline
Index paved the way for future versions by banning non-Catholic authors,

even if their individual works did not include sufficient references to religion to condemn them on this ground alone. It also banned authors who were 'not congruent' with religious and moral precepts, anonymous works – instantly deemed dangerous – and the entire output of certain printers. Another class of prohibition was '*libri omnes*', cumulative condemnations against entire categories of books whose level of danger had to be established by individual inquisitors.

Bans affected works written in the vernacular above all; as Cardinal Carlo Borromeo wrote about the text of the Bible in 1582, there was a risk of 'the mysteries of Holy Scripture' being 'indifferently read and examined by all people; then that, due to their stature, and the inexperience of many, simple souls can easily fall into error, and remain oppressed'.[7] Indeed, vernacular translations of the Bible were absent from the list of permitted reading for a long time, at least in Italy and Spain. However, the interdictions did not only concern works of a religious or doctrinal nature, but all written production, of which the Inquisition was the only judge. In this way, condemnations were meted out to Aretino and Rabelais for their obscenity, Machiavelli for his anticurialism, the *Decameron* for its immorality and so on with much of the sixteenth-century vernacular output. Ultimately, any work that could cause intellectual anxiety was identified as dangerous; it was no longer simply a question of doctrinal heresy. As Archbishop Beccadelli claimed, when in doubt, it was better to ban 1,000 innocuous books than allow one dangerous book to be published (474).

The 1559 *Index* also raised the question of expurgation procedures. The inclusion of a huge number of literary works implicitly posed a significant problem: was it possible to impose a total ban on reading Boccaccio, Berni, Pulci, Lando, Della Casa, Aretino, Bracciolini and similar authors? With regard to the grey areas of censorship, there was growing interest in the idea that certain works could be 'saved' from interdiction by being amended to varying degrees.

The Tridentine *Index* was promulgated in 1564, drawn up by a commission of bishops appointed within the Council of Trent, whose debates were referred to by Sarpi in the initial quotation above. The new *Index* stressed that it was possible to modify some texts – indicated as *donec corrigantur* or *donec expurgantur* – and allow them to be read after correction. In this way, certain works – including those by Erasmus – that had been included in the first category in the 1559 *Index* had some chance of limited distribution. In general, the new instrument was characterized by a certain degree of clemency; the condemnations were more or less the same, but the general overview changed, with the establishment of ten rules of prohibition that broadly characterized Catholic censorship over the following four centuries. Bans were handed out to all heretical or superstitious texts, all New Testament editions by heretics and obscene books, except for the ancient classics. The seventh rule wholly proscribed 'those books that explicitly treat, relate or teach lascivious or obscene matter'.[8] There were still three categories, as in the previous *Index*, but some authors moved from the first to the second group, so that only certain works were banned rather than their entire production. The condemnation of heretical authors also now only affected works of a religious and faith-based nature, instead of all their works indiscriminately. Nevertheless, works of heresiarchs were subject to a total ban.

The Tridentine *Index* was reprinted several times and officially remained in force until 1596. Although it was not always enforced with the same level of rigour, the situation started to change in 1565 with the election of Pius V. The new pope had been General Commissioner of the Congregation of the Sant'Uffizio and had also been involved in drawing up the 1559 *Index*. The return to the spirit of the latter was marked in 1567 by a definitive ban on printing vernacular editions of the Bible, which had started again after the Council. Pius V set up a special Congregation in 1571 with the aim of drawing up a new catalogue, and the Congregation of the *Index* was officially founded in the following year.

After a long and tortuous preparation period, Clement VIII promulgated the new *Index* in 1596. It was probably the greatest single effort implemented by Rome to combat the spread of books deemed dangerous. At the same time, it marked the moment of transition from a flexible phase for drawing up rules, which might remain subject to ongoing debate, to a phase where the rules were consolidated and systematically enforced. Unlike the two previous indices – the first compiled by the Inquisition and the second by a special congregation of bishops appointed by the Council of Trent – the Clementine *Index* was the fruit of the labours of the newly created Congregation of the *Index*, initially assisted by the Sant'Uffizio and the Master of the Sacred Palace. The Congregation had been at work for 25 years, taking account of the experience of half a century of censorship practice. Open opposition came from Savoy, and indeed from Venice, where it was only accepted after lengthy diplomatic negotiations ending in an agreement that to some degree safeguarded jurisdiction in the Veneto and the printing industry.

Although it was presented almost as a supplement to the 1564 *Index*, the Clementine *Index* recaptured the severity and spirit of the 1559 Pauline

Index, to which an appendix was also added containing the prohibition of the complete works of 682 authors (including Rabelais and Aretino), 185 individual titles by named authors, and 276 anonymous works. A total of 116 authors and titles – such as Folengo – were provisionally banned awaiting expurgation, which in some cases replaced absolute interdiction in the previous *Index*. Works published after 1564 were added and the ten Tridentine rules were supplemented by some directives on the prohibition, correction and printing of books. Collected in an *Instructio*, they formulated, reaffirmed or clarified the previous rules and acted as guidelines over the following decades. There were some liberal elements, especially with regard to humanism and literary production, but these were compensated for by a series of somewhat harsh regulations, above all the rule whereby booksellers had to swear compliance with the provisions of the *Index* before a bishop or inquisitor, undertaking not to accept those suspected of heresy in their profession. In this way, as booksellers and printers had to swear an oath to a non-secular authority, they became papal subjects. Furthermore, the *Instructio* contained inflexible clarification of previous condemnations, including those regarding astrological literature, the *Talmud* and Jewish texts in general, and vernacular translations of the Bible, the latter thanks to the work of the Sant'Uffizio. However, papal nuncios were granted a certain degree of flexibility in banning the Bible in the vernacular immediately after promulgation. This discretion was implemented above all in areas such as Bohemia, Poland and Dalmatia, where Catholics lived in close contact with Protestants.

Furthermore, the category of censored books included not only *donec corrigantur*, pending revision, but also works by authors that had not been declared heretics, or works by heretical authors which did not deal with religion and, due to their technical character, were in demand in universities or professions. The eighteen Clementine rules *de prohibitione, de correctione* and *de impressione librorum* also definitively established the characteristics of censorship intervention, at the same time increasing the number of works subject to revision. The *donec corrigantur* category was retained, but was only used to designate a scant number of explicitly mentioned volumes. Most books were covered by general rules, whether from Trent or *de correctione librorum* in the new *Index*, increasing the propositions and subjects that were held to clash with faith and morality and could therefore scandalize Catholics. As rule VIII stated, books whose principal argument was good could just be expurgated of any specific content amounting to heresy, impiety, divination or superstition. No literary genre outside the theological field was spared from this extension of censorship intervention.[9]

Moreover, as Antonio Possevino stated in *La coltura de gl'ingegni* (1598, a translation of the first book of *Bibliotheca selecta* from 1593), 'purgation' was required to 'remove sinister feelings and intelligence, heresy and dishonesty and obscene things'.[10] It did not matter where they were found and, most importantly, it was not only a question of suppressing sentences or words deemed dangerous by making cuts of varying sizes. Indeed, the operation became more complex when entire passages essentially had to be rewritten to instil orthodoxy, or when it involved distributing works conveying opposite messages to the author's original intentions. To this end, Sarpi underlined that any amendment to an author's thinking was more serious than prohibiting it completely: 'writings... have been changed to the opposite of what the author meant through additions, subtractions and other alterations'.[11]

The 1596 *Index* probably represented the pinnacle of the Church's attempt to control consciences by prohibiting or neutralizing books, marking a turning point with regard to publishing output. The boundaries of Catholic censorship were clearly defined and there was a widespread idea that only a limited group of the faithful should have direct access to books, especially those in the vernacular. As Pope Clement VII had said, the others would have to make do with saying rosaries.

Sarpi's attack in the passage from *History of the Council of Trent* quoted above seems to be clear, articulated with rhetorical irony towards the Council fathers (474–475). There was a long tradition of the motif of prohibiting food because of its potential effects; it expressed one of the most unbearably patronizing features of the Church of Rome in the eyes of the Reformed churches. However, it is an attack that in some way conceals Sarpi's deep-rooted idea of censorship. As he wrote in a well-known passage in *History of the Inquisition*, 'The matter of bookes seemes to be a thing of small moment, because it treats of words, but through these words comes opinions into the world, which cause partialities, seditions, and finally warres. They are words, it is true, but such as in consequence draw after them Hosts of armed men.'[12]

It is a fundamental passage because it shows Sarpi as anything but 'liberal' with regard to texts. He saw some books as dangerous, meriting restricted distribution as they could be seditious and spread dissent. Others were prohibited by the Church to disproportionately extend its sphere of influence over the secular government. The state needed to act to halt this ecclesiastical 'deviation' and limit it within its boundaries.[13]

Therefore, Sarpi felt that the main problem was not so much the need for censorship as the extent to which censorship should apply, which texts should be banned and who should act as the censoring body. From this point of view, papal censorship was understandable and justifiable; in his opinion there was originally no form of prohibition in the church except what was self-imposed by the pious fathers. Councils could therefore recommend avoiding certain books, but it was up to emperors and popes to prohibit them officially. However, these prohibitions should have been exceptional cases, whereas instead they were increasing uncontrollably. Above all, censorship was a danger when used for political ends. Sarpi felt that the prohibition of books was increasingly affecting works through which the secular authority could defend itself against interference from the Church. The problem was therefore primarily jurisdictional in nature and not so closely related to the relative lawfulness of the practice of censorship.

Sarpi's attack started to take shape as soon as censorship was used as an instrument of political aggression by popes against state structures and secular authorities. It prompted him to write that 'a better mystery was never found, then to use religion to make men insensible' (473). He also saw it as evident that the *Index of Prohibited Books* contained a growing number of books unrelated to doctrinal or heretical issues.[14] The Church was therefore increasingly operating in the field of the state, acting not only to prohibit, but also to expurgate: 'They have gelded the bookes of ancient Authors by new printing of them, and taken out all which might serve for Temporall Authority.'[15]

The ambiguity of Sarpi's position can be understood most clearly in his *Consulti* – 'opinions' voiced to the government of the Venetian republic regarding individual issues. Sarpi's political nature is more apparent in these, emphasizing the importance of intervention against certain types of books and the opportuneness of allowing others to be distributed. In this sense, Sarpi has a pragmatic attitude – it is pointless, for example, to only consider the past, as he wrote in his *Consulto* 'On prohibiting pernicious books to the good government' on 17 August 1615: 'When new dangers are discovered, new ways of defending oneself need to be found.' Sarpi claimed that the interests of inquisitors and the state had coincided until around fifty years previously, because 'the inquisitors made sure that things against religion or the good government were not printed'. However, matters had changed by 1615, when he was writing what would become *History of the Council of Trent*: 'The government today can no longer trust the inquisitors as before, as they have totally conflicting interests. However, the prince needs to have his own censorship structure.'[16]

These were therefore positions that could vary over time – during Rome's Interdict against Venice and what is called the 'war of writings', the opportuneness of distributing books was evaluated on a case-by-case basis, just like the evaluation process to decide if it was opportune to respond to writing attacking the government that slipped through the censorship net. This shows one of the fundamental characteristics of the long-term effects on Catholic culture, especially in Italy. Nobody questioned the system of censorship, due to the shared premise that knowledge should be denied to the majority and reserved to extremely small groups that could manage the explosive nature of liberty. The problem was not whether prohibition was appropriate, but who to include in this highly select community. This had a negative effect on social harmony, which only ended when the ties between repressive structures and dominant classes became even closer. Therefore, the way in which censorship worked established an integrated 'system' of mediation, attitudes and relations with power structures that are still surprisingly entrenched.[17]

Areopagitica's Adversary: Henry Parker and the *Humble Remonstrance*

Geoff Kemp

[F]oreasmuch as irregular Printing, hath of late been the fewell in some measure of this miserable Civill-Warre, by deceiving the multitude, and hath brought into both Church and State, sundry other mischiefs and miseries, as well as poverty and desolation upon the Corporation of Stationers. It is most humbly prayed, That some speedy course may be taken for such a perfect regulation of the Presse, as may procure the publike good of the State, by the private prosperity of the Stationers Company.[1]

On the final page of the most celebrated denunciation of pre-publication press censorship in the English language, John Milton refers to a petition to Parliament which, he says, procured the press licensing ordinance that prompted *Areopagitica*. Milton portrays the petition as the work of monopolists and royalist sympathizers in the print trade, seeking to make rival publishers their 'vassals' and ensure 'malignant books' dominate. He then turns his back on the petition's 'sophisms' and concludes his own printed address to Parliament by saying that the chances of 'errors in a good government and in a bad are equally almost incident', but a virtuous and wise government will open itself to advice and redress errors, not rule that 'liberty of Printing be reduc't into the power of a few'.[2]

Milton was not to know that the petition came from the pen of one of the most controversial political writers of the early English Civil War period, an unseen adversary who shared his view at this time that good government was parliamentary and bad government was absolute monarchy. Printed anonymously as *To the High Court of Parliament: The Humble Remonstrance of the Company of Stationers*, a copy was duly inscribed 'By Henry Parker Esq' by Parker's friend, the bookseller George Thomason, who added the date

'April 1643', seven months into the first civil war between Charles I and his parliament.[3] On 14 June, Parliament fulfilled the *Remonstrance's* main aim by passing an ordinance (in lieu of statute with royal assent) for 'the Regulating of Printing', the censorship measure to which *Areopagitica* responded the following year. Parliament's order declared an intention to suppress 'the great defamation of Religion and Government' and mandated the pre-publication licensing of books and pamphlets by parliamentary appointees, binding this 'public service' to the Stationers' private interest by empowering the company to police the print trade.[4]

In this chapter, I consider *The Humble Remonstrance* in relation to Parker's other writings and to *Areopagitica*. It should be admitted at the outset that the *Remonstrance* suits the chapter's brevity, being a short, hack piece without a particularly engaging case. However, although a scant cipher, it promises clues to understanding the censorship debate of the period and to interpreting the brief encounter of Parker and Milton, two writers harnessed by recent scholarship to a republican theory of liberty as 'non-dependence'. In Quentin Skinner's influential account, Parker and Milton are foremost proponents of a paradigm of 'republican' or public liberty, holding that freedom is subverted by the presence of arbitrary political power, whose ultimate opponent is Thomas Hobbes in *Leviathan*. Others, following Skinner, have argued that aversion to dependence leads Milton to oppose formal censorship as inherently enslaving in *Areopagitica*.[5] I suggest that the divergence of Parker and Milton points to the vagaries of theory in practice but also argue that a shared aversion to dependence can help explain their separation on censorship, inclining Parker to trust the state more and Milton to trust it less. In the final analysis, however, both were exercising a liberty to contribute to public counsel as a means to avoid arbitrariness in political decision-making.

Parker's *Remonstrance* does not discuss liberty directly. Its core contention, as the quotation above suggests, is that the 'public good' coincides with the private prosperity of printers and booksellers given due regulation of the press (71). Well-governed states advance through gains in knowledge, facilitated by secure rewards for good books and foreseeable punishment for bad books within a framework of licensing and registration, which Parker believed would curtail the anarchic upsurge of printers and printing seen in the early 1640s. 'Parliament wants no power to punish', he declared, and the Stationers had the ability to effectively prosecute its measures, along with the requisite 'good affection' to Parliament to curb delinquents (66–67). Parker depicted a current 'Confusion or Community of Copies' which dis-incentivized established printers and authors while encouraging indigent others to publish error and heresy, necessitating 'severe Examiners for the licensing of things profitable, and suppressing of things harmfull' (66, 69).

The *Remonstrance*'s complaint that printing had been the fuel of 'miserable civil war' was a pregnant parting shot in view of Parker's more incendiary political writings at this time (71). Several of his works featured in a blacklist of rebellion-fuelling tracts later drawn up by the Restoration censor Roger L'Estrange, citing their 'seditious' doctrines that monarchical power derived from the people, was conditional on serving the public good, and if necessary for the safety of the public could be displaced by the authority of Parliament as the 'whole body of the State'.[6] In 1642, Charles I had singled out Parker's *Observations upon some of his Majesties late Answers and Expresses* as an example of Parliament's failure to restrain the 'Scandalous, Seditious and Traitorous Pamphlets against Our Self and Our Government'. In the month following the *Remonstrance*, Parker 'the Observator' produced *A Political Catechism* on Parliament's authority, which seized on apparent concessions in Charles's *Answer to the XIX Propositions* accepting 'Regulated Monarchy'.[7]

Although a hired pen, Parker can be taken to have believed what he wrote, or at least to have self-censored no more than other political writers. He believed in limited monarchy and press restraint. The 'republican' label was applied, then and now, for the implications and associations of his argument that when monarchy spurned regulation by parliamentary influence, becoming arbitrary, Parliament could govern without the monarch. Milton at this time was not dissimilar, though on press control, unlike Parker, he rejected the presumption in favour of censorship that extended across the political spectrum.

The divergence of Parker and Milton on licensing policy invites underestimating affinities in their thinking but also overstating their differences on censorship. Neither man saw the issue as being primarily about political dissent but rather about encouraging 'the advancement of wholesome knowledge', particularly the securing of religious truth (66). Neither writer saw cause to question post-publication punishment or to protect 'seditious' and 'libellous' books, the pamphlets of royalist 'malignants' and 'incendiaries', or religious-political 'popery' (66, 68, 96, 108, 123). The protestant 'neighbouring differences' defended by Milton, between impiety and 'perverted' Arminius, were not immeasurably wider than Parker's proposed path between 'the poyson of Socinus and Arminius' to the puritanism of Sibbes and Preston (66, 69, 104, 123). Both men attacked the anti-puritan censorship regime of the previous decade (both used Sarpi's *History of the Council of Trent*), both saw episcopacy's campaign against print and in print as a cause of the civil war, and both feared the growing censorious influence of the bishops' former presbyterian targets.[8]

It is no small matter, of course, that Parker's tolerance was narrower than Milton's, or that he believed 'severe examiners' would advance knowledge more than Milton's open contest of ideas. Their differences will be approached here, however, in the light of their kindred thinking on 'publick liberty', or political liberty.[9] To Hobbes, the public liberty claimed by writers like Parker and Milton was a chimera, because 'whether a Common-wealth be Monarchical, or Popular, the Freedome is still the same'.[10] Such writers, he believed, confused the freedom of individuals within a state to act without interference, within limits determined by monarch or assembly, with a liberty of the whole state which was only exercised by the sovereign (in foreign affairs). They repeated the empty rhetoric of Greek and Roman authors who encouraged a popular belief that popular government involved additional liberty, intrinsically rather than at most instrumentally, drawing on ideas such as Aristotle's twofold description of democratic liberty as freedom to act without constraint and freedom to engage in governing.

In recent scholarship, Parker and Milton are among those thinkers taken to have identified public liberty not primarily with instrumentally achieving extra 'negative' freedom from constraint, or with a 'positive' liberty to participate politically, but with a 'neo-Roman' notion that sees an intrinsic link between independence from arbitrary political will and a 'negative' freedom to act and speak. As Skinner puts their case, merely the existence of a discretionary royal power to impose or veto policy and laws poses the danger that 'the body politic will be moved to act by a will other than that of the nation as represented in parliament'; but 'for a body to be subject to any will other than its own is for that body to be enslaved'.[11] As Parker had argued against Charles I's ship money levy, 'Where the meere will of the Prince is law ... wherein doe we differ from the most abject of bond-slaves?'; or as Milton later wrote, if we live in the gift of royal prerogative then we are 'no Common-wealth, nor free' but 'a multitude of Vassalls'.[12]

Skinner observes that cowed subjects of arbitrary executive government will be inclined to self-censor their words or actions, though the cause of their unfreedom is not themselves but the form of government, as the source of their condition of servitude and radical uncertainty.[13] A corollary is that such self-censorship would disappear under non-arbitrary government, though another implication, ironically, would then seem to be that the will of the nation represented in Parliament could justify formal state censorship (and, paradoxically, perhaps need censorship more, in lieu of self-censorship). This is the assumption that underpins the *Remonstrance*.

Parker's underlying position is illuminated by one striking difference between the *Remonstrance* and *Areopagitica*. Milton devotes the early part of his treatise to contending that, historically, licensing was spawned by the papacy and favoured by no 'well instituted State', while avoiding mention of his own country's censorship history until the recent persecuting prelates (95–100, 105). Parker points out that 'England was not heretofore without a regulation in Printing' and lists several 'Wholesome Ordinances', including the Elizabethan Star Chamber decree of 1586 (66), the forerunner of the 1637 Star Chamber decree, both decrees having served Charles I's censorship regime. The *Remonstrance* notes the loss of Star Chamber, whose abolition led to the explosion of uncensored print and ultimately the 1643 ordinance, which largely reimposed the licensing provisions of 1637. Milton calls Parliament's order 'the immediate image' of the Star Chamber decree (124–125).

The *Remonstrance*, then, not only does not condemn a royal censorship decree but condones one closely tied to Charles I's arbitrary tyranny. The possibility of an explanation can begin with Parker's use of the example of Star Chamber alongside ship money in his *Observations*. He argues that 'the Law of Prerogative' is subordinate to the paramount law of *salus populi*, the people's safety or welfare, a core argument for Parliament at this time. Parker contends that if either ship money or Star Chamber is against the public good its removal is a duty, not an act of royal grace, 'granting Prerogative to be but mediate, and the Weale Publike to be finall'.[14] The contention is not that Star Chamber is against the public good *because* it is a prerogative court but that 'if' it does not serve the public good it should be abolished.

Viewed from a public liberty perspective, the suggestion is that the existence of prerogative need not be enslaving if it is directed towards the public welfare, since then by definition it is not arbitrary – it is the will of the prince but not his 'meere will'. The will becomes arbitrary when not determined by its proper end, the public good, which can occur if the prince denies that duty or does not adopt the means needed to rightly guide his will. The royalist response was to concede the duty but insist that God was the required guide; Parker and the parliamentarians insisted it was Parliament, as the king's 'public counsel' which, if ignored, could assume the exercise of the public will.

Parker's position, argued in the *Observations* and elsewhere, is that power originates with the people, who confer authority on the prince for protection and other benefits of executive government, but 'public consent' is ultimately with

Parliament as the supreme representative of the people. Parker's avowed view was that 'Parliament is Infallible', which has seen him labelled a 'parliamentary absolutist', relying on the same tenet of *salus populi* associated with monarchical absolutism.[15] However, his conception allowed for royal rule up to a point when Parliament decided that its counsel was being actively ignored, endangering the nation. Skinner argues that insistence on the royal veto, the king's 'negative voice', was the crucial tipping-point but, in effect, this was because it marked the rejection of Parliament's voice – its counsel, judgement and, crucially, consent.

Turning back to the *Remonstrance*, it can be seen why Parker could support a Star Chamber decree imposing press licensing – he supported it up to a point. He says that decrees regulating printing emerged 'as well knowing that the publike good was very much concerned in that Art, and that no act did more depend upon the publike Care' (A1v). We can say that he endorsed licensing when Parliament (the king-in-Parliament) accepted that it served the public good, for political, religious and 'private' or trade reasons. But when the king and Parliament (Lords and Commons) differed on the matter – as they did about Star Chamber latterly – the judgement of Parliament was decisive. To Parker, both possibilities accorded with the avoidance of arbitrary political will, as did Parliament's subsequent reimposition of licensing.

We have seen that Parker did not simply support parliamentary censorship and oppose monarchical censorship, but this does not explain the contrast with Milton's clear opposition to both. This explanation can start by examining the suggestion that Milton's aversion to dependence led him to reject the 'potential persecution' represented by licensing, under which even an approving imprimatur could appear a mark of slavery.[16] *Areopagitica* is dotted with references to servitude and vassalage, including his memorable protest against the writer's work appearing, like a child with a guardian, under the 'censors hand' – one of the very first uses of 'censor' in its modern sense (110).

However, it is questionable whether Milton's association of licensing with slavery is sufficient to explain his opposition to the 1643 ordinance in terms of a political theory of non-dependence, and it cannot explain his divergence from Parker. The dependence identified is essentially that of subjection to the licenser's discretion rather than immediately to arbitrary political will. If licensing is wrong for reasons other than being imposed by arbitrary political power, this will remain the case whether the government is monarchical or parliamentary, but then it is not clear why Milton's demonstration of reasons why censorship is wrong means it is ruled out by a political theory of non-dependence, at least directly.

The further step required is intimated by a small addendum to the variant historical account of censorship offered by *Areopagitica* compared to the *Remonstrance*. Milton, in concluding that no well-instituted state has favoured licensing, adds in confirmation that there is no 'Statute left us by our ancestors' (9). The intimation is not so much that Parliament alone embodies the well-instituted state, since a statute is an act of king-in-Parliament. It is that Parliament has shown itself to be a source of superior judgement on the case for and against censorship: a royal decree may be tacitly accepted by Parliament, as Parker suggested, but a statute implies full deliberation and accord. Censorship decrees were based on flawed reasoning but the correct judgement will be reached by Parliament giving full consideration to the reasons against licensing, which is where the intimation becomes the entire, openly-declared purpose of *Areopagitica*.

Parker and Milton both believe that men are treated as slaves when subjected to arbitrary will; a will is arbitrary when it is not determined by a due process of will-formation to achieve its end, and for political authority the end is the public good and the process is one of public counsel. Both men hold that the king's will is arbitrary when it does not heed Parliament, with Parker in particular hammering home the point that Parliament is the king's 'public counsel', contrasted with the 'private counsel' of courtiers. But Parker and Milton differ in their degree of assurance that Parliament's judgement can be non-arbitrary.

Parker, for political as well as intellectual reasons, specifically his immersion in Parliament's paper warfare with royalism, elevates the claims of Parliament's counsel to the point where its view is held to be intrinsically non-arbitrary, making it 'infallible' and self-sufficient in deliberation. Parker cannot concede that Parliament may infringe the liberty of the people by imposing dependence through its measures and appears blind to the practical dependence Milton identifies in licensing. Ideas of non-dependence help lead him to trust Parliament to censor for the public good. Milton, less immersed in the disputes between king and Parliament, believes that Parliament ensures its will is not arbitrary by heeding wider public counsel, importantly including the information conveyed by liberty of printing from men like himself, who although 'in a private condition' publish to 'advance the publick good'. Ideas of non-dependence help lead him to see why Parliament might otherwise act arbitrarily.

The case being made is not that Milton sees the need for published political counsel as itself the main argument against licensing: rather, liberty of printing facilitates the process of bringing the main reasons to the attention of Parliament, avoiding an arbitrary decision. Equally, licensing-as-dependence may be a key reason to avoid licensing because a government committed to political non-dependence would not impose dependence at other levels, but it is the process of reasoning, not the absence of licensing as such, that makes the political authority non-arbitrary. Relatedly, Parker's faith in a non-arbitrary Parliament cannot be a complete explanation of his support for licensing, since clearly he too weighed reasons, presumably concluding that the damaging 'discretion' he identified in anti-puritan censorship was outweighed by concerns over religious and political instability, the needs of trade interests conducive to learning, and a conviction that discretion differed under parliamentary licensers.

This leads to a final point, which is that Parker's *Remonstrance*, and not only Milton's *Areopagitica*, represented practical engagement in a process of reason-giving and public counsel through print. Parker's explanation of Parliament's infallibility was that 'the multitude hath onely a representative influence', not just because 'the people' cannot speak except through a representative but also in the sense that Parliament mediates their many voices such that 'they are not likely to sway, and yet some influence they have, and that enough to preserve themselves from being overswaid'. The 'absolutism' in his published writings was coupled with their purpose as contributions to securing non-arbitrary political conclusions, with Parker as a 'privado' writing to the public and to Parliament, cementing the 'Democraticall advantages' of Parliament as a representative.[17] The *Remonstrance*, like *Areopagitica*, was addressed to Parliament as the people's proxy – the classical idea of the senate as the public – but, as Milton observed, writing in print was 'more publick' than a speech and was potentially to 'publish to the world' (116). Parker's tract on censorship was not his finest hour, but neither was it simply a 'fraud' to make men 'vassalls', as Milton claimed (125). It was a public appeal for public censorship.

Text and Image: William Marshall's Frontispiece to the *Eikon Basilike* (1649)

Helen Pierce

On the morning of 30 January 1649, King Charles I of England stepped out of the Banqueting House on London's Whitehall and onto a hastily assembled scaffold dominated by the executioner's block. One onlooker reported that as the king's head was separated from his body, 'there was such a grone by the thousands then present as I never heard before and desire I may never hear again'; subsequent images of the scene produced in print and paint show members of the crowd weeping and fainting, as others reach forwards to salvage drops of the king's blood as precious relics.[1]

The shaping of Charles's posthumous reputation as royal martyr may appear to have originated with the relic-hunters at the scaffold, but both its catalyst and its fuel was the publication of a book. Copies of *Eikon Basilike: The Pourtraicture of His Sacred Majesty in His Solitudes and Sufferings* were circulating in the capital within days of the regicide.[2] A collection of prayers, reflections and meditations attributed to the king, the *Eikon Basilike* assumed an immediate and essential role in the development of a distinct royalist hagiography. It was a work the regicide regime would have liked not to exist but also one that was difficult to suppress, for practical and also political reasons. This chapter considers the artist William Marshall's (literally) iconic visual frontispiece as a crucial part of the process of royal myth-making and suggestive of the problem of censoring 'sacred majesty'.[3]

The book was first published in octavo format by Richard Royston, a prolific bookseller and long-standing freeman of the Stationers Company. Royston was also a staunch supporter of the crown who had spent time in the Fleet Prison in 1645 for the publication of an anti-Parliamentarian satire. Attempts were initially made by the Commonwealth's Council of State to curb Royston's printing and distribution of the *Eikon Basilike*: according to Dr William Denton, Charles's former physician and a later advocate of liberty of the press, 'the King's booke … hath beene much supressed, the first printer and impression plundered and presses broken'.[4] The Council's actions, however, were ineffective. They merely led Royston to publish the *Eikon Basilike* on a press beyond the city boundaries, from which 2,000 copies were swiftly distributed within days of the regicide, followed by two further reprints of Royston's edition. By the middle of March 1649, three new editions in the smaller, duodecimo size had been printed from the private press of William Dugard, headmaster of the Merchant Taylors School in London. Dugard was arrested and questioned by the Committee for Scandalous Pamphlets, but he was not dissuaded from issuing a further edition upon his release. Later editions published in the second half of 1649 for John Williams were smaller still, with the introduction of miniature versions of the king's book developing a relationship between text and reader that was increasingly personal, private and portable.[5]

The interventions by the Council of State did little to curb the enthusiasm of royalist publicists. A total of thirty-five English editions of the *Eikon Basilike* were published in 1649, with their number supplemented by English and foreign-language versions printed at Cork, Amsterdam, Rotterdam, Paris, Rouen and Copenhagen, serving the interests of both supportive residents and royalist exiles. Further foreign imprints were issued during the 1650s, together with four editions printed in England with a false imprint of The Hague. In 1649, it was not until 20 September that earlier parliamentary printing orders were strengthened by an 'Act Against Unlicensed and Scandalous Books and Pamphlets, and for Better Regulating of Printing', too late to prevent the multiplying editions of the king's book. It is significant that this Act, albeit belatedly, makes reference to 'any scandalous or libellous Books, Pamphlets, Papers or Pictures whatsoever' and to the seizing of both unlicenced printing presses and rolling presses, which were used for the publishing of letterpress and engraved images respectively; the *Eikon Basilike*'s own scandalous content encompassed both text and image.[6]

The role and status of the *Eikon Basilike* has its own historiography within broader debates over politics, print and propaganda. Less attention, however, has been paid to how the pictorial elements of this book, particularly its frontispiece, contributed to the novel fashioning of Charles I as an English martyr-king, whose image invited continuing reverence by both his supporters and, uneasily, by his critics.

The title *Eikon Basilike* translates from the Greek as 'the royal portrait', highlighting the importance of the visual in promoting a particular posthumous identity for the king. The book's frontispiece was a vital tool in this public relations campaign. An illustrated frontispiece will usually look to draw the reader in and then provide that reader with an initial means of engaging with the accompanying text by encapsulating its broader narrative or messages within an image. That of the *Eikon Basilike* is no exception.

The illustration promotes Charles as a martyr-king through a combination of emblematic, mnemonic devices. The king is placed at the centre of its composition, set within a barrel-vaulted chamber; he kneels in prayer and contemplation of the heavenly crown above him as his hand reaches firmly for a circle of thorns, which contrasts with the earthly crown at his feet. Charles's identity is indisputable to a broad audience: the profile format recalls the more familiar forms of royal representation on coins and medals, while ermine-lined robes and the discarded crown confirm his status and authority. Behind the king, an open landscape sees a rock steadfast in the middle of a stormy ocean, and in the foreground, the weights attached to the fronds of a verdant palm tree are ineffective, with the fronds springing upwards as rolling banners proclaim the unmoved and triumphal nature of the rock ('*Immota, triumphans*') and the virtue that cannot be outweighed ('*Crescit sub pondere virtus*'). Further Latin inscriptions clarify the meaning of individual elements, in the recognizable manner of an emblem book. William Dugard's editions of the *Eikon Basilike* saw an explanatory text in Latin and English inserted beneath the image, signed G. D. (Gulielmus Dugard), of which a number of subsequent versions and variants exist.

The artist William Marshall (fl.1617–1649) was tasked with the production of this original image. Marshall was a prolific engraver who worked primarily for the London book trade. Although it is difficult to assign particular political sympathies to Marshall on the basis of his output, it is likely that the *Eikon Basilike* commission had its origins in earlier works that he produced for royalist patrons, such as illustrations to Francis Quarles's *Emblemes* (1635) and *The Shepheards Oracles* (1645). The former, one of the earliest emblem books published in England, may well have provided inspiration to both the engraver and his employers in their development of the frontispiece content of the king's book. The *Eikon Basilike*'s design was carved by Marshall onto a copper plate using a cutting tool called a burin. The plate could then be inked and passed through a rolling press multiple times to reproduce multiple copies of that image. Marshall's design is known in seven slightly different states – an indication that the image was in great demand, with a plate being worn down by the continual printing process and re-engraving many times over. Multiple English and overseas editions of the *Eikon Basilike* resulted in five additional frontispieces based on the original design, signed by contemporary engravers and etchers including Wenceslaus Hollar, Thomas Rawlins and Robert Vaughan, together with numerous unsigned versions by unknown artists, after Marshall.

The power and influence of this image of Charles as martyr-king can be seen not only in the ubiquity of the frontispiece in manifold editions of the king's book but also in its existence beyond the material object of the *Eikon Basilike* itself. William Somner's 1650 pamphlet *The Frontispice* [sic] *of the King's Book Opened* accompanies Marshall's design with a lengthy verse explanation and panegyric of the picture and book ('By Heav'n 'tis Licenc'd, and may not goe downe, Though, as a Booke it wants men's *Imprimatur*.') The image was subsequently bound into *Reliquiae Sacrae Carolinae*, a collection of Charles's writings printed in 1651 by William Dugard and for Richard Royston in 1657. As well as forming an integral part of the *Eikon Basilike*, the frontispiece is also easily detached from the book. Its striking and persuasive emblematic content ensured that it was able to exist independently as a distinct piece of royalist visual polemic in a single sheet, particularly in those impressions from Dugard's press onwards, which were accompanied by a written 'explanation of the Emblem'. Excerpts from the *Eikon Basilike*'s text were copied down in manuscript form by loyal royalists; so too Marshall's engraving was disseminated beyond print, through copies in paint and needlework.[7]

Further illustrations sporadically joined the frontispiece in various editions of the *Eikon Basilike*: these were primarily engraved portraits of the king and of the prince of Wales taken from existing plates rather than newly commissioned compositions. Engraved plates are printed using a rolling press rather than a common or hand press; text and image are transferred to the page using two distinct printing processes, and it is likely that the *Eikon Basilike* would have passed through the workshops of several printers. The inclusion of Marshall's illustration and its later derivatives, together with supplementary images, would have added both time and cost to the production of the book; the retention of this illustration across multiple editions therefore underlines its value and importance to the broader project of royal martyr-making.

Marshall's design was not the only persuasive image of Charles in circulation in the wake of the regicide. A continued and positive presence of the king in visual form across the Interregnum can be understood as representing a challenge to government and initially provoked forms of censorship in response. A spate of iconoclastic attacks was carried out on public statues of Charles in London during the early 1650s, under the orders of the Council of State; sculptures were removed from public display, and the king's likeness at the Royal Exchange was decapitated. However, such actions ran counter to a more general, unspoken unwillingness among his critics to visually denigrate Charles or censure his visual image. English prints purporting specifically to show, let alone celebrate, the regicide, were unknown during the Interregnum. Although the bibliophile George Thomason was able to acquire an engraving of the execution scene, represented in eyewitness form, this was produced by the German engraver and publisher Sebastian Furck.

John Milton was the most notable of a number of authors to comment disparagingly on Marshall's frontispiece, observing how 'the Picture sett in Front would martyr him [Charles] and Saint him to befool the people…' and seeing the bewitching nature of the image highlighted as troublesome, belying its portrayal of the personal qualities of the individual pictured.[8] Milton's *Eikonoklastes* ('image-breaker'), first published in October 1649, presented a government-endorsed, written response to the *Eikon Basilike* which sought to justify the king's trial and its ramifications, as well as to justify its own appearance in opposition to the royal bestseller.

In Milton's view, the frontispiece purported to present a simple picture of harmless piety but its very nature as an accessible and iconic image drew the 'Image-doting rabble' into a 'civil kinde of Idolatry' which could then be used to revive royalist ambitions. In effect, it was a political message that worked by not involving political thought. He contended that those who could 'read' the image included many too illiterate to read rightly the book's Latin sign-off, 'prayers may give what war denies' ('*Vota dabunt qua Bella negarunt*'). As a key to the image, Joseph Jane's royalist defence *Eikon Aklastos* insisted that the Latin conveyed the pacifist message that the king would receive his reward in heaven; to Milton, it implied that Marshall's imagery of prayer and *Eikon Basilike* generally were intended to succeed where the royalist war effort had failed: the image of the pious king could help bring final victory.[9] Later claims for the importance of *Eikon Basilike* to the restoration of monarchy in 1660 – when *Eikonoklastes* was among the first books banned – did little to prove him wrong.

At the Restoration, the *Eikon Basilike* was subject to further, approved publication by the new regime; it was also included in the *Basilika*, a collection of writings attributed to Charles, first published in 1662 by Richard Royston. In this form, the work encountered criticism from a quite different confessional perspective to that of Milton and his contemporaries. A copy of the *Basilika* was seized by the Portuguese from an English ship en route to Lisbon in 1670 and subjected to some severe annotations on the orders of the Inquisition.[10] Any written references to Charles as a Christian martyr, or defender of the Protestant faith, were expurgated, with the text of the *Eikon Basilike* suffering particular damage. Its frontispiece image, a version of Marshall's design by the Dutch engraver Abraham Hertocks, saw only the heavenly crown, which the king gazes up at, struck through in ink. But with the single stroke of a pen, the meaning of the image was changed: the king's body remains unsullied and the authority of monarchy unchallenged, yet his martyr-status has been comprehensively removed – a rare example of literal 'image-breaking' within the king's book which does not seem to have been repeated by English readers, at home or abroad, during the Interregnum.

Already by the time of these criticisms, however, an anonymous work, *Eikon Alethine* ('the truthful image'), had questioned the authorship, and thus the authority, of the king's book. The attribution of the *Eikon Basilike* continues to generate debate today, with scholars generally conflating the king's contributions with those of John Gauden, Dean of Bocking in Essex and later Bishop of

Worcester.[11] The *Eikon Alethine* points immediately to the involvement of a mysterious clergyman. Its own frontispiece illustration shows a hand pulling back a curtain theatrically, to reveal what the accompanying verses describe as a 'Presumptuous Preist' who plots to 'make his King his Bastard Issue owne'. Charles himself does not feature within the composition, with the viewer encouraged to direct their censure at this generic, clerical figure who has dared to assume the voice of the king. A royalist riposte soon appeared, in the form of *Eikon e Piste*, which took the frontispiece to the *Eikon Alethine* and inverted its imagery: a similar curtain is lifted away, this time to reveal the king seated at a table, surveying his 'own' book. A critical figure, presumably the author of the *Eikon Alethine*, attempts to replace the king's crown with a cleric's cap; his efforts are thwarted, however, by a dynamic cavalier who instead places a jester's hat on the intruder's head. Amidst this action, Charles is again a model of thoughtful contemplation and authority.

This respectful treatment of the king's body in illustrated form was continuing a pattern of restraint established during the 1640s. Controversial individuals closely linked to Charles, such as Thomas Wentworth, the Earl of Strafford and Archbishop William Laud, found themselves ridiculed in both cheap printed images and more refined engravings and etchings in the wake of the abolition of Star Chamber in the summer of 1641. Printing restrictions and controls collapsed as the monopoly and authority of the Stationers' Company faltered, and critics of the king's autocratic rule across the 1630s were granted a novel voice in print, though often couched as criticism of royal counsellors rather than the king himself. The iconography of kingship itself remained unimpeachable: reports emerged in 1642 of an illustrated broadside picturing Charles standing outside the closed city gates at Hull, observed by its governor, Sir John Hotham, on horseback upon the city walls. Hotham had indeed refused the king admission into Hull, on the orders of the House of Commons; yet when the sheet was brought before the Commons, it was uniformly condemned and orders were issued that all known copies of the image were to be publicly burned.[12] In contrast, Laud's visual image was treated with notable hostility and a generous measure of irreverent, slapstick humour by critics of his ecclesiastical regime; he is shown variously in the act of vomiting, having his nose held to a grindstone, and with a noose around his neck, in pamphlet and broadside illustrations.

The continuing availability of conventional printed portraits of Charles I during the 1650s suggests that the royal image remained a popular and marketable genre. In 1654, the prolific London printseller Peter Stent published an advertisement of stock available from his premises at the White Horse in Guiltspur Street; here, interested parties could acquire a portrait of the king 'in a Laurel' etched by Wenceslaus Hollar after an original painting by Anthony Van Dyck; further prints of 'The King, Queen & children'; and the 'King & Queen standing', together with a 'great sheet' of Charles on horseback – all alongside portraits of Oliver Cromwell and Thomas Fairfax.[13]

Although attacking the royal image appears to have been off limits to supporters of the Republic, as I have discussed further elsewhere, royalist polemicists demonstrated no such charity to their counterparts.[14] A stream of acerbic illustrated broadsides criticizing the regicide and Cromwell's subsequent Protectorate also emerged from continental and, in particular, Dutch presses, during the 1650s. Such imagery sought to damage reputations through bodily exaggeration. Cromwell was pictured variously with a monstrous tail, a false beard and moustache, or with a pipe-smoking, bespectacled owl at his shoulder. Following Cromwell's death, his son Richard was reportedly 'confined to his chamber' following the publication of a mocking woodcut printed in London showing 'His Highnesse' as half man and half owl.[15]

At the Restoration, copies of Milton's *Eikonoklastes* were burned by the public hangman; in contrast, paintings based on Marshall's frontispiece were distributed around the country to be placed on public display.[16] The frontispiece to the *Eikon Basilike* was a powerful tool in shaping an image of the late king as Christian martyr, which helped preserve the continued pictorial treatment of the royal body with respect during the 1650s.

Rara temporum felicitas: Spinoza's Theological-Political Treatise

Edwin Curley

Since we happen to have that rare good fortune (rara felicitas) – *that we live in a republic in which everyone is granted complete freedom of judgment, and is permitted to worship God according to his understanding, and in which nothing is thought to be dearer or sweeter than freedom – I believed I would be doing something neither unwelcome, nor useless, if I showed not only that this freedom can be granted without harm to piety and the peace of the republic, but also that it can't be abolished unless piety and the peace of the republic are abolished with it.*[1]

There is a line in Tacitus which radical thinkers in the early modern period liked to quote, probably for purposes quite different from those of Tacitus. At the beginning of his *Histories*, dealing with the period from 69 to 96 CE, Tacitus says he is postponing for his old age the history of his own, happier times, the reigns of Nerva (96–98) and Trajan (98–117). That would be 'a richer and less perilous subject … because we have the rare good fortune (*rara temporum felicitas*) to live in an age when it is permitted to think what you wish, and to say what you think'.[2]

Benedict de Spinoza took this line as formulating an ideal of freedom of thought and expression. In his *Theological-Political Treatise* (1670), he claims to show that this is what a free state permits its citizens to do: think what they like and say what they think. That formula provides the title of Chapter XX (239). In the preface to the *Treatise*, from which the quotation above is taken, Spinoza even says that his own society has realized this ideal. This is not true, of course. No doubt Spinoza thought he would be doing something welcome and useful if he defended freedom. But though the Dutch Republic had a commitment to freedom unusual for its time, it did not allow everyone complete freedom of judgement and worship in matters of religion. If it had, Spinoza would not have felt the need to publish his work anonymously, with false information on the title page about the identity of the publisher and the place of publication. If it had, he might not even have felt the need to write his book in the first place. Explaining his aims in a letter to Henry Oldenburg in 1665, he said one reason he was taking up the theological issues of his book was that he wanted to defend 'the freedom of philosophizing, and saying what we think. Here the preachers suppress it as much as they can with their excessive authority and aggressiveness'.[3]

The Dutch Republic was, by the standards of its time, a remarkably free place. But the qualification is crucial. The standards of seventeenth-century Europe were not those of twenty-first-century European or North American states.[4] The Republic had a public church, the Dutch Reformed Church, whose buildings and ministers the state were paid for with public funds. Attendance at the services of this Calvinist church was not mandatory, but for anyone who held public office, membership was mandatory.

It is a mark of the Dutch commitment to religious liberty that they permitted most other Protestant denominations to build their own churches and hire their own pastors. It shows the limits of that liberty that dissident Protestants could do this only under certain conditions: first, they had to pay the state for the privilege of having their own churches; second, there had to be nothing in their teachings or manner of worship prejudicial to the interests of the state; and finally, they had to submit to state monitoring of their services to ensure that the second condition was satisfied.

Catholic worship was not officially permitted. Spain's brutal rule in the sixteenth century had left bitter memories. When the seven rebel provinces agreed in the Union of Utrecht (1579) on the principles which would govern the new state they aimed to set up, one of the most fundamental of these was that there should be, as Sir William Temple put it, 'no particular or curious Inquisition into the Faith or Religious Principles of any peaceable man who came to live under the protection of their laws'.[5] *De facto* the Catholic minority was permitted to hold services, provided they were discreet. They had to meet in quarters which did not look like churches and could not advertise their services. Sometimes they had to bribe public officials to look the other way.

In some places – chiefly Amsterdam – even Jews were permitted freedom of worship, though under conditions somewhat more onerous than those imposed on dissident Protestant denominations. They were, for example, forbidden to belong to most of the guilds, or to intermarry with Christians, or to convert Christians.[6] The Calvinist clergy were not happy about granting the Jews this freedom, but the Regents were generally inclined, in the tradition of Erasmus, to emphasize ethical conduct over dogma and to not worry too much if a minority religion disagreed with the public church about theological matters, particularly if that minority was industrious and an economic asset to the community. The Socinians (ancestors of those we nowadays call Unitarians) were an odd exception to this toleration. Their worship was not permitted under any conditions. Evidently it was tolerable to deny the doctrine of the trinity if you were a Jew; but if you claimed to be a Christian, you were outside the bounds of toleration if you found that doctrine incredible.

Such were the policies which were sufficient, in seventeenth-century Europe, to earn a country a reputation for being exceptionally tolerant of different religions. But freedom of religion was one thing. The freedom of philosophizing which Spinoza advocated was something else. Not only did Spinoza argue on purely secular grounds for freedom of thought and expression – contending that such freedom is necessary both for the material prosperity of society and for its flourishing in the arts, sciences and philosophy – he also contended that religion itself allowed this freedom (174, 179–180). When God revealed himself to the people of Israel at Mount Sinai, he did not teach them to have true beliefs about his nature. An unprejudiced reading of the Pentateuch would show that even Moses, the prophet traditionally supposed to have surpassed all others in his knowledge of God (Numbers 12:6–8; Deuteronomy 34:10), had a very inadequate conception of God, not realizing that he is omniscient, or that he directs all human actions by his decrees, or that he is free of human affects, or that he is incorporeal, or even that he is the only god (38–39). Contrary to what had long been believed, Moses was no monotheist.[7]

Religion – *true* religion, the kind an intelligent, critical and unprejudiced reader of the Jewish and Christian scriptures would find to be consistently taught in both sets of sacred texts – does not require true belief, Spinoza argued. It requires only obedience. And not obedience to *all* the commands of scripture either but only to those that scripture consistently teaches throughout: to practice justice and loving kindness; and to do the things which clearly follow from these fundamental requirements, such as aiding the poor, killing no-one and not coveting the things that belong to others (165–166). If scripture is inconsistent (as, for example, in its teachings about divorce), then its commands do not bind us.[8]

This is all very congenial to those modern readers who find the ethics of scripture, read selectively, more appealing than its theology. But it does have its problems. For one thing, the Christian scriptures do sometimes require that we believe certain theological propositions in order to be saved. It is not only Paul who says this, as Spinoza tends to suggest (157–158).[9] It is also Jesus, at least as portrayed in the gospel of John.[10] So, it is no wonder that the credal statements which defined the faith of the Dutch Reformed Church also committed its members to this view.[11] The necessity for Christians to have some sort of special belief about Jesus can hardly be denied without denying the reliability of scripture and the authority of those churches which claim to base their teachings on scripture. Spinoza did that. He denied both the need for true beliefs about God and the reliability of scripture when it dealt with speculative matters.

But what may be more important – since it affects even Jews, who don't accept the authority of the New Testament, and whose religion tends to be less credal – is that Spinoza makes the concept of obedience to God problematic. In Chapter IV of the *TTP*, he argues that God cannot be adequately conceived as a lawgiver (62–65).[12] His argument is that a lawgiver is someone who prescribes rules to people which they can either obey or disobey (subject to certain rewards for obedience and punishments for disobedience). But if God is omnipotent, his relationship to humans cannot be like that.

If God prescribes laws to his people, then he wills that they behave in certain ways. A law is an expression of the will of the person who makes the law – the sovereign, whether this is an individual or a corporate body. But if an omnipotent being makes a law, the people to whom he gives the law will necessarily behave as the law requires them to. No one can thwart the will of an omnipotent being. That is what it means to be omnipotent. So the notion of God as an omnipotent lawgiver involves a contradiction. An omnipotent being cannot issue a law which those subject to the law can disobey. When Spinoza says that true religion requires only obedience, we are not to think of that 'obedience' as conforming our behaviour to laws issued by God. By all means, observe the requirements of justice and love your neighbour. But don't imagine that by doing so you are obeying a law prescribed by God.

It should surprise no one, then, that Spinoza's book went beyond the limits of what was permissible in the Dutch Republic in the late seventeenth century. Within months of its publication, the elders of the Reformed Church in several Dutch cities – notably, Amsterdam, Utrecht, Leiden, and Haarlem – had all proclaimed it blasphemous, dangerous and even obscene.[13] In the view of the South Holland Synod, it was 'as foul and blasphemous [a work] as any that are known of or that the world has ever seen'.[14] This judgement may strike some twenty-first-century readers as absurd, but that just shows how far we have come since then. At any rate, when the elders appealed to the civil authorities to suppress Spinoza's work, under a law enacted years earlier which forbade the printing and distribution of irreligious books, they apparently did the best they could to comply. It has often been said that in spite of the efforts of the Reformed Church, the civil authorities permitted the *TTP* to circulate freely in the Dutch Republic for several years. But Jonathan Israel has argued persuasively that this is not true, that the circulation of Spinoza's work owed more to the difficulty of a really thorough suppression, given the institutional structure of the Republic, than it did to the authorities' unwillingness to suppress the work.[15]

Was it an act of homage to Spinoza when Hume quoted that passage from Tacitus – the one beginning with *Rara temporum felicitas* – on the title page of his *Treatise of Human Nature*? It would be pleasant to think so, and just conceivably it was. Certainly Hume would have had no sympathy with Spinoza's doctrine that there is only one substance, even if it is clear that the abuse he heaps on Spinoza's 'hideous hypothesis' of monism is feigned, a device designed to embarrass those who think the soul is immaterial. Those people, he argues, hold a position 'almost the same' as that of the infamous atheist, Spinoza.[16] The more tar he can brush on Spinoza, the more there will be to rub off on the orthodox. But no less certainly Hume would have liked Spinoza's psychological analysis of superstition in the Preface to the *TTP*, with its argument that superstition arises from the uncertainties of life, from people's vacillation between hope and fear, and from their desperate desire to control their future.[17] Surely he would have appreciated how deftly Spinoza makes the slide from his account of the causes of superstition to an attack on the clergy for using the human liability to superstition to secure for themselves positions of status and power. Alas, I know of no hard evidence that Hume ever read the *Theological-Political Treatise*. It is not even clear that he read the *Ethics*. What he says about Spinoza's metaphysics in his own *Treatise* could all have come from Bayle's well-known (and very misleading) article on Spinoza in his *Historical and Critical Dictionary*.[18]

However that may be, one thing is tolerably certain. Spinoza and Hume both appreciated the uses to which Tacitus could be put. Like Spinoza, Hume knew that before speaking candidly, he needed to calculate carefully the possible costs of such speech. As he was preparing his *Treatise* for publication, he was most anxious to get Bishop Butler's opinion of his work. Before he could solicit that opinion, he felt obliged to delete from the manuscript his discussion of miracles.

His position was less radical than Spinoza's. He did not deny the metaphysical possibility of miracles, just the possibility of ever having adequate evidence for them. Still, he was concerned enough to write to his friend, Henry Home, who was acting as an intermediary between Hume and the Bishop: 'I am at present castrating my Work, that is, cutting off its noble parts, that is, endeavouring it shall give as little offence as possible; before which I cou'd not pretend to put it into [Bishop Butler's] hands. This is a piece of Cowardice, for which I blame myself; tho I believe none of my Friends will blame me'.[19] Indeed, when Home read Hume's discussion of miracles, he advised total suppression of the argument. This was the policy Hume followed for nearly ten years, until he finally included his essay on miracles in the *Enquiry Concerning Human Understanding.*

What is the function of these allusions to Tacitus in Spinoza and Hume? When Tacitus himself wrote the lines from which we began, it seems that he wrote them without irony, as a conventional way of assuring his readers that he had no reason not to say what he thought, that they could trust him to speak the truth as he saw it. He began his *Annals* with a similar passage, promising to treat the reigns of Augustus and Tiberius *sine ira et studio*, without anger and without partiality, motives for which he said he had no cause.[20]

When Spinoza and Hume quote Tacitus, though, the irony should be plain, even to a reader who does not have the advantage of being able to consult the author's personal correspondence. Were these men really writing in times when they would pay no price for saying what they thought, if what they thought was apt to offend the powerful? In Spinoza's case the answer is clearly 'no'. If we know that, and think Spinoza must have known it too, then the quote from Tacitus functions as a warning: it is a rare piece of good luck when an author is perfectly free to speak his mind; the author of this book is not that lucky; he must make some nice judgements about what he can say without inviting more trouble than he is willing to accept; so you must be on guard when you read him; things may not be what they seem.

In Hume's case, the situation may appear different. It is true that he did 'castrate' his *Treatise* by deleting his essay on miracles. But then he published it nine years later, in the *Enquiry*, commenting to a friend: 'I see not what bad consequences follow, in the present age, from the character of an infidel; especially if a man's conduct be in other respects irreproachable.'[21] Doesn't that mean that Hume had no reason to fear speaking his mind? Or at least, that if he was confident that his conduct was otherwise beyond reproach, he believed he had no reason for such fear? But really, he ought to have known better. Even at this point in his life, he had already been denied a chair of philosophy at the University of Edinburgh because his religious views – unless some of his friends had spoken indiscreetly, these must be the views of the expurgated *Treatise*! – were deemed unacceptable. After the publication of the *Enquiry*, he was to lose yet another chair, at the University of Glasgow.[22] In the end he did secure an academic appointment which he found satisfactory but as a librarian, not as a professor of philosophy. Mossner's comment on these affairs will provide a fitting conclusion: 'While Professor Clow [James Clow, the successful candidate at Glasgow] … remains as insignificant as Professor Cleghorn [William Cleghorn, the successful candidate at Edinburgh] … Scotland's most distinguished philosopher never held a philosophy chair.'[23] Bad consequences did follow from Hume's candour, not only for Hume personally but for Scotland as well.

Roman Censorship, Spartan Parallels and Modern Uses in Rousseau's *Social Contract*

Melissa Lane

Just as the general will is declared by the law, public judgment is declared by Censorship. Public opinion is the kind of law of which the Censor is the Minister .... Therefore the censorial tribunal, far from being the arbiter of the people's opinion, merely declares it, and as soon as this body departs from that opinion, its decisions are useless and ineffective.

There is no use in distinguishing between the morals of a nation and the objects of its esteem, for all of these things stem from the same principle and are necessarily intermingled. Among all the peoples of the world, it is not nature, but opinion that determines the choice of their pleasures. Reform men's opinions and their morals will purify themselves ....

A people's opinions arise from its constitution. Although the law does not regulate morals, it is legislation that gives rise to them. When legislation weakens, morals degenerate, but then the judgment of Censors will not be able to do what the force of law has not done. It follows from this that Censorship can be useful for preserving morals, but never for reestablishing them. Establish Censors when the Laws are in full vigour. As soon as the laws have lost it, the situation is desperate; nothing legitimate has force any longer when the laws no longer have any.

Censorship maintains morals by preventing opinions from becoming corrupt; by preserving their rectitude through wise application; sometimes even by determining them when they are still uncertain ....

I have said elsewhere that since public opinion is not subject to constraint, there must be no vestige of constraint in the tribunal established to represent it. The art with which this mechanism, altogether lost among modern peoples, was set to work among the Romans and better still among the Lacedemonians cannot be sufficiently admired.[1]

In this text, Jean-Jacques Rousseau draws a parallel between a special kind of common judgement that constitutes the general will to assent to fundamental laws and a more diffuse kind of 'public opinion' which is expressed in the mores and customs that a Censor – in the ancient Roman sense – can uphold. In choosing to focus here on 'censorship' in its ancient Roman sense of the arbiter of mores, Rousseau did not do so out of unfamiliarity with censorship in the specific modern sense of prohibition or restriction on publication. Both his native city of Geneva and his long-time host France deployed censors of the press. Rousseau had sought to avoid such interference where possible, for example by not submitting his *Discourse on the Origins of Inequality* to the Genevan government for censorship in advance.[2] Yet, ironically, both *Du Contrat Social* and *La Nouvelle Héloïse* would be subjected to censorship in this sense, being placed on the Vatican's *Index Librorum Prohibitorum* (Index of Prohibited Books) listing the books that Catholics were forbidden to read.

Yet, while Rousseau was well aware of these contemporary institutions and practices of press censorship, his reflections on censorship in his theoretical writings about politics are for the most part focused instead on the ancient Roman institution of the Censorate – together with the ancient Spartan institution of the Ephorate that Rousseau (like many other authors) assimilated in function to the Roman one – and on their roles as political models. This is the theme of his chapter 'On Censorship' in the *Social Contract* (book IV, Chapter 7), from which the quotation above is drawn. To distinguish, I will use 'Censorship' for his theoretical discussions derived from these ancient models, and 'censorship' for publishing prohibitions.

The line between the ancient and specific modern usages is not absolute, of course. The Roman institution is the original source of the term that was adopted by the Church and later by modern governments for the specific meaning of press censorship. Moreover, common to the ancient institution and this more specific meaning is the role of 'censoring' *mores*, the customs of a people that would be at risk of corruption by the prohibited institutions or publications. The ancient application of such censorship in the form of sanctions on luxury, in particular, would also be broadly associated with 'censorship' in modern conditions, even though the problem of luxury and the problem of press censorship became separate and distinct.

Despite his occasional embroilment with press censorship, Rousseau's reflections on ancient Censorship depart from discussions primarily focused on that topic in two distinct ways. On the one hand, his understanding of Censorship was in many ways faithful to the ancients. On the other hand, in sketching how ancient Censorship might be emulated in modern institutions, he drew on the ancients in one particular way – the purported absence of compulsion – that was less true to them than to certain contemporary practices in France and to his own ideas about the nature and power of public opinion. We will consider these aspects of his reflections on Censorship – the more historically faithful and the more theoretically original – in turn.

Consider, first, Rousseau as an avid reader of the ancient historians and philosophers, one familiar with the actual duties of the ancient institutions in ways that many of his modern readers are not.[3] He knew that the Romans charged their Censors with evaluating and sanctioning not publications but persons and contracts. The two Censors elected to a dual magistracy every five years had the power to sanction grossly licentious or immoral behaviour. But they did so not by prohibiting publications or ideas. Rather, the most powerful sanction available to them was demotion of the status of an individual, specifically 'expulsion from the Senate or the equestrian order'.[4] This power derived from the original and primary function of the Censors, which was to carry out a quinquennial census of population and property, assigning each person a status related to their birth and property.

The Roman Censors also had a traditional role of regulating the morals of the people in areas including marriage and childbearing. Accompanying this was a set of sumptuary laws from 217 BCE onward, continuing into the reign of Augustus. Note that these were laws passed by the people, not rules imposed by the Censors. But the most famous censor of antiquity, 'Cato the Censor' (Marcus Porcius Cato, or Cato the Elder: see Chapter 1) extended the role of such a moral regimen by 'a distinctive and seemingly unprecedented application when he systematically overvalued particular categories of property and then imposed a special tax upon them'.[5] His goal was to prevent luxurious consumption from undermining the simplicity, uprightness and hardihood of republican citizens.[6] Many writing before Rousseau, for example Montesquieu in *The Spirit of the Laws*,[7] had stressed the role of the Roman Censors in proposing sumptuary laws to be passed by the Roman people, especially those directed at keeping women frugal.

Rousseau's own proposal for taxes on luxury goods, made in his *Discourse on Political Economy*, published in 1755 in the fifth volume of Diderot and d'Alembert's *Encyclopédie*, bears a striking resemblance to Cato's measures. He argues that taxes on luxury will rightly fall more heavily on the rich than on the poor. The result will be either that the rich give up their luxuries, in which case 'the tax base will have produced the effect of the best sumptuary laws' and will simultaneously decrease the expenses of the state in dealing with corruption in society; or else they won't, in which case the public revenues from the luxury taxes will support the increased state expenditures needed to cope with a more corrupt society.[8] It has been observed that with this proposal, Rousseau pointedly rejected the existing sumptuary laws in patrician-dominated Geneva that were framed according to a threefold division of property classes, in which some luxuries were permitted to 'people of quality' (the top group) only while taxes were more consistently imposed on staple food rather than on luxuries.[9] Indeed, in preferring luxury taxes over sumptuary laws in this text (though not everywhere in his writing), Rousseau can be seen to be mirroring Cato's Roman innovation while at the same time modernizing the republican concern with luxury that had become mired in class-dominated and ineffective sumptuary laws.[10]

Yet for all his concern with the corrupting effects of wealth, inequality and luxury, Rousseau did not make these the primary focus of his reflections on censorship. Instead, his primary concern with Censorship was the one expressed in the head quote: that Censorship is the expression of public opinion and judgement, serving to complement the law in maintaining *mores*. We will expand upon this role of Censorship in Rousseau's thought, as he explored it in diverse contexts. In all of them, it is crucial to note that this function of Censorship expresses the second and more original aspect of his reappropriation of the ancient institutions: for he stresses that the Censorship he recommends must be exercised by an institution using 'no vestige of constraint' (215). Whereas the ancient Censors had powers of sanctioning persons, limited though they were to demoting men from the Senate or equestrian order, Rousseau envisages a variety of new models of Censorship that all abstain from any use of coercive force.

In the chapter on Censorship in the *Social Contract*, Rousseau gives four examples, omitted for space from the opening quotation above, that we must now consider. The two that conclude the chapter from which the text is taken are drawn from ancient Sparta (or Lacedemonia, as Rousseau refers to it). Apart from their general executive duties, the role of the Spartan Ephors that fascinated Rousseau was their overseeing of mores, embodied in various functions (about which Rousseau's admired Plutarch recounts many stories, although we know too little that is certain): overseeing the educational system for all Spartan boys; important religious functions; and the sort of general injunction to all Spartans 'to shave their moustaches and to obey the laws'.[11] In this same chapter of the *Social Contract*, Rousseau recounts two stories in which the Spartan Ephors used clever means of honour and shame, rather than coercive sanction, to criticize bad morals (those of a particular Spartan and of drunkards from another Greek city). In an earlier pair of examples in the same chapter drawn from more recent times, he first suggests that the same kind of non-coercive judgement of honour was successful in abolishing the use of seconds in duels by the French king. But whereas that edict, describing the use of seconds as cowardly, succeeded in determining the public's judgement because in fact it anticipated the public's inchoate view, an attempt to abolish the actual fighting of duels by describing it also in an edict as cowardly failed, because in that case (the second example), 'the public scorned this decision, upon which its judgment was already formed' (215).

The absence of coercion in Rousseau's description of this aspect of ancient Censorship, and in his wish to reappropriate it in new variants, is striking – in that it is so different both from the press censorship of his day (ecclesiastical and civil alike) and also from the way that his discussion of 'censorship' is often understood by scholars, who tend to read it precisely as involving the very kind of coercion that he here explicitly abjures. Scholars also tend to think of 'censorship' in Rousseau as something that can establish good morals, whereas he is very clear in the quotation that opened the present chapter and elsewhere that it cannot. It can only maintain good morals, not establish them in the first place or correct them once corrupted. Occasionally the Censor may be a tiny bit ahead of public opinion, as in the example of abolishing seconds in duelling, but Rousseau insists that they will never succeed in contravening public opinion that is firmly formed, as in the example of failing to abolish duelling that follows. As he remarks in one of his *Political Fragments*: 'With regard to Peoples once they have been corrupted, it is very hard to see what could be done to make them better. I do not know what Laws could perform this miracle, but I do know very well that everything is irremediably lost once it is necessary to have recourse to the gallows and scaffold.'[12]

We may illustrate these points with the two most extensive discussions of a role for Censorship (and its confusion with press censorship) outside the *Social Contract*: in the *Letter to d'Alembert* and in *On the Government of Poland*. Discussion of the former by scholars often manifests a more subtle form of confusion of Rousseauian Censorship with what is often misunderstood as a variant on press censorship, to wit, Rousseau's suggestion to prevent a theatre from being established in Geneva.[13] This is not a suggestion to ban any particular play, on a par with Plato's suggestion that major chunks of Homer and Hesiod should be banned from Kallipolis in the *Republic*; nor is the restriction of reading material in Emile's education, in *Emile*, a suggestion to ban publication of any particular book, although this is sometimes misunderstood. What Rousseau proposes in his letter to d'Alembert is rather that a public theatre should not be opened in Geneva at all. While this would prevent plays from being performed in practice, shielding Genevan citizens from them, it would not infringe the authors' ability to write or publish.

In this context Rousseau does discuss the informal role of public opinion in maintaining Censorship in well-ordered virtuous cities (all individuals in small cities are 'born censors of one another'; women 'almost perform the role of censors in our city [Geneva]').[14] But Rousseau is clear that an institution of Censorship would not be able to rectify the dissolution of mores that he argues the establishment of a theatre, and the attendant presence of actors in the city, would impel. As he observes, the Genevans already have both ecclesiastical and civic Censorship institutions (the Consistory and the Chamber of the Reformation). Yet he asks rhetorically: 'if the whole force of this tribunal barely suffices to maintain us as we are, when we have added a new inclination to the penchant of morals, what will it do to arrest this progress?'[15]

Finally, in *Considerations on the Government of Poland and on Its Planned Reformation*, written in 1771–1772, Rousseau returns to the original and primary function of the Roman Censors, that is, in enrolling the citizens by means of the census and assigning them to property classes (something he also discusses briefly in the *Social Contract*). He proposes the establishment of a 'censorial or beneficent committee' of the elect of each province who are not yet deputy senators, together with those priests 'judged most worthy of this honour' and perhaps also 'the elders and notables of all stations'.[16] Each of these provincial committees would have several functions, including assembling reports on the conditions of the province and providing for welfare out of freely-given donations by the rich. Their key duties for our present purposes would be making lists of those whose conduct is worthy 'of honour and of recompense', of which the most important list, as Rousseau himself qualifies it, would be of the most virtuous peasants, from whom a number (fixed by law) are to be chosen by the Diet for enfranchisement, and similarly to ennoble or honour a certain number of the bourgeoisie. Rousseau insists that these committees 'would never be occupied with punishments or reprimands, but only with benefits'.[17]

This is a fascinating extension of the principles of ancient Censorship to fit the conditions of a modern country still burdened by peasant serfdom, on the one hand, but also featuring an ambitious and impatient bourgeoisie, on the other. Rousseau here appropriates the Censor's role, which in Rome was to demote unworthy citizens to a lower rank, to the purpose of a gradual enfranchisement and ennoblement that will allow peasants to become free men, suitable to serve in the militia, and the bourgeoisie to become represented in the Diet and so attached 'by affection to the fatherland and to the maintenance of the constitution'.[18] Rousseau is all too aware that such a 'department of beneficence ... to the shame of Kings and of peoples, has never yet existed anywhere', and reinforces again that, as these censorial committees would be composed of citizens not yet advanced to magistracies, they 'would not be vested with any coercive power'.[19] This is consistent with a note to the *Second Discourse* in which Rousseau had observed that the full powers of magistracy in Roman Censorship could not be tolerated by modern men, who are willing to allow the magistrates to determine the ranks of citizens only on the basis of 'the real services that they render to the State' rather than directly on 'personal merit'.[20] His sense of the difference between ancient and modern mores is summed up in the same note thus: 'Only morals as pure as those of the Ancient Romans can bear Censors; such tribunals would soon have overthrown everything among us'. Instead, he observed, it should be not a coercive magistracy but rather a body expressing 'public esteem' that is made responsible 'to establish the difference between evil and good men'.[21] The Censorial committees proposed in *On the Government of Poland* exemplify the kind of non-coercive mobilization of public opinion for which my *Social Contract* opening quotation calls, in the form of a mechanism to be supplied to 'modern peoples' imitating that of the 'Romans and ... the Lacedemonians' (215). It would be a tribunal bringing public opinion to bear with 'no vestige of constraint' (215), which is a parallel example to that offered in *On the Government of Poland* of 'the manner in which one can proceed so that ... virtue might be capable of opening all the doors that fortune is pleased to close'.[22]

Censorship from Rulers, Censorship from Book Piracy: The Strategies of Immanuel Kant

John Christian Laursen

I have placed the main point of enlightenment – mankind's exit from its self-imposed immaturity – primarily on religious matters since our rulers have no interest in playing the role of guardian to their subjects with regard to the arts and sciences and because this type of immaturity is the most harmful as well as the most dishonourable. But the manner of thinking of a head of state who favours such enlightenment goes even further and sees that even with regard to his own legislation there is no danger in allowing his subjects to make public use of their reason and to lay publicly before the world their thoughts about a better formulation of this legislation as well as a candid criticism of laws already given. We have a shining example of this, in which no monarch has yet surpassed the one we honour.

But only a ruler who, himself enlightened, does not himself fear shadows, and at the same time has at hand a large, well-trained army as a guarantee of public peace, can say what a republic cannot dare: argue, as much as you want and about whatever you want, only obey![1]

The German philosopher Immanuel Kant (1724–1804) is well known for his contribution to the debate about the meaning of Enlightenment in an article entitled 'What is Enlightenment?' of 1784. He is perhaps less well known for his strategies for dealing with censorship, although some of them appear in the article. The ruler he honours in the passage quoted above was Frederick II of Prussia, known as Frederick the Great. It was true that the latter possessed a large army, and that he did not often interfere in German intellectual life via censorship. But some years after he published the paragraphs cited above, Kant was the subject of censorship by the king who succeeded Frederick on the throne. Kant was also very aware of a threat to writers that could amount to censorship broadly construed: book piracy, which deprived writers of royalties and thus of a way to make a living from their writing. As we shall see, he developed several strategies for working around censorship in its various forms.

One of Kant's strategies is disingenuousness. This includes flattery, heading off censorship by currying favour with the authorities. Asserting that the ruler is himself enlightened and does not fear shadows is designed to appeal to his vanity and his desire to be seen as brave and self-confident. Only the weak would need to use censorship. And there is more to Kant's appeal here. He has indeed devoted most of the article to justifying criticism of religion, but that is not entirely because, as he says above, religious immaturity is the most harmful and dishonourable. Rather, it is because Kant knew that Frederick was not very respectful of religion and would approve of criticism of it. Kant's justification of criticism of religion serves as an entering wedge for criticism of other matters such as the ruler's own laws. Indeed, mention of criticism of the ruler's own laws is limited to the paragraph cited above, which is the second to last paragraph in the article. Kant's most subversive point is undeveloped, all but hidden, just suggested at the end of the article.

Kant is also somewhat disingenuous when he asserts that rulers have no interest in supervising the arts and sciences. He knows that changes in the hearts and minds of people and their rulers caused by progress in the arts, sciences and enlightenment in all of its forms will eventually change their attitudes towards laws and governments. Note also that in the passage quoted above Kant appears to take the side of monarchism by disparaging republics for being unable to afford true liberty. Some scholars have taken this as part of a flirtation with enlightened despotism, the strategy by which an all-powerful ruler is persuaded to accept enlightened values and reform his country accordingly. This was the tactic of Voltaire and Diderot at times.[2] This was also the strategy of Johann Friedrich Struensee, a German physician who became Prime Minister of Denmark in 1770 and almost immediately declared unlimited freedom of the press – the first in the world to do so.[3] However, the enemies he made by many other well-intended reforms and his dalliance with the queen led to his overthrow in 1772 and the reimposition of police controls over the press. Press freedom by despotic fiat was subject to the revocation of press freedom by fiat. In 'What is Enlightenment?', Kant remarked that a change of those in power brought about by a revolution will not change the way they do business unless their hearts and minds are also changed (59).

In any case, by the time of his political writings of the 1790s, Kant was fully in favour of a republican government as a requirement of reason. In *Perpetual*

Peace of 1795 he asserted that the civil constitution of every state should be republican. In *The Contest of Faculties* of 1798, he updated the Platonic ideal republic as 'the idea of a constitution which is compatible with the natural rights of man, so that those who obey the law should also act as a unified body of legislators', called it 'the eternal norm for all civil constitutions' and asserted that we have a duty to work towards this condition. But it cannot be created overnight; so meanwhile 'it is the duty of monarchs to govern in a republican (not a democratic) manner, even although they may rule autocratically'. If they do, 'violence will gradually become less on the part of those in power, and obedience to the laws will increase'.[4] If a ruler can be persuaded to govern in a republican way, then we are on our way to actually having a republic.

At least one republic of Kant's day had declared a right to freedom of the press. The Virginia Declaration of Rights of 1776 declared: 'That the freedom of the Press is one of the greatest bulwarks of liberty, and can never be restrained but by despotick Governments'.[5] The Bill of Rights of the fledgling United States, proposed in 1789 and ratified in 1792, had provided that 'Congress shall make no law … abridging the freedom of speech, or of the press'.[6] But a right to freedom of the press enforceable against a ruler was not available to Kant because, as he argued in 1793, subjects cannot have rights that imply a right to coercion against the ruler without becoming, in effect, the real rulers. One could only try to persuade the ruler to do the right thing, as we have seen Kant doing in the passage quoted above. 'Thus freedom of the pen is the only safeguard of the rights of the people', he wrote in *Theory and Practice*.[7]

In our passage, Kant repeats his definition of enlightenment earlier in the article as 'mankind's exit from its self-incurred immaturity' (58). This was the meaning he read into the slogan he borrowed from Horace, *Sapere aude*, dare to know, or 'have the courage to use your own understanding!' (58). As he puts it in this article, one must think for oneself. But this is also a bit disingenuous because we know that in Kant's overall understanding of thinking one cannot think alone. In another article two years later, 'What is Orientation in Thinking?', he argued that one cannot think only by and for oneself:

> We do admittedly say that, whereas a higher authority may deprive us of freedom of speech or of writing, it cannot deprive us of freedom of thought. But how much and how accurately would we think if we did not think, so to speak, in community with others to whom we communicate our thoughts and who communicate their thoughts to us![8]

One of the purposes of ending censorship is to enable us to think in common. This is the meaning of his stress on the public use of reason in our passage above, by which he means the use of reason in print.

In 1792, one of the royal censors in Berlin refused permission to Kant to publish book two of his *Religion Within the Limits of Reason Alone* because of its heterodox religious implications. Rather than leave it unpublished, he sent it on with books three and four to a different censor in a different city, received approval and published it. In 1794, King Frederick William II, who took an interest in religious matters, rebuked Kant for this evasion of the censor, ordered him to refrain from publishing on religion in the future, and demanded a commitment from him. Kant wrote an elaborate defence of his writings, and pledged: 'As your majesty's most faithful subject, I hereby solemnly declare that I will entirely refrain from all public statements on religion, both natural and revealed, either in lectures or in writing.'[9] Yet after Frederick William II died in 1797, he published again on religion, reasoning that the promise not to publish applied only as long as he was 'your majesty's faithful servant', i.e. as long as his majesty was alive. It is probably safe to say that the king did not realize that Kant's pledge was for his lifetime only, and that Kant must have known that. So yet another of Kant's strategies for getting around censorship was equivocation about words.

Kant's disingenuousness and his refusal to admit rights against rulers are part of his usual strategy of step-by-step reform rather than calling for revolution. One scholar has argued that his political theory is best understood as 'provisional theory for an uncertain world'.[10] Kant knew that he would not have the beneficial effect he wanted to have if he openly denounced the authorities of his time for their violations of the rights of reason and demanded radical change. He knew he needed to massage them into making incremental improvements that may amount to substantial change in the long run.

Kant's strategies of flattery, disingenuousness and misrepresentation in his efforts to persuade rulers and the public to eschew censorship stand in contrast to his contemporary as a writer in defence of freedom of the press, Carl Friedrich Bahrdt, who became known as 'the notorious Dr Bahrdt'. Bahrdt expressed in-your-face opposition to the rulers. In *On Freedom of the Press and its Limits* of 1787, he wrote:

> Oh, you tyrants of humanity who keep and protect the iron sceptre of violating conscience! Step forward…I will make things so clear to you, that only an extreme level of stupidity or the blindest dependence on prejudices will be able to keep you from being persuaded. It is true, your minds are armoured with

metal and your backs are covered with Russian leather, but I will smash the bronze and tear the skin.[11]

We can ask ourselves which strategy, Kant's or Bahrdt's, was more likely to be more effective at that time and in that place. A later proponent of wide press rights in Prussia, Frederic Ancillon, argued for them respectfully from within the absolute monarchy, and later became Minister of Foreign Affairs for the years 1831–1837. Some of his best arguments for freedom of the press include the point that no government is qualified to draw the line between truth and error ('there is some truth in all errors, and some error in all truths') nor to decide when an idea is really dangerous and when it is not (which must be always in flux).[12]

Kant's incrementalism and indirect approach to political problems can also be observed in his treatment of one of the biggest threats to authors of his time: book piracy, or the unauthorized reprinting of books. Book piracy amounted to a sort of censorship because it meant that booksellers could not pay authors much of a royalty because their competitors could then reprint the book without having paid more than the cost of a copy. If booksellers could not pay royalties, authors could not make a living from their writing and thus were discouraged from writing. In Kant's day, this may have been more of a systematic impediment to freedom of the press than the sporadic interventions of the authorities. We know this was an important issue because one publisher brought out a book in 1794 with his comments on a debate on this issue consisting of more than sixty books, pamphlets and journal articles which had appeared in the previous decades.[13] Some of them made the point that not only were writers discouraged from writing because they could not make a living from it but the public was thus deprived of what may have been good ideas.

Kant responded to book piracy in a magazine article of 1785 entitled 'On the Wrongfulness of Unauthorized Publication of Books' and in a small section of his great work on legal philosophy, *The Metaphysics of Morals* of 1797.[14] Kant's strategy concerning book piracy was not that of some contemporaries who tried to attribute to purchasers an implicit agreement not to reprint books. This would have been an author's right, enforceable against buyers. But that would have required judges to find an implied right where no one had found one before and where no book buyer thought he or she was buying with that implied contractual obligation, and it left it up to the author to sue a bookseller who violated the implied contract. It was unlikely that most authors would be in a position to hire a lawyer to sue the book pirate. Other contemporaries sought legislation by the enlightened rulers, which might have required a long campaign of persuasion. Kant's strategy was subtler: it was to construe the author/publisher relationship as a matter of agency law, according to which the publisher acted as an agent for his or her authors, and thus it was the publisher's right that was violated and it was the publisher that could sue. Kant argued that this was part of natural law and needed no new legislation if judges could be persuaded that this right already existed, so publishers could sue right away, without waiting for political change. And by making it a publishers' right, he made it more likely that it would be enforced simply because publishers were wealthier on average than authors and thus in a position to sue. So, Kant is arguing for a change in the way things are understood by judges which might have a real effect on the way things are done rather than for changes in what all book buyers are thinking or in legislation. Once again, he was looking for the path of least resistance.

By the time Kant's *Metaphysics of Morals* appeared, the legal status of book piracy had begun to change. The Prussian Code of 1794 contained one of the first provisions for copyright in European law, and this was followed over the following decades with copyright legislation in many countries. Eventually the Berne Convention established an international copyright union in 1887. Authors and publishers could now make such arrangements as they wished for assigning copyright, but as a matter of practice over time it seems likely that more publishers than authors have actually brought legal action against pirates. If that is the case, it accords with Kant's strategy for preventing censorship by book piracy.

Kant's responses to political problems like censorship were never openly revolutionary. As we have seen, he preferred an indirect approach, persuading people, including rulers, to do the right thing. In the process, he resorted to disingenuousness, equivocation and also creative legal interpretations. In doing so, he was drawing on the strengths of the intellectual and philosopher, and those of a pragmatist. He was not a heroic revolutionary in political life, although his ideas eventually worked a revolution in people's minds.

The 'Censorship of Public Opinion': James Madison, the Sedition Act Crisis and Democratic Press Liberty

Robert W. T. Martin

The essential difference between the British government, and the American constitutions, will place this subject [the freedom of the press] in the clearest light. ... In the United States ... the people, not the government, possess the absolute sovereignty. The legislature, no less than the executive, is under limitations of power. Encroachments are regarded as possible from the one, as well as from the other. Hence, in the United States, the great and essential rights of the people are secured against legislative, as well as against executive ambition. They are secured, not by laws paramount to prerogative, but by constitutions paramount to laws. This security of the freedom of the press requires, that it should be exempt, not only from previous restraint by the executive, as in Great Britain, but from legislative restraint also; and this exemption, to be effectual, must be an exemption not only from the previous inspection of licensers, but from the subsequent penalty of laws.[1]

Amidst an undeclared naval war with France in 1798, President John Adams and his allies in the United States Congress passed a law banning seditious libel. They justified this provision of the Sedition Act by drawing on long-standing English legal norms and the eminently reasonable argument that wartime conditions made critiques of the government even more dangerous than usual. Indeed, only six years prior, an English jury had found Thomas Paine guilty of seditious libel for his arguments in *The Rights of Man, Part Two*, despite the able defence provided by Thomas Erskine. What is remarkable, then, about this particular moment of censorship is not that an established government would pursue it with some public support, but rather the fact that James

Madison, Thomas Jefferson, and eventually the mass of the American people would reject this logic so completely and embrace a theory of free expression of unprecedented breadth and depth.

Despite being arguably the freest government in European history, England in the late eighteenth century was still a monarchy, if a limited one, and the prohibition against seditious libel remained a pillar of the common law. Respect for, and deference to, the government was seen as a necessary condition for public order; accordingly, seditious libel (that is, criticism of government) had the damaging tendency to bring government officials into disrepute, undermining the needed deference. Some legal scholars even argued that any truth in such criticism of government officials would actually make matters worse, because though the public might well ignore dubious accusations of official corruption, accurate claims would be more likely to reduce deference and even bring popular unrest.

Adams's 'Federalist' party was thus on fairly solid ground when it criminalized 'any false, scandalous, and malicious writing against the government of the United States, or either House of Congress, or the President, with intent to defame, or bring either into contempt or disrepute' (20). They argued, with considerable plausibility, that the new American legal system still drew in many ways on the English common law, despite achieving independence two decades earlier. From this perspective, the law was simply formalizing these traditional legal principles. What is more, the Federalists believed they were adapting those established legal norms to American conditions when they made two changes that seemed to open up avenues for legitimate political dissent. First, the law gave defendants the right to prove the truth of their allegedly false libel and, second, it gave the jury the power to decide whether the published words really amounted to seditious libel (rather than limiting the jury to determining only whether the defendant was indeed the author of the libel, as did some English precedents). Admittedly, the First Amendment (1791) to the American Constitution (1787) declared that 'Congress shall make no law…abridging the freedom of speech, or of the press', but the Federalist Congress was only codifying what 'freedom of the press' properly meant.

At issue, then, were the theoretical foundations of the novel notion of popular sovereignty that the United States was modelling for the world. But the moment was not limited to questions of philosophical fundamentals: Federalist officials – and juries packed with their supporters – would spend the next two years prosecuting and jailing newspaper editors who had opposed the Adams administration by publishing articles critical of the government. The partisan purposes of the law were unmistakable. Federalist critics of Jeffersonian members of Congress would never face even the hint of prosecution, and the law notably failed to criminalize criticism of the Vice-President, Thomas Jefferson. Moreover, the Act provided for its own expiration at the end of Adams's term in office.

For James Madison, who had split with the Federalists years earlier and was now the leading spokesman of the opposition, the biased enforcement was not nearly as important as the debate over the very meaning of popular government. The nature of the American government was, in his view, something altogether new. The people, not the legislature, were sovereign. And this sovereignty was not merely some philosophical postulate, a conceptual proposition meant to remain in the theoretical background. Defending the Virginia legislature's 1798 Resolutions criticizing the Sedition Act – resolutions he had drafted – Madison articulated his long-standing notion of an active popular sovereignty rooted in democratic power. Indeed, it was not only the right of citizens to discuss and criticize governmental policies and practices, it was their 'duty' to 'control [government proceedings] by the censorship of public opinion' (225). This 'censorship' would not be legal or institutional, but public sentiment would be no less effective, if broad-based enough.

This unprecedented power of the citizenry to genuinely rule their government had been no more evident than when public debate ratified a new understanding of constitutional foundations in 1787–1788. The Federalist approach to the freedom of the press misunderstood the demands of truly meaningful popular sovereignty, according to Madison. For starters, lacking a monarch, and given the comparatively limited powers of the US president, the threat of governmental overreach was now also, or even especially, likely to emerge from the legislature. While this might seem a fairly simple deduction from the new claim of popular, rather than parliamentary, sovereignty, it was, in fact, a monumental step for democratic theory. When John Adams observed in 1776 that a 'democratic despotism is a contradiction in terms', he was merely expressing the then common understanding that a people could not oppress itself.[2] Madison's explication of a constitution as the supreme articulation of popular sovereignty, however, newly recognized the dual threats posed by popularly elected legislatures: both when they act counter to the popular will (aggrandizing themselves) and when they act following the majority's desire to tyrannize the minority.

Whether the Sedition Act was indeed an example of majority tyranny was, for Madison, ultimately to be decided by public opinion, which in turn would be informed by public discourse, including Virginia's Resolutions and Madison's *Report*. But for this public opinion to be most effective, there must be practical mechanisms for its expression, especially meaningful elections. But these elections in turn relied on the very freedom of the press that the Federalists' Sedition Act was undermining.

'The right of electing members of the government', Madison explained, is 'the essence of a free and responsible government'. But for this right to have any real value, the public must have an 'equal freedom ... of examining and discussing [the] merits and demerits' of both incumbents and challengers (227). And between elections, a free press is the only channel that can circulate 'an adequate knowledge' thereby giving 'efficacy to [government's] responsibility to its constituents' (224).

Madison's concern with majority as well as minority tyranny and, especially, his novel theory of an ongoing public discourse via an effective mass media (newspapers, broadsides, pamphlets) were significant developments in the theory of democratic press liberty. But, drawing on the Anti-Federalist critics of the proposed Constitution of 1787–1788 and various democratic radicals of the 1790s, Madison went even further. Because true popular sovereignty required continuous public accountability, which in turn required a robust democratic public sphere, only eliminating 'previous restraint' (prior censorship by some government licenser) was not nearly enough protection. Citizens must feel confident that they are safe also from subsequent punishment, such as the fines and imprisonment threatened by the Sedition Act. If an author had to worry that his political criticism might result in punishment, he would likely think twice before publishing. The law would thus induce a kind of self-censorship, what we now call a 'chilling effect', which effectively restrains the critic and thus undermines public debate. This 'mockery', Madison insisted, simply can 'never be admitted to be the American idea' of freedom of the press (220).

Political speech, then, must be free from all criminal sanction. Only overt acts, actual 'resistance', can be proscribed and punished (219). Did not this mean that even false accusations might go unpunished? Yes, insisted Madison and other members of the emerging Democratic-Republican party. The Federalists' Sedition Act convictions amply demonstrated the futility of allowing defendants to prove their innocence by permitting evidence of the truth of their statements, Madison explained. Even 'simple and naked facts' are, in actual practice, rarely provable 'with the full and formal proof necessary in a court of law'. More importantly, in political discourse, opinion is 'in many cases inseparable from the facts', or – more likely – it is the statement of opinion that is deemed libellous.

And opinions simply 'cannot be the subjects of that kind of proof which appertains to facts, before a court of law' (226).

For Federalists then, and many critics today, this expansive notion of press liberty is too extreme, virtually guaranteeing abuse of this freedom and a host of resulting ill effects. Neither Madison nor his Jeffersonian colleagues disagreed. He explicitly conceded that 'some degree of abuse is inseparable' from the proper use of the political press. But 'it is better to leave a few of its noxious branches to their luxuriant growth, than by pruning them away, to injure the vigour of those yielding the proper fruits'. Despite its dangers, the unprecedented expansiveness of American press liberty was on balance advantageous to democratic governance. Indeed, 'to the press alone, chequered as it is with abuses, the world is indebted for all the triumphs which have been gained by reason and humanity, over error and oppression'. More specifically, the press had made the United States a 'free' nation and 'improved [its] political system' (222).

As radical as Madison's theory was, other Democratic-Republicans would take the argument even further. The New York lawyer Tunis Wortman, for example, would follow Madison in asserting that only actual conduct should be punished. But Wortman took the Sedition Act crisis as an opportunity to develop an exhaustive theory of democratic press liberty in his important book *A Treatise Concerning Political Enquiry and the Liberty of the Press* (1800). Here, he shared Madison's concern with any laws that might chill political speech but went into further detail, specifying that even civil suits for harm to the reputation of a maligned politician had to be strictly limited or the law would 'constantly damp the energy of Public Spirit and awe the timid and the irresolute into an abdication of their rights'.[3]

Wortman also took free speech theory further by analysing the other threats to a democratic public sphere. Any existing administration, for example, would have a great many practical advantages in public debate, not least a coterie of friends in the press and elsewhere that sought personal advantage by cozying up to those in power. Economic clout was another way in which existing elites could minimize public challenges to their position: 'Wealth exerts a pernicious empire over Manners and Morals'.[4] The goal of press liberty for Wortman was a public sphere that allowed all sides to be heard, despite Federalist judges who rejected such thinking, declaring from the bench that the 'truth has but one side, and listening to error, and falsehood is indeed a strange way to discover truth'.[5] For Wortman even more intensely than Madison, a public sphere of robust dissent 'produces Collision, engenders Argument, and affords exercise and energy to the intellectual powers; it corrects our errors, removes our prejudices, and strengthens our perceptions; it compels us to seek for the evidences of our knowledge, and habituates us to a frequent revisal of our sentiments'.[6] Ultimately, it allows for all of society to influence the public opinion that rules in a democracy.

For all of Wortman's advances, it was Madison's like-minded associate Thomas Cooper who developed the most thoroughgoing theory of the place of political dissent in democratic press liberty. A British expatriate and naturalized American citizen, Cooper argued during the Sedition Act crisis for a concept of press liberty that not only tolerated falsity but actively encouraged dissenting views, whether they were true or not. In a series of political essays – some written with Elizabeth Ryland Priestley, the daughter-in-law of his old friend, the famed chemist Joseph Priestley[7] – Cooper espoused a novel appreciation of the centrality of dissent to democracy. He maintained that even if an author's 'opinions be false, still it *may* be of importance and *can* be of no detriment that they should [be published]. At all events the greater is the chance of settling the point in question, and of striking out collateral knowledge during the discussion.'[8] Nor was this mere theory for Cooper: he was convicted in 1800 of seditious libel and punished with a heavy fine and six months in jail.

However, the example of Cooper's radical theory of press liberty is telling in more ways than one. Though he had been an outspoken critic of the slave trade in his youth, Cooper moved to South Carolina in 1819 to take up a professorship and eventually changed his views, espousing scientific racism and states' rights. These changes occasioned shifts in his approach to press liberty, and by 1826 he argued that untrue statements are punishable. More broadly, nineteenth-century America would see state-based (rather than federal) laws limiting political expression and even occasional mob violence against printers.

But if these examples demonstrate that conceptualizing American press liberty involves ongoing moral and political struggles, Madison's own practice suggests that this radical approach is practically possible as well as philosophically robust. As the US president during the War of 1812 against the British, Madison saw a great many threats to the fledging republic. Many of his critics were nearly treasonous in their opposition to the war and their support for the British (by late 1814, there was even a movement towards secession in New England). Moreover, this was a genuinely existential threat, as enemy soldiers occupied various parts of the country, even burning much of Washington, DC, including the White House. Yet, in the face of all these threats, Madison never considered legal efforts to silence the press, thereby demonstrating practically the viability of his political theory.

The theory of democratic press liberty espoused by Jeffersonians during the Sedition Act crisis, and elucidated by Madison in his *Report*, was the most expansive conception the world had ever seen. And to this day, America maintains a distinctively broad approach to political press liberty. The Sedition Act itself expired at the end of Adams's term and was never formally overruled. But the Supreme Court in 1964 famously maintained that 'the attack on its validity has carried the day in the court of history'. The 'lesson' of this episode was clear: 'restraint ... imposed upon criticism of government and public officials [is] inconsistent' with freedom of the press and democratic government.[9]

The 'Spirit of Independence' in Benjamin Constant's Thoughts on a Free Press

Bryan Garsten

What, indeed, is the outcome of all attacks made on freedom of the pen?
They embitter against the government all those writers possessed of that
spirit of independence inseparable from talent, who are forced to have
recourse to indirect and perfidious allusions. They necessitate the circulation
of clandestine and therefore all the more dangerous texts. They feed the
public greed for anecdotes, personal remarks, and seditious principles. They
give calumny the appearance, always an interesting one, of courage. In sum,
they attach far too much importance to the works about to be proscribed.[1]

A key moment in the debates about censorship and freedom of press in
France occurred in 1814–1815, when the restoration of the monarchy raised
fundamental constitutional questions. The first Treaty of Paris, which ended the
fighting of the Napoleonic Wars in the spring of 1814, restored the Bourbon
monarch Louis XVIII to the throne but required him to provide the French
people with a constitution or 'charter'. Granted to the people in early June of that
year, the royal Charter included as its eighth clause a statement that indicated
the wariness with which freedom of the press was endorsed, even by people
who favoured it: 'Frenchmen have the right to publish and to have printed their
opinions, while conforming with the laws, which are necessary to restrain abuses
of that liberty.'

In spite of the cautionary language about 'abuses', the immediate effect of
the statement was to initiate a period of new openness, in contrast with the
strict restrictions that Napoleon had instituted. A host of new political journals
sprung up right away, and debate about the Charter was energetic during
that summer. By the fall, however, the monarchy began to fear 'abuses' and
by October it had issued a set of more restrictive censorship laws, so that any

pamphlet less than twenty pages long now required prior approval by censors before it could be printed. The next spring, Napoleon marched back onto the scene and regained power during the famous 'Hundred Days' until his more decisive military defeat at Waterloo in June 1815, which was followed by a second Treaty of Paris. In the aftermath of that episode, the (again) restored monarchy of Louis XVIII issued an even more restrictive set of censorship laws designed to restrain public opinion from the kind of mistakes that were thought to have prepared the ground for the recent turn against the king.

During this year of intense debate about press freedoms, and the years of reflection that followed as the issue continued to be discussed, liberals of all stripes shared a strong endorsement of freedom of the press in principle. They differed among themselves, however, on the question of exactly when the principle should be turned into law, what form such a law should take and what the ultimate purpose of a free press was. In this brief essay, I highlight the distinctiveness of Benjamin Constant's position on these questions, in 1815 and in his earlier *Principles of Politics*, from which the chapter's opening quotation is drawn (106). I contrast Constant's position with two alternatives: the position articulated at roughly the same time by François Guizot and, more briefly, the position elaborated a bit later by Alexis de Tocqueville. The distinctiveness I mean to emphasize is the value that Constant placed on individuality and therefore on the practice of political disputation among individuals. Unlike Guizot and Tocqueville, Constant did not subordinate individuality and contestation to a process of finding a shared public reason for all nor did he understand its usefulness primarily as a spark to associational life and joint social action.

Guizot, a so-called 'doctrinaire' who would later take significant posts in government, wrote a pamphlet in 1814 endorsing freedom of the press but insisting that its application must always depend upon circumstances and, in particular, upon the readiness of the French people to wield the freedom responsibly. He began the pamphlet with arguments friendly to increasing freedoms. He argued that the French mood was at that moment better prepared for such freedom than it had been during the height of the revolutionary period. The French were tired of controversy, he noted, suspicious of passions in politics and thirsty not for new ideals but for effective, peaceful government. The public could hardly be less susceptible to the enthusiasms of demagoguery than in this moment of exhaustion after the Revolution and Napoleon's imperial ideology. 'The time of dreams has passed', wrote Guizot: 'We speak of nothing but moderation … We mistrust eloquence and enthusiasm; anything that takes such a tone inspires in advance an unfavourable prejudice. We are disposed to regard vehemence as the language of error, and a man who tries to move the passions, to seize the imagination, obtains little trust.'[2] Given this general exhaustion, he argued, freedom of the press would not be likely to result in dangerous crusades against the government.

At the same time, Guizot thought that the public had become too suspicious of government. Napoleon had dissolved any sense of trust citizens might once have had for the institutions. Napoleonic propaganda had accustomed the public to dismissing as euphemisms all that appeared in the press; it had neutered the power of the newspapers and journals and therefore stood in the way of the development of public enlightenment and reason that such publications should encourage. As a consequence, the public could hardly conceive of the love of country, and the willingness to make personal sacrifices for the nation, that France would need if it was going to escape Napoleon's legacy and rebuild itself into a sustainable constitutional monarchy. A mere change of regime would not be enough to tie the people to the government or produce trust in it, Guizot remarked; the people would need to be persuaded, and a free press was crucial to producing such persuasion or trust.

Even at this moment, decades before Guizot ascended to high posts within government during the years leading up to 1848, he demonstrated his affinity for ruling and his tendency to take the ruler's point of view. At the end of the pamphlet, when he summarized his argument in a peroration, he returned to this point, noting that only a properly functioning free press would make it possible for the people to 'make common cause with' the government.[3]

If that was the purpose of press freedoms, then their implementation had to be carefully regulated so as to ensure that abuses did not override benefits. Thus Guizot, noting deficiencies in the current state of public opinion and the press, endorsed a temporary regime of censorship in his 1814 pamphlet. He aimed to restrain and moderate the censorship by suggesting that no single censor should have exclusive dominion over any set of texts but instead should only be empowered to recommend 'suspension' of publication to a committee. The judgements of that committee would in turn be overseen by a rotating set of senators and representatives who could, every five years, request changes in the censorship regime to reflect the evolution of the French public.

Guizot envisioned a gradual move toward greater freedom of the press, as society became better educated, better accustomed to distinguishing among the many arguments and facts they would hear from the press, and better able to disregard harmful speech. To unleash full freedom of the press prematurely, however, would in his view have been rash. In language similar to the Charter's

concern about 'abuses' of press freedom, Guizot was willing to speak of the
harmful effects of 'the licence of the press' and to recommend that liberty be
tried gently (*doucement*).[4] He acknowledged that the censorship regime he was
content to accept might delay the publication of important truths, but he
argued that such delay was no great loss, if the truths were lasting ones: 'A few
pamphlets suppressed. A few passions reduced to silence. I don't see anything
terribly regrettable', he remarked, calling such delays merely an 'inconvenience'.[5]
His judgements were based on his view that the purpose of a free press was
to contribute to the long-term development of a public opinion unified in its
enlightenment.

Benjamin Constant, like Guizot, was an opponent of Napoleon (except
during his infamous about-face during the Hundred Days, when Constant
agreed to help draft a Constitution for Napoleon in the hope that he could
institutionalize liberal freedoms). Like Guizot, Constant hoped for a
constitutional system protective of liberty; both admired the English settlement
of 1688 and hoped for something similar in France. Thus it is striking that
Constant argued for a different position: full freedom from censorship and
prior restraint, for all publications, no matter how short. Some of Constant's
arguments were quite practical. He pointed out that eliminating certain
periodicals would require sealing the borders of France against journals
brought from outside, invasively searching people as they entered the country;
the circulation of printed materials across Europe was by then a fact of life,
and France could not ignore the circulatory quality of public opinion. He also
noticed that delays in publication such as the ones that Guizot accepted were
not without consequence, since they would tend to deprive legislators of all
the benefits that public debate about potential laws could provide during the
period of considering and amending those laws. And he remarked on the
absurdity of allowing only works over a certain number of pages to be printed
without prior restraint, since the effect would simply be to encourage people
with one thought 'to clog it with a heap of useless explanations, or of idle and
irrelevant digressions', simply to put themselves over the page qualification for
uncensored publication.[6]

Constant also pointed to another set of damaging consequences that a
regime of prior censorship and licensing would tend to produce: when the
government had the power to interfere with the publication of an article but
did not actually do so, readers would assume that the government positively
supported the sentiments expressed in it. The net result of the intertwining
of government with editorial decisions would therefore be to deprive the

journals of the independence that was the source of their legitimacy: 'That a man may be trusted when he says any thing, we must know that he had the power of saying the reverse, if such had been his opinion', wrote Constant. 'Unanimity always suggests an unfavourable suspicion, and with reason: for in important and complicated questions, there never was unanimity without slavery.'[7] In describing the unanimity of a censored public opinion as a form of 'slavery', Constant indicated how much he valued the back and forth of political controversy and debate. In this argument we can begin to see the ways in which his understanding of the function of a free press differed from Guizot's.

While Guizot hoped a free press would help produce, over time, a public opinion unified around 'truth, reason and justice', thus giving to representative government the legitimacy that came with public reasoning, Constant emphasized to a much greater degree the importance of suspicion and disagreement, and the legitimacy that came with transparency, surveillance and contestation. He thought a public sphere full of debating journals would produce citizens who were more accustomed to sorting through a messy world of conflicting opinions and even conflicting facts, who would learn to judge for themselves and to take the opinions of editorialists with a grain of salt. The proliferation of political opinions, like the proliferation of religious sects which Constant also endorsed, would have the effect of casting individuals back on the resources of their private judgement and the associated 'spirit of independence'. Lucien Jaume has described the contrast between Guizot and Constant on this point as indicative of two broad strains of post-revolutionary liberalism in France.[8]

Constant had viewed freedom of thought and expression this way at least since 1806, when he penned the original draft of *Principles of Politics*, his major work of political theory. There he had claimed that the need for a free press arose particularly in large, modern states in which citizens, living far away from one another, would not otherwise share any common understandings or even a common set of facts. Citing a well-known episode from Livy's history of Rome, Constant turned freedom of the press into part of his familiar thesis about the distinctiveness of modern politics, in comparison to the ancient world:

> Collatinus could expose Lucretia's body in the public square in Rome and everybody was apprised of the outrage done to him. The plebeian debtor could show his indignant fellow citizens the wounds inflicted on him by the greedy patrician, his usurious creditor. In our era, however, the vastness of states is an

obstacle to this kind of protest. Limited injustices always remain unknown to almost all the inhabitants in our huge countries. (110–111)

Without a shared public forum, freedom of the press to some extent took the place of political rights (121). A free press did not fully eliminate the distance between individuals that the scale of modern politics produced, but it provided those individuals with common materials necessary to make judgements about matters of shared concern.

When Constant argued that 'the question of press freedom is … the general one about the development of the human mind' (112), he did not primarily mean the development of a shared sense of reasonability. Instead, he was concerned with the conditions under which individuals could fully develop their personal capacities. Citing an intellectual torpor that he thought had accompanied press restrictions in parts of Europe and in China, he argued that curbs on intellectual debate would infect all areas of human achievement, since, as he put it, 'All men's faculties go together' (121). He elaborated, nature's 'design was that all our faculties should be in intimate liaison and that none should be subject to limitation without the others feeling the effect. Independent thinking is as vital, even to lighter literature, science, and the arts, as air is to physical life' (119).

Constant concluded his discussion by observing that limitations on the expression of thought would turn the most ambitious and important individuals against the state. Noting that 'nature will not be stopped from giving birth to men of talent and their active side will, indeed, have to be exercised' (124), Constant predicted that if free expression were stifled, such men would find themselves either turned into opponents of the regime or diverted into the 'egotism' of private accumulation. Constant insisted that such brilliant types had a 'right' to express themselves in political activity because 'celebrity, renown, and glory are the human race's patrimony. It does not belong to a few men to rob their equals of them. It is not permitted to them to make life wither by depriving it of what gives it its brilliance' (124). In his pamphlets *The Spirit of Conquest* and *Usurpation*, issued in 1813 just before the Bourbons' (first) restoration, Constant reproduced these passages in a chapter titled 'The effects of arbitrary power upon intellectual progress', turning them into an indictment of Napoleon for stifling brilliant figures. Presumably he had in mind examples such as Germaine de Stael, whose work Napoleon had ordered burned, or Constant himself, who had been punished with exile.[9] His arguments built a romantic appreciation of individual talent and genius into the case for representative government, constitutionalism and the free press.

Behind Constant's approach to the issue was not merely a certain romanticism about talented individuals but also a conviction that public opinion could not be marshalled and dominated by institutions without corrupting its essential character as a circulating and independent force. He thought that opinions would lose their power if harnessed by governing institutions, just as religious opinions did. Indeed, the fundamental dynamic driving the whole human history of religions, on his elaborate account, was a tendency for opinions to grow stale and stagnant once institutionalized, and eventually to break free from institutional fetters and take on new life. Constant's account of public opinion had the same structure. Both public opinion and religious sentiment were most vital when left free and open to the private judgement of individuals, on his view; newspapers and journals were valuable insofar as they facilitated that judgement.[10]

Constant's fundamentally individualistic approach to public opinion can therefore also be contrasted with the remarks that Alexis de Tocqueville made on newspapers some years later. While in the first volume of *Democracy in America* Tocqueville had offered a qualified defence of press freedom similar to the one advanced by other liberals, he offered a more distinctive argument in the second volume. He noticed there that newspapers functioned not only or even primarily as a means of communication among all citizens at once but as the linkage among particular groups of citizens who shared an interest in certain issues, localities or interests, but who were separated by geography or, more fundamentally, by the withdrawal into private life, the *individualism*, that democratic societies tended to produce. Given the dispersed nature of modern democratic citizenship, he concluded that 'if there were no newspapers there would almost never be common action'.[11] Newspapers, he argued, were necessary to create associations, those crucial intermediate bodies that Tocqueville thought saved society from its otherwise anonymous, vast, formless and passive homogeneity. Newspapers brought individuals together and so helped to give society its structure, coherence and agency.

Guizot, then, saw public opinion as a resource for the state, while Tocqueville linked public opinion to the art of association outside the state. Compared with both perspectives, Constant's arguments stand out for their emphasis on the individual and his talents. Whether that emphasis on individuality would lead to a corrosive individualism, as Tocqueville feared it might, was a problem that liberals at the time were only beginning to grapple with and arguably one they still have not fully sorted out.

The Royal Shambles (1816): Hiding Republicanism in Plain Sight

Jason McElligott

Have we no *men* in France? —
No they all died with *y* Republic!
Who is that dragging the ___ ?
He is of a Nation that once *put* their
Tyrant to death but they *forget*!

Unfurl that Banner & to the
right about face!

not time yet!

rue's wife

In August 1816, an obscure London bookseller named William Hone, who traded from small premises at 55 Fleet Street, published a visual print entitled *The Royal Shambles or the Progress of Legitimacy & Reestablishment of Religion & Social Order -!!! -!!!.*[1] A detail from the print serves as this chapter's opening 'quotation', with the whole image reproduced over the page.

The sheet, measuring 21.8 centimetres high and 55 centimetres long, was drawn by the leading caricaturist of the day, George Cruikshank, who was both a personal friend and business collaborator of Hone, who as publisher commissioned the work and guided the print's content. *The Royal Shambles* exists in two different states: uncoloured and hand-coloured. The price of a coloured sheet seems to have fluctuated between three and four shillings. An uncoloured sheet is reproduced in this essay. A study-quality copy of the image is available on the website of the British Museum.[2] *The Royal Shambles* was one of about 20,000 satirical or humorous visual prints produced in London during the years between 1770 and 1830. Taken as a whole, these visual prints testify to a remarkably vibrant culture of political polemic and invective which pulled no punches in terms of challenging good taste, social graces and sexual propriety.[3]

The Royal Shambles is a burlesque parody of the celebration which took place in Paris on 8 July 1816 on the anniversary of the occupation of the city by Louis XVIII.[4] It is a satire against royalism in France and the role played by England and its allies in securing the restoration of the Bourbon monarchy. Unlike most of the British political nation, which welcomed the defeat of Napoleon and the end of the war, Hone was evidently unhappy at the return of the Bourbons. *The Royal Shambles* is an explicit attack on the political settlement in France, but, it will be suggested, it also hides in plain sight a desire for the rebirth of the French Republic, in a format sensitive to the dangers of censorship.

In the print, King Louis XVIII processes through the capital on a cannon inscribed with the words *Jure Divino*. The pageant is led by monks, and followed by acolytes, and the cannon is drawn along by the Duke of Wellington in military attire. The procession tramples on the prostrate bodies of men, women and children: the people of France. Wellington plants the spiked sole of his jack-boot on the head of a prostrate man. Louis grasps Wellington's sword and is told by the Duke: 'Hold fast & never fear – but if you let go my swoard you'll fall *head fore most*.' Behind the cannon comes an ass inscribed with the word 'Legitimacy', which carries the two nephews of Louis XVIII and their wives. An 'Odour of Sanctity' emanates from the rear of the animal. The route of the procession is flanked by soldiers with crosses and priests with bayonets. All but one of the civilians standing at the back shouts not 'Vive le Roi' but 'Vive l'oie', or 'long live the goose'. The vast majority of 'the people' are at the front of the print: dead or dying.

The woman standing between the cannon and the ass is identified in the print as Madame Pleignier. During the procession of 8 July 1816, she had petitioned Louis XVIII to spare her husband, Jacques, who had been sentenced to death for his part in a plot to seize Paris, overthrow the monarchy and invite Napoleon Bonaparte back to the capital.[5] The poor unfortunates being mutilated and executed on the raised ground behind the procession represent those like Jacques Pleignier and his comrades who were decapitated at the Place de Justice on 27 July 1816 after having their right hands cut off. In this print, the word 'shambles' has a deliberate double meaning. It can be taken to refer to the confused, disorderly and shambolic nature of the royal procession but also to the 'shambles': a noxious, unpleasant area within a city where fish were gutted and animals were killed and slaughtered. Pleignier and his comrades were only a fraction of the total number of French former citizens who would die as subjects in this royal shambles.

However, *The Royal Shambles* goes beyond expressing an unpatriotic dissatisfaction with Britain's role in imposing a monarchical settlement on France. The vignette consisting of five soldiers in the top right-hand corner of the print seems to pine for the return of the French Republic. These men, one officer and four soldiers, wear the uniforms of the defeated army of Napoleon. They are dejected and down-cast, and a broken cannon lies in front of them. This piece of ordinance may represent Bonaparte's fortunes: he began his military career as an artillery officer.

One soldier holds erect a furled tricolour flag surmounted by that quintessential symbol of the Revolution: a Cap of Liberty. The officer, on the left, addresses this man: 'Unfurl that Banner & to the right about face!' The soldier answers: 'Not time *yet*!' The other three say to each other:

> Have we no *men* in France?
> — No they all died with ye Republic!
> — Who is that dragging the [----]?
> — He is of a Nation that once put their Tyrant to death but they *forget*!

The '[----]' refers to the king, although this could always be denied in court. The man dragging the king is, of course, the Duke of Wellington. Wellington was born in Ireland, but the comment that 'He is of a nation that once put their Tyrant to death' is evidently intended to refer to England in particular, or Britain in general. The tyrant put to death by the British must surely be read as a reference to Charles I, executed in 1649. This scene on the hill is a favourable comment on regicide in British history, a statement of regret for the loss of the Republic in

France, and a hope that it will be reborn in time. The shouts of '*vive l'oie*' – (long live the goose) – give a hint of how that rebirth is to be achieved: geese were usually harvested by bringing a blade down upon their necks. This explains why Wellington warns Louis that British military forces prevent him falling '*head fore most*'. It is not accidental that at the centre and top of the print, above all the squalid slaughter of the royal shambles, stands Madame La Guillotine: clean, quiet and supremely effective. The basket in front of the machine waits to be filled. The shambles of 1816 consists of those being killed by kings. At some point in the future – 'Not time *yet*!' – the tide will turn.

This reading of *The Royal Shambles* contradicts everything that we think we know about William Hone and his politics. Hone played a minor role in the struggle for the reform of Parliament during the 1810s, but was catapulted to national prominence in December 1817 by the decision of the Attorney General to try him for blasphemous libel for publishing three parodies of the Anglican liturgy which attacked the corruption, venality and cruelty of the government. Hone faced three trials on three consecutive days, and on each occasion his rousing speeches to the jury (which have been described by E. P. Thompson as among the best ever made in an English court) convinced them to acquit him.[6] This unprecedented defeat for the authorities meant that he became the most prominent polemicist in favour of Reform in England. Between 1818 and 1821 his satires and squibs sold in their tens of thousands.

The modern literature on Hone presents him as a sensible, moderate radical – a reformer – who actively eschewed violence.[7] Hone's polemics are consistently placed within a constitutionalist idiom which condemned current abuses but tended to place the blame on one person or a small clique of ministers and implied that the system could be successfully reformed once this person or clique had been removed from power. Hone was certainly at pains to stress his moderation and reasonableness in both his public utterances and private correspondence. It is natural to assume that this position represents Hone's actual politics, and it would go too far to see him as a violent republican, but there are occasions when one can detect decidedly radical undertones in his work, and he consciously adopted particular forms of publication in order to circumvent punishment by the state.

During this period even moderate, peaceful reformers were often subject to harsh penalties. One of the reasons that Hone confined his condemnation of the settlement in France to a visual print must surely have been the traditionally wide degree of latitude given to these items, partly because of the high social status of those expected to purchase such expensive items, but also due to the difficulty of proving the transgressive nature of any print or portion of a print. A defendant could always argue that: a prosecutor had read a meaning into a print which was never intended to be there; a particularly grotesque rendering of an individual was not actually intended to represent that individual; or that an objectionable idea simply represented the thoughts of those drawn in the print.

In 1817, Hone mistakenly calculated that attacking the government through printed parodies of the Anglican liturgy would protect him from prosecution. At exactly that time a government rattled by recession and economic unrest was anxious to teach the radical press a lesson, and Hone was carefully selected for punishment because it was believed that it could be suggested that his offences were not against the government, but against God and the Church. It is intriguing, though, that in court Hone expressed bewilderment that he had been prosecuted because, he argued, parodies were as old as printing itself, and there had never been a prosecution for parody in an English court.[8] The absence of any previous prosecution in connection with a parody must have been a factor in determining his decision to deploy this genre against the government during that very dangerous year.

Between 1818 and 1821, Hone collaborated with Cruikshank to produce a series of wonderfully comic satires against the regime in Britain. Many of these best-selling squibs aped the form, look and language of children's rhymes, stories and songs. This was at least partly to render ridiculous any potential prosecution: what rational person could possibly take offence at childish rhymes and ditties? A key example, *The Man in the Moon* of 1820, blends together a host of influences from popular chapbooks, ballads, songs, lullabies, catches and rhymes.[9] It is ostensibly nothing more than a witty satire against the Prince Regent. There is nothing particularly seditious about the pamphlet until one reads the two epigrams at the start of the text in their original context. The first, on the title-page itself, is from Shakespeare's *Cymbeline*, Act III, Scene I, when the Roman official Caius Lucius informs the British King Cymbeline that he has not paid the necessary yearly tribute to his Overlord, Caesar. Cymbeline's son Cloten speaks the words quoted by Hone – 'if Caesar can hide the Sun with a blanket, or put the Moon in his pocket, we will pay him tribute for light'. – as a way of asserting that his father should refrain from prostrating himself before the tyrant. Cymbeline then asserts that it is fitting for a 'warlike people, whom we reckon/Ourselves to be' to throw off Roman tyranny, and draws encouragement from the other peoples of the Roman Empire who 'for/Their liberties are now in arms'.

The theme of armed resistance to tyranny is continued in the second of the epigrams quoted at the start of *The Man in the Moon*:

Is there not
Some hidden thunder in the stores of heaven,
Red with uncommon wrath, to blast the men
Who owe their greatness to their country's ruin?

These words are from Act I, Scene I of Joseph Addison's 1713 play *Cato*, which portrayed the Roman senator Cato (95–46 BCE), descendant of Cato the Censor, as the noble, heroic and high-minded defender of the republic, who committed suicide rather than surrender to the victorious tyrant Julius Caesar. Addison's play opens with Caesar marching on the beleaguered members of the Roman Senate in the north African town of Utica. The odds are heavily against Cato but he is determined to fight 'the cause/Of honour, virtue, liberty, and Rome', and he tries to rally his supporters with a speech which ends with a rousing call to arms: 'A day, an hour of virtuous liberty,/Is worth a whole eternity in bondage'. At the end of the play, with the fall of Utica imminent, Cato commits suicide, but as he dies news arrives that Spain has risen against Caesar. One of Cato's sons is left to lament: 'Were Cato at their head, once more might Rome/Assert her rights, and claim her liberty.' As with the first epigram, there is hope for the future even in the most difficult of times because there are brave souls in Europe in arms against tyranny.[10]

It is hard to delineate the exact contours of Hone's political ideology. He embraced constitutionalism in his printed polemics and tended to campaign under a series of broad slogans: 'liberty', 'freedom', and an end to 'tyranny'. He was also adept at embedding his polemics within formats and genres which he believed were less likely to be censured than traditional printed texts. His surviving private correspondence is very measured and careful, partly because he knew that the authorities commonly intercepted and read such communications. It would be foolish to argue that Hone was 'really' a republican who contemplated the use of violence to achieve his goals. However, this short essay has examined two of Hone's publications in which one can detect oblique praise of revolutionary violence if one focuses on the margins of the texts.

These works display a tension between the desire to communicate a dangerous idea and the need to restrict the number of those who were conscious of its presence. Most who saw *The Royal Shambles* would undoubtedly have laughed at Louis XVIII. Many would have felt sympathy on a human level with Jacques Pleignier and the other condemned men, but it is not clear how many properly understood the small vignette of the Napoleonic soldiers, and probably only those already sympathetic to republicanism. The same might be said of the epigrams in *The Man in the Moon*, which are perhaps even more oblique. So perhaps these asides are best thought of as functioning not as a means of winning over a wide audience, but as a 'code' for a select group of like-minded friends and comrades 'in the know'.

Censorship was a very real danger for Hone and its presence forced him to adopt strategies to minimize his personal risk. There is, however, a more insidious reason why Hone's revolutionary asides have long been overlooked. During the second half of the 1820s he moved away from radical politics, and built a national profile for himself as a peddler of apolitical books built around entertaining historical snippets and tales. He now actively re-wrote his earlier radical career to downplay or erase his involvement with a number of his most famous pamphlets, including *The Man in the Moon*.[11] During the 1830s Hone's political trajectory led him to publicly oppose parliamentary reform, embrace a politically conservative form of evangelical Christianity, and portray his life before being saved by Jesus as that of an 'infidel'. This double censorship – first having to hide radical messages in texts and then choosing to rewrite his early life – ensured that historians have long overlooked the extent of Hone's radicalism during the turbulent years between 1816 and 1821.

Mill and Censoriousness

Gregory Claeys

*In our times, from the highest class of society down to the lowest, every one
lives as under the eye of a hostile and dreaded censorship. Not only in what
concerns others, but in what concerns only themselves, the individual or
the family do not ask themselves – what do I prefer? or, what would suit my
character and disposition? or, what would allow the best and highest in me to
have fair play, and enable it to grow and thrive? They ask themselves, what
is suitable to my position? what is usually done by persons of my station and
pecuniary circumstances? or (worse still) what is usually done by persons of a
station and circumstances superior to mine? I do not mean that they choose
what is customary, in preference to what suits their own inclination. It does
not occur to them to have any inclination, except for what is customary. Thus
the mind itself is bowed to the yoke: even in what people do for pleasure,
conformity is the first thing thought of; they like in crowds; they exercise
choice only among things commonly done: peculiarity of taste, eccentricity
of conduct, are shunned equally with crimes: until by dint of not following
their own nature, they have no nature to follow: their human capacities are
withered and starved: they become incapable of any strong wishes or native
pleasures, and are generally without either opinions or feelings of home
growth, or properly their own. Now is this, or is it not, the desirable condition
of human nature?*[1]

John Stuart Mill's *On Liberty* (1859) is today justly famous for offering the
most vigorous defence of the individual's right to be left alone in matters
which concern only themselves, and it is chiefly for this argument that Mill is
usually regarded as our most important liberal political philosopher. The chief
reason for the vehemence of Mill's defence lies in the idea of the 'tyranny of the
majority', which he largely inherited from Alexis de Tocqueville's *Democracy in*

America (2 vols, 1835–1840). In vol. 1, ch. 15 of his famous work, Tocqueville had dilated at length upon the 'effects of the tyranny of the majority upon the national character of the Americans', describing this as a new and worrying tendency in democracy and complaining that 'I know no country in which there is so little true independence of mind and freedom of discussion as in America.' Such was the overwhelming power of public opinion in the United States, Tocqueville lamented, that 'freedom of opinion does not exist in America'.[2] Mill, who had never visited the US, took this to heart, reviewing Tocqueville's volumes as they appeared. *On Liberty* was in part a direct reaction to Tocqueville's paradox that greater democracy might fatally undermine liberty of thought and that the power of public opinion was sufficiently great generally to be the source of the 'love of glory; the love of praise; the love of admiration; the love of respect and deference; even the love of sympathy'.[3] This chapter will take up two aspects of Mill's discussion of these issues: the question of freedom of speech in relation to religion; and the issue of 'moral coercion' to improve or restrain behaviour in everyday life. I will try to show that while Mill was very averse to 'censorship' in the sense of interceding with free speech, he in fact encouraged 'censoriousness' in the sense of censuring behaviour deserving of moral disapprobation but not legal restraint. The spectrum and type of interventions suggested by Mill were thus quite different from those often associated with liberalism.

In chapter 2 of *On Liberty*, 'On the Liberty of Thought and Discussion', Mill tried to meet these problems head-on, in the recognition that social intolerance might be even more stifling than legal repression in preventing the free play of opinion and thus the emergence of truth. Tying freedom of speech closely to his general theory of progress, he proposed a regime of far greater toleration, official and unofficial, than existed in either Britain or the US at the time. He famously contended that even 'If all mankind minus one, were of one opinion, and only one person were of the contrary opinion, mankind would be no more justified in silencing that one person, than he, if he had the power, would be justified in silencing mankind' (33). We could, he insisted, never be sure that an opinion being stifled was in fact false, and the presumption of infallibility which accompanied the stifling was itself wrong. But we might well reflect that even if it were, false opinions served the vital purpose of sharpening the truth of their counterparts. With respect to liberty of the press, he here took up an issue, tyrannicide, which remains highly relevant to us today, albeit under the label of 'terrorism'. Mill argued that abstract discussions of the principle itself should not be deemed punishable, but 'the instigation to it, in a specific case, may be a proper subject of punishment, but only if an overt act has followed, and at least a probable connexion can be established between the act and the instigation' (32).

Mill's chief concern, however, was with more common instances of the suppression of free speech. Here religion was Mill's particular example, from the killing of Socrates to the persecution of Jesus (whom Mill admired) to the gaoling of Mill's friend George Jacob Holyoake, to the refusal of contemporaries to swear an oath on the Bible in court. Bypassing the issue of the truth content of any particular religion, and offering a radically relativist and environmentalist conception of religious truth instead, Mill contended that religious beliefs were a function of upbringing. Thus the same causes which made someone 'a Churchman in London, would have made him a Buddhist or a Confucian in Pekin' (35). As an agnostic (a label he usually preferred to atheist, though he admitted he had never believed in a deity), Mill believed that religion played a major role in inhibiting the progress of rational argument, particularly where practical morality was concerned, and led to a host of unreasonable restrictions (sabbatarian legislation, diet) which were unjustifiable on any other grounds than mere prejudice. Indisputably he defended here his own particular cause; he was reluctant to trumpet his agnosticism too loudly, but he did state that 'a large proportion of infidels in all ages have been persons of distinguished integrity and honour' (55–56). Heresy had the virtue of challenging the propositions of every religion, and its advantages had to be acknowledged as such. Social heresies, too, such as Rousseau's critique of civilization, had to be met head on rather than suppressed.

Religion was thus the paradigm of unquestioned dogma, whose criticism was an essential element in the progress of rational opinion generally even if the process was hemmed in at times by prudential considerations. Mill's defence of freedom of opinion was correspondingly almost unbounded, and certainly went well beyond the limit of 'offence' which is currently common in public debate, particularly where religious belief was concerned. Within certain boundaries (speech before an agitated crowd, for instance, in which 'speech' and 'act' were nearly proximate), Mill clearly would have permitted such criticism even in the face of the hypersensitivity of some zealous onlookers. 'Harm' thus did not usually translate into 'hurt', defined subjectively as 'offence', where opinions were concerned. To bow to either majority or minority voices in such matters in order to avoid 'offence' would be a retrograde move. If we assume 'offence' to entail hurting someone's feelings, or causing them to feel angry, resentful or irritated, we can safely say that Mill would have regarded these responses as a reasonable price to pay for intellectual freedom.

Current legislation, however, is remarkably loose respecting these issues. In Britain, the Public Order Act (sections 4a and 5, 1986) deems it an offence where threatening, abusive or insulting words or behaviour causes or is likely to cause another person harassment, alarm or distress (in 2012 the removal of the word 'insulting' was proposed). In addition the Racial and Religious Hatred Act (2006) makes it an offence to use threatening words or behaviour intended to stir up religious hatred, with up to seven years imprisonment if convicted. As has often been pointed out, the problem with such legislation is that 'alarm', 'distress', indeed even 'religious hatred' are almost entirely subjective categories. One person may tolerate an open debate which impugns the first principles of their religion; the next may deem it offensive to question in any way any precept they hold. To the one, rational discussion can be countenanced; to the other, every such discussion strikes at the heart of psychological identity and is a deep wound. Close textual scholarship to demonstrate the historical rather than divine formation of religious beliefs may be deemed unacceptable. In the clash of two rights, that of free speech and freedom of religious expression, the latter clearly must take second place.

Mill would doubtless have been unhappy about this. His own position seems to have been that 'the free expression of all opinions should be permitted, on condition that the manner be temperate, and do not pass the bounds of fair discussion' (95–96). He insisted that 'if the test be offence to those whose opinion is attacked ... experience testifies that this offence is given whenever the attack is telling and powerful, and that every opponent who pushes them hard, and whom they find it difficult to answer, appears to them, if he shows any strong feeling on the subject, an intemperate opponent' (96). Attacks on principles were thus to be permitted, those on persons as such, not. The emergence of the 'faith school' in Britain, and the near-coercion of parents to feign religious belief in order to secure places for their children at schools, would moreover have offended Mill even more as promoting intolerance, narrow-mindedness and bigotry, which were in fact the qualities he most associated with the modern 'revival of religion' (57).

The realm of opinion was however quite different from that of action. Mill's response was complicated by the fact that he wished society to be guided morally in part through interventions respecting the behaviour of others. Here it is actions, particularly in public, which are at issue, rather than opinion. At the outset of *On Liberty*, he introduced the famous 'harm principle' in contending that 'the only purpose for which power can be rightfully exercised over any member of a civilized community, against his will, is to prevent harm to others. His own good, either physical or moral, is not a sufficient warrant' (22). Just what Mill meant by 'harm' here, and what impact this has for 'paternalistic' legislation and social interference, has been the subject of much controversy. But clearly he did intend to minimize occasions when government and/or public opinion interfered with behaviour which was in his view essentially only 'self-regarding'; that is to say, it did not harm others directly, either physically or through their rights or interests. Mill has been taken to have wished the state to relinquish inquisition in the bedroom and in regard to intoxication, among other issues, provided no obvious injuries to others resulted from any activity. Clearly, however, there are many difficulties with establishing just when 'harm' occurs, and where consequently lines are to be drawn between behaviour which is permissible and that which is not. Non-self-regarding behaviour in Mill's view included bearing children whom one was unable to support, and in some cases he believed the state could compel individuals to labour to maintain their offspring.[4] Yet the 'harm' distinction was intended only to apply to *physical* interference in people's behaviour, not extra-judicial chastisement of the sort which routinely occurs in everyday life. But Mill was clear that we had a right 'to act upon our unfavourable opinion of any one, not to the oppression of his individuality, but in the exercise of ours'. This might involve avoiding someone, cautioning others against them, 'if we think his example or conversation likely to have a pernicious effect on those with whom he associates', and giving 'a preference over him in optional good offices, except those which tend to his improvement'. 'In these various modes', Mill conceded, 'a person may suffer very severe penalties at the hands of others, for faults which directly concern only himself; but he suffers these penalties only in so far as they are the natural, and, as it were, the spontaneous consequences of the faults themselves, not because they are purposely inflicted on him for the sake of punishment' (139). In Mill's view it was quite right to expect the better educated and/or publicly minded to play a monitory role of this type, in keeping with his aversion to hero-worship but acknowledgement that following wiser or nobler individuals was often a matter of course. It is equally clear, however, that for those not susceptible to social pressure of this kind, little result could be expected.

This aspect of Mill's theory has been given much less attention than other features of his theory of liberty.[5] Yet it has led some authors to accuse Mill of projecting a form of 'moral totalitarianism' in the assumption that promoting an image of man as a 'progressive being' meant imposing a particular form of utilitarianism upon society generally and regulating individual conduct in everyday life accordingly. Thus in Maurice Cowling's view, Mill 'wished to moralize all social activity' in proposing that utilitarianism, and more specifically Auguste Comte's even narrower conception of the 'Religion of Humanity', would supplant the role currently played by Christianity. Mill's liberalism was thus 'a dogmatic, religious one, not the soothing night-comforter for which it is sometimes mistaken'.[6]

Upon reflection, it is certainly unclear whether all social activity is not in fact already generally 'moralized' in civil society, in the sense of being valued or not valued, although social mores can of course alter swiftly, along with immunity to chastisement. But equally this argument presses us to clarify what patterns of intervention are justified in respect of what categories of behaviour. How then did Mill conceive that the principles of non-intervention on the basis of the harm principle and intervention on the basis of justifiable moral intervention could be reconciled? When, in other words, was 'censoriousness', or the proclivity to criticize the behaviour of others, to be condemned, and when to be lauded? Mill clearly opposed most forms of traditional censorship, for instance, of the press. Yet as I have argued elsewhere, he clearly felt that 'the moral coercion of public opinion', as *On Liberty* puts it, had a positive role to play in regulating behaviour in the public space, and in particular in 'stimulating each other to increased exercise of their higher faculties, and increased direction of their feelings and aims towards wise instead of foolish, elevating instead of degrading objects and contemplations'. Mill permitted 'advice, instruction, persuasion, and avoidance by other people if thought necessary by them for their own good' as 'the only measures by which society can justifiably express its dislike or disapprobation' of an individual's conduct (168–169). The trick here, he thought, was that exhortation and advice 'offered' or 'obtruded' had necessarily to fall short of 'the evil of allowing others to constrain him to what they deem his good'.[7] Yet, clearly, public opinion is here to act not upon opinion, but upon actions which are in some sense morally reprehensible without being actually harmful. And 'constraint', if a milder term than 'coercion', is still not free of ambiguity any more than 'liberty' itself is. Distinguishing between 'force' and 'pressure' in non-coercive behavioural regulation is thus an essential starting-point.

The issue here in part is that, as Joseph Hamburger has indicated, Mill did not describe how such censure was to operate. In Hamburger's view Mill proposed 'social controls that could legitimately restrict individual liberty', including 'expressions of distaste and contempt and other pressures of opinion he sanctioned for certain self-regarding actions'. Thus a problem resulted here 'for anyone wishing to portray Mill as a friend to an ample individual liberty'.[8] Yet is it 'liberty' which is being interfered with here? Depending on how they are defined, such 'social controls' would not necessarily restrict liberty so much as hint at the bounds of social propriety, and remind us that in the grand collision of rights we have a duty to protect the rights of others. (There are many possible examples; but think of someone shouting loudly down their mobile phone at the table next to mine in a restaurant: I look reprovingly at them in the hope not that they will necessarily cease their conversation, but in the probably vain expectation that they will reduce the volume so as not to impinge upon my right to enjoy my meal in relative peace.) 'Liberty' to Mill did not mean unlimited 'licence' to do whatever one wanted. It meant behaving with a due regard to the rights of others as well as a due regard to the necessity for society to move voluntarily towards an improvement in virtue; towards a strengthening of social ties; and a stronger sense of the need both to identify and to uphold the common good. 'The liberty of the individual must be thus far limited; he must not make himself a nuisance to other people', Mill insisted (101). Mill can here clearly be construed as inhibiting extremely unsocial behaviour but not liberty unduly.

We have seen in this chapter that Mill, far from being a libertarian who favoured unlimited individual expression in both thoughts and actions, established clear boundaries for both freedom of opinion and, in a more complex manner, freedom of action. Mill did not accept 'offence' as a ground for suppressing opinions, particularly where religion was concerned. And while he proposed the 'harm' principle to attempt to distinguish between acts which might be interfered with by society and the state and those which should be left alone, he left a large but usually unexplored domain for social intervention in self-regarding acts which nonetheless had potentially harmful implications. In the realm of language, while Mill was clearly opposed to the censorship of written texts, spoken words aiming at censoriousness which wounded the feelings of others by causing 'offence' were doubtless still permissible in his view. The caveat that such expressions be 'temperate', which implies not being emotionally charged, is nonetheless an important one. He was accordingly much less interventionist on the one hand, and rather more on the other, than our own climate of opinion indicates. Here, his general line of thought may be described in terms of a positive paternalism aiming to promote good, rather than an effort to reduce harm as such, though in both cases his views remain controversial. These observations leave many questions unanswered but certainly prove the case for Mill's recurring relevance.

'Every Idea is an Incitement':
Holmes and Lenin

Sue Curry Jansen

Holmes: *Persecution for the expression of opinions seems to me perfectly logical. … But when men have realized that time has upset many fighting faiths, they may come to believe even more than they believe the very foundations of their own conduct that the ultimate good desired is better reached by free trade in ideas – that the best test of truth is the power of the thought to get itself accepted in the competition of the market, and that truth is the only ground upon which their wishes safely can be carried out. That at any rate is the theory of our Constitution. It is an experiment, as all life is an experiment.*[1]

Lenin: *[In] capitalist usage, freedom of the press means freedom of the rich to bribe the press, freedom to use their wealth to shape and fabricate so-called public opinion. In this respect, too, the defenders of 'pure democracy' prove to be defenders of an utterly foul and venal system that gives the rich control over the mass media. They prove to be deceivers of the people, who, with the aid of plausible, fine-sounding, but thoroughly false phrases, divert them from the concrete historical task of liberating the press from capitalist enslavement.*[2]

The year 1919 has been described as a year that 'changed the world'.[3] The Treaty of Versailles redrew the map of Europe and imposed war reparations against Germany, creating conditions that would lead to World War II. Russia, which had withdrawn from the Allied effort after the Bolshevik Revolution, was an anomaly; perceived as a potentially dangerous outlier in 1919, its vision of worldwide proletarian revolution disturbed the peace of many a capitalist. Across the Atlantic, anarchists sent a series of letter bombs to American public officials, including one addressed to Supreme Court Justice Oliver Wendell Holmes Jr. that was intercepted by the postal service and another that damaged the home of Attorney General Mitchell Palmer. With the support of Congress, Palmer responded with a series of violent raids, arrests and deportations of anarchists and leftists in 1919 and 1920, a period that was dubbed 'The Red Scare'. It would later become known as America's 'First Red Scare': its sequel, the virulent 'red-baiting' of the early Cold War era, produced an even more chilling blight on the life of the mind.

In terms of censorship, the two 1919 texts reproduced above, from Justice Holmes's dissenting opinion in *Abrams v. US* and Russian revolutionary leader Vladimir Ilyich Lenin's Speech at the Opening Session of the First Congress of the Communist International, have been retrospectively elevated to iconic representations of competing visions of the role markets play in the circulation of ideas. From a twenty-first-century vantage point, they seem to capture in starkly reductive terms the East-West/communist-capitalist ideological visions that defined most of the twentieth century.

Torn from history and reduced to propaganda, Holmes's statement is now misinterpreted by many as a defence of capitalist free markets and of markets as the chief arbiters of truth as well as, by extension, trustworthy censors of bad ideas. Conversely, Lenin's speech frames capitalist marketplaces of ideas as rigged: controlled and censored by the rich, who use the mass media to deceive the people and manipulate public opinion to advance their own ends. The task of 'liberating the press from capitalist enslavement' therefore requires censoring capitalist censors.

For sixty years, endless variations on this oppositional – either/or – rendering of freedom and censorship supported powerful master narratives within each sphere of influence which, except for a brief strategic respite during World War II, proscribed any breaching of borders. From 1961 to 1989, the Berlin Wall cemented the divide. The fall of the Wall signalled the beginning of the end for the Soviet Union as well as the unmooring of these seminal documents from their respective orthodoxies.

Restoring these texts to their historical contexts permits us to recover some of their lost resonance as well as to interpret them more lucidly through the lens of the present. It also exposes some revealing conundrums. Many current champions of Holmes's market metaphor are, for example, unaware that he actually deployed it in defence of the free expression of self-proclaimed Russian revolutionaries and did so against the prevailing opinions of the American public, the Congress, the Justice Department and the majority of the Supreme Court. Holmes's contemporary critics claimed the dissent contradicted his earlier decisions and ran counter to the entire tradition of First Amendment case law as it had developed up to that time. In short, Holmes' opinion failed the test of the marketplace of ideas in his own time although it acquired salience much later.

Lenin's argument is also fraught with complexity. We now know too well the tragic historical consequences of his censorial logic. Yet, Lenin's solution to the problem of the liberal press – censoring the censors – draws on an enduring flaw in Enlightenment-based defences of free expression: their Achilles' heel, the absence of any reliable universal principle securing liberalism's enfranchisement of free expression. Every liberal defence of free expression contains what journalist Walter Lippmann called 'a weasel clause' which limits its range.[4] Holmes himself, despite his expansive support for allowing expression of 'opinions we loathe and believe fraught with death', drew the line at views that 'so imminently threaten immediate interference with the lawful and pressing purposes of the law that an immediate check is required to save the country' (277). But even this narrowly conceived weasel clause has proven remarkably elastic under the US national security state.

Bringing these two censorship moments together, instead of cloistering them in opposition, will not yield the Holy Grail of a universal principle for securing free expression, but it will demonstrate why the problem of censorship is so intractable.

Justice Oliver Wendell Holmes Jr. (1841–1935) has been widely mythologized in America: the favourite son of an internationally famous author of patrician lineage, he was a thrice-wounded Civil War veteran who possessed exceptional eloquence of both pen and voice. He was the subject of a bestselling semi-fictional biography shortly after his death, *Yankee from Olympus*, as well as a hit Broadway play and film, *Magnificent Yankee*. The first full biography, which revealed some of his less laudable beliefs and behaviour, did not appear until 1989.[5] By then popular interest in Holmes had waned and the patina of the myth was too well burnished for it to be tarnished. Today, Holmes is most often remembered for his 1919 Abrams dissent, which provides the philosophical foundation for modern interpretations of the First Amendment.

In 1919, the First Amendment of the US Constitution, which prohibits Congress from abridging freedom of speech and the press, was little more than fine-sounding phrases. Emergency wartime measures, including the Espionage Act of 1917 and its 1918 amendment, the Sedition Act, had in fact abridged both freedoms. The Sedition Act, for example, made it a crime for anyone to 'utter, print, write or publish any disloyal, profane, scurrilous, or abusive language about the form of government of the United States, the Constitution of the United States, or military or naval force of the United States, or the flag ... '.[6] The Act carried a penalty of up to twenty years in prison and/or a fine of $10,000.

In a 7–2 decision, the majority of the Supreme Court upheld the convictions of Jacob Abrams and four other defendants, all Russian émigrés who had been charged with four counts of conspiracy under the Espionage and Sedition Acts and sentenced to twenty years in prison. Few Americans today, including the highly educated, are aware of the events that incited the émigrés' actions: the Polar Bear Expedition, the US's ill-conceived 1918–1919 invasion and occupation of Northern Russia and Siberia in attempts to aid anti-Bolshevik forces and secure US ordnance intended for those forces. Cold War-induced historical amnesia effectively erased this fact from collective memory.

Abrams and the other émigrés had printed and thrown two leaflets from a window of a building in New York City. The first denounced sending US troops to Russia, claiming that 'German militarism combined with Allied capitalism to crush the Russian Revolution' and the 'common enemy' of all capitalists, the working class; it was signed 'The Rebels'. The Russians added a note to the leaflet claiming that calling them pro-German was absurd, avowing: 'We have more reasons for denouncing German militarism than the coward of the White House.' The second leaflet, written in Yiddish, denounced the war and American intervention in the Russian Revolution; it used what Holmes describes as 'abusive language', referring to the Allies as 'hypocrites', and urged Russian émigrés and 'friends of Russia in America' not to participate in producing weapons 'to murder not only the Germans, but also your dearest, best, who are in Russia and are fighting for freedom'.[7]

Holmes dismissed the first two conspiracy counts as unfounded and the third because the prosecution did not prove intent on the part of the defendants. He focused on the fourth count, arguing that the defendants' objective was 'not to impede the United States in the war that it was carrying on' with Germany but rather 'from the beginning to the end that the only object of the paper [the second leaflet] was to help Russia and stop American intervention there against the popular government' (275). Holmes contended that 'the defendants had as much right to publish as the Government has to publish the Constitution of the United States now vainly invoked by them'; and he concluded the defendants were 'deprived of their rights under the Constitution of the United States' (277).

The Abrams dissent marked a radical departure in Holmes's approach to free expression. Before Abrams, the 78-year-old jurist voted to protect speech in only three of the eleven cases that came before the Supreme Court; after Abrams, he voted fourteen times in its favour and only twice to deny. Historians contend that the young progressives he socialized with in his old age played a role in transforming Holmes's judicial philosophy. Progressives certainly contributed to mythologizing Holmes and the importance of the Abrams dissent, which became 'a rally[ing] point for resistance to the Red Scare'.[8]

Although the phrase 'marketplace of ideas' is indelibly linked to Holmes today, he never actually used it: Justice Douglas invoked it in 1953 as did Justice Brennan in 1965. Since then, thousands of lower court cases and commentaries have used the metaphor and linked it to the Abrams dissent. Legal scholars generally trace its genesis to Socrates, John Milton, Adam Smith, John Stuart Mill and more immediately to the influence of Holmes's friends and associates, including Harold Laski, Learned Hand, Zechariah Chafee, Louis Brandeis and the editors of *The New Republic* magazine.[9]

In embracing and literalizing Holmes's metaphor, free market fundamentalists ignore Holmes's actual judicial record: he supported government regulation of business and the rights of labour to organize, strike and to sponsor boycotts. Moreover, in illustrating the meaning of his metaphor, Holmes repeatedly used political, not economic, examples. However, a subtle shift in meaning occurred when the metaphor evolved from Holmes's 'free trade in ideas', which implied dialectics – testing the logic and value of propositions in arguments – to a 'marketplace of ideas', which denotes a physical space dedicated to commercial exchanges.[10] Commerce was not involved in the Abrams case; however, it has been involved in many, possibly most, post-1953 First Amendment cases.

Writing in 1928, Holmes's fellow pragmatist, philosopher John Dewey, interpreted Holmes's trade metaphor as referring to a forum in which 'intelligence would prevail' – similar to contemporary social theorist Jürgen Habermas's concept of the ideal speech situation.[11] There is a substantial body of legal scholarship persuasively challenging literal interpretations of the market metaphor; legal research also demonstrates that even if the metaphor is taken literally, commercial markets for ideas are so radically different today that they no longer meet Holmes's standard of 'free'.[12] That is, media markets now are dominated by vast global conglomerates that have reach and penetration that far exceed anything Holmes or Lenin could have envisioned in 1919.

If this is not enough to convince free market fundamentalists that Holmes was not of their tribe, in *Gitlow v. US* in 1925 the Justice went so far as to assent to the possibility that 'free trade in ideas' might lead to the triumph of Bolshevism:

> If in the long run the beliefs expressed in proletarian dictatorship are destined to be accepted by the dominant forces of the community, the only meaning of free speech is that they [Bolsheviks] should be given their chance and have their way. (323)

Despite red-baiting by his enemies, Holmes was no Bolshevik sympathizer. Aristocratic by disposition, conviction and heritage, he thought socialism was a flawed ideology that would lead to mediocrity. It is, however, reasonable to assume that the historic Holmes's concept of free expression drew more inspiration from Socrates' dialogic misadventures in the Athenian marketplace than from any concern for Mr. Rockefeller's accounting ledgers.

If Holmes was mythologized, Lenin (1870–1924) was elevated to the role of a secular saint after his death: officially venerated as both theoretician and revolutionary hero in the Soviet Union, he was also long romanticized by the Western left. Disabled by a series of strokes, Lenin died just three years after the end of the Russian Civil War, succeeded by Stalin's totalitarian regime. Lenin's early death engendered much utopian speculation about what might have been.

A voracious reader and prolific writer (his collected works run to forty-five volumes), once in office Lenin proved remarkably flexible in revising his theories as situations demanded. To deal with the scarcity of food, for example, he restored some levels of free enterprise among peasants, which, ironically, led his leftist critics to charge that he was actually 'an agent of Wall Street bankers'. Lenin's strategic realism along with his final 'Testament', in which he critiqued his own past errors and recommended removing Stalin as General Secretary of the Party, fuelled the Lenin myth.[13]

However, Lenin's affirmation of terror as a revolutionary strategy as well as his centralized leadership model – whereby the proletariat ruled in name only through its proxy, the Central Committee of the Communist Party, which, in turn, was subject to the iron discipline of the supreme leader – created the structural conditions that would secure Stalin's brutal regime. That is, Lenin was directly responsible for the conditions that made possible the developments that he regretted in his final days.

The same must be said of his approach to censorship. In his youth, Lenin loved languages and literature and only developed an interest in revolutionary ideas in his late teens after his older brother was executed by tsarist forces. Although Lenin began university studies with a strong academic record, he was expelled after only a few months for participation in proscribed student political groups and was forbidden to matriculate in any Russian university in the future. His petitions for release from the educational ban were repeatedly denied, but he undertook a rigorous programme of self-study, and he was allowed to take examinations as an external student in jurisprudence and was awarded a degree with honours from St Petersburg University. He then briefly practised as a lawyer before his political activities led to imprisonment, exile to Siberia and then forced emigration.

The son of educators, Lenin believed in the transformative power of ideas: so much so that he contended that revolutionary re-education could produce a 'New Man'. In that respect, he was actually more of a Hegelian than a Marxist, emphasizing politics over economics and consciousness over class position. He promoted universal literacy, public schools and free public libraries. In his 1901 article, 'Where to Begin', Lenin ascribed a crucial role to the press in developing revolutionary consciousness, famously arguing: 'The newspaper is not only a collective propagandist and a collective agitator, it is also a collective organizer.'[14] That is, the material conditions required to organize, produce and distribute a newspaper – especially an outlawed newspaper like *Iskra*, produced abroad and smuggled into Russia – creates a network that can be used to develop disciplined revolutionary activity.

In his own incarnation as a journalist in exile, Lenin published extensively in obscure revolutionary papers and from 1900 to 1903 served as one of the editors of *Iskra*, the first Marxist newspaper with a national circulation in Russia. During the period of liberalization beginning in 1905, Bolshevik papers were allowed to publish in Russia. Lenin published hundreds of articles in *Pravda*, which became the most important Bolshevik newspaper.

Censorship was a given in tsarist Russia; as a journalist, Lenin faced many struggles with censors. In his pre-revolutionary writings, he did not advocate censorship. After the October 1917 revolution, however, he immediately imposed censorship as 'a temporary measure'. The Decree on the Press declared, 'the bourgeois press is one of the mightiest weapons of the bourgeoise' that cannot be allowed to undermine the revolution. In large cities, Commissars for the Press shut down hostile publications and acted as censors in printing houses. By mid-1918, the Party tightened its control to suppress 'counterrevolutionary agitation', shutting down most of the remaining Socialist Revolutionary and Menshevik newspapers (234 newspapers, of which 142 were socialist).[15] By the end of the year, all non-Bolshevik papers were suppressed. Several agencies, including one headed by Lenin's wife, Nadezhda Krupskaya, supervised publishing, literacy education, development of schools, libraries, reading rooms and the banning of 'obsolete literature' from public libraries.

With the end of the civil war, new literary organizations and some private publishing houses appeared. Under Lenin's New Economic Policy (1922), censorship was formally instituted to more effectively supervise the emerging literary scene; and The Main Administration for Literary and Publishing Affairs, commonly known as Glavlit, was established. Its mission was to prevent the publication and distribution of works that (1) contained anti-Soviet propaganda; (2) revealed military secrets; (3) incited public opinion with false information; (4) aroused nationalistic or religious extremism; or (5) contained pornography. During almost seventy years of operation, Glavlit even censored some of Lenin's own writings when they failed to conform to current orthodoxies.[16] Glavlit continued to operate until August 1990 when Mikhail Gorbachev's Press Law abolished official censorship.

In *Gitlow v. US*, Holmes maintained that 'Every idea is an incitement' (323). Those who care passionately about ideas, as both Holmes and Lenin did, worry most about the seductions of oppositional ideas; and when they have the power to silence them, they are sorely tempted to do so. Holmes worried about Bolshevism, but in Abrams he resisted the temptation to censor. Abrams's activities did not rise to the high standard he set for suppression.

If we grant some legitimacy to Bolshevism after the October Revolution, Lenin's 'temporary' 1917 censorship may have met Holmes's standard, given that Russia was involved in both World War I and a civil war at the time. If so, however, Lenin's subsequent 1918 suppression of all competing newspapers and imposition of permanent censorship grossly violated Holmes's limited franchise.

If we take Holmes at his word – that his belief in free speech was stronger than his will to preserve capitalism – then we must concede that he set an even higher standard of tolerance for himself than for the country. Unlike Lenin, who suffered the consequences of his own incitements, Holmes was never called upon to face the consequences of his fine-sounding idea, the idea that free speech might topple capitalism.

Orwell: Liberty, Literature and the Issue of Censorship

Stephen Ingle

In this country intellectual cowardice is the worst enemy a writer or journalist has to face, and that fact does not seem to me to have had the discussion it deserves. ... At this moment what is demanded by the prevailing orthodoxy is an uncritical admiration of Soviet Russia. Everyone knows this, nearly everyone acts on it. Any serious criticism of the Soviet regime, any disclosure of facts which the Soviet government would prefer to keep hidden, is next door to unprintable. And this nation-wide conspiracy to flatter our ally takes place, curiously enough, against a background of genuine intellectual tolerance ... [It is] the kind of censorship that the English literary intelligentsia voluntarily impose upon themselves....[1]

Despite this clear declaration of interest in the notion of censorship in the essay 'The Freedom of the Press', since identified as a proposed preface to *Animal Farm*, George Orwell would have been intrigued to find himself included in a collection designed to explore any political concept, even something so close to his heart. Although, as Richard Rorty argued, Orwell's writing is a sure guide to an understanding of twentieth-century politics – and arguably twenty-first-century politics – he was not primarily a political thinker: conceptual analysis was not his forte. Orwell was first and foremost a writer and it was as a writer that he approached all aspects of politics, including individual liberty, truth telling and censorship.

He was concerned with censorship at two distinct but interconnected levels. The first level was an immediate concern: he found it impossible sometimes to get his own work published. This caused him to reflect on the nature of censorship in both totalitarian and liberal societies. The second was more general and indeed more substantive. It focused on the relationship between 'truth telling' – the prime responsibility of any writer, he believed, but especially a novelist – and the nature of language itself. These two concerns come together most tellingly in Orwell's last and most widely read novel *Nineteen Eighty-Four*, though of course their origins can be traced back to earlier work. We shall explore each of these levels separately and then examine their interconnection.

Orwell's early writing offered an acerbic critique of British imperialism and of what he considered to be Britain's quasi-imperialist social structure. Nonetheless, he clashed with official state censorship only once, when in 1940 two detectives came to his cottage in Wallington from the public prosecutor's office to seize all the books he had received through the post. The detectives, he reported, were 'very nice about it' and the public prosecutor later wrote to him returning *Lady Chatterley's Lover* but not *Tropic of Cancer*.[2] Orwell subsequently made it clear that he did not oppose official censorship in principle, especially in time of war: he was willing to work within its confines when producing programmes for transmission to India in the Eastern Service of the BBC from 1941 to 1943. His letter of resignation states clearly that he was allowed 'very great latitude' in compiling his programmes and that he was never once required to 'say anything on air that I would not have said as a private individual'.[3]

What increasingly concerned Orwell, however, was what he identifies as voluntary censorship in the above quotation (101). He had no more trouble getting *Burmese Days* published in 1935 than any young author might, despite its explosive nature. But the publication of *The Road to Wigan Pier*, the product of an empirical study of unemployment and poverty in Yorkshire and Lancashire, turned out to be more problematical. The manuscript comprised two separate sections – the first largely descriptive of what Orwell saw, the second an analysis of the shortcomings of British socialism. The publisher Victor Gollancz, who had commissioned Orwell's study, did his best to 'persuade' Orwell to drop the second half. He stood firm, however, and to Gollancz's chagrin, the published book drew a stream of protest from many on the left.

In a sense, voluntary censorship is a misleading description because, as Orwell acknowledges, the agent of this self-denial is not always or even usually an individual but an unofficial literary establishment, an intelligentsia that is both social and ideological. As Orwell came to maturity as a writer the prevailing orthodoxy of this intelligentsia was pro-Soviet socialism, an ideology that for obvious strategic reasons gained wide support after 1941 and Operation Barbarossa, but which had been highly influential for almost a decade before then. In *Wigan Pier*, Orwell referred to two kinds of socialist whom he despised: the 'dull, empty windbags' (a category others might have labelled as ethical socialists) and the more scientific socialists, like George Bernard Shaw or Harold Laski, who have a 'hypertrophied sense of order' and who see socialism as a set of reforms that 'they', the clever ones, are going to impose upon 'them', the lower orders.[4] While he views the first group with obvious distaste, the second group fills him with foreboding because of its 'strong tendency towards totalitarianism'.[5] It is they who form the leftist intelligentsia with the power to invoke 'voluntary censorship' and they are generally in thrall to the Soviet Union. Shaw, for example, in answering criticisms about the Soviet Show Trials, declared that the revolutionary old guard who proved inadequate have to be pushed off the ladder with a rope around their necks. From before 1936, then, Orwell believed that his brand of socialism – democratic socialism – was under threat not just from fascism but from the pro-Soviet socialism championed by the Western intelligentsia. Though he clearly recognized the existence of this intelligentsia early in his writing career he failed initially to appreciate its increasingly hegemonic influence. To many observers, he was himself a member of that intelligentsia, if a rather idiosyncratic one.

What opened Orwell's eyes to the extent of that hegemonic influence was his experience in the Spanish Civil War, or more precisely his experience subsequently when he tried to publish his reflections on the war. Almost by accident, Orwell had joined and fought with the POUM brigade, a disparate group of Catalan trade unionists, anarchists and Trotskyites. He had acquired first-hand experience of the attempts of the Communist government, under Moscow's instructions, to eliminate POUM; indeed in Barcelona he came close to being eliminated himself. On his return to Britain he sought to expose Soviet duplicity in his writing. He turned – where else – to the socialist *New Statesman* and its editor Kingsley Martin. The latter refused an article and later a review by Orwell because they 'controverted the political policy of the paper'.[6] But he offered to pay Orwell for the article all the same!

For Orwell this was no mere ideological dispute. He had seen 'the most terrible things' in Barcelona.[7] What, above all, turned Orwell from hostility to Soviet communism into what Bowker calls a 'deep dyed loathing of it' was the death in Communist custody of the idealistic young Glaswegian Bob Smillie. Smillie, whom Orwell described as a 'brave and gifted boy' had fought with Orwell on the Aragon Front but was later seized and thrown into prison by the Communists where, according to Orwell, he was left to die 'like a neglected animal' – a fate that might well have overtaken Orwell himself had he not engineered a successful escape from Barcelona.[8] Orwell found outlets for his writing but not the ones he wanted or indeed felt entitled to expect. He was vilified by British Communists like Harry Pollitt, who had never forgiven him for *Wigan Pier* and who called him a disillusioned bourgeois with no grasp of political reality and who certainly should not be writing about politics. Orwell might have expected this; but the fact that the majority of the left-wing establishment sided with this position came as a shock. Indeed his publisher Victor Gollancz, after initial enthusiasm, made it clear to him that he would not publish the book Orwell had begun to write; it would, he said, harm the struggle against fascism. When eventually *Homage to Catalonia* was published by Warburg, there was an initial print run of only 1,500, of which more than half remained unsold until after Orwell's death. Orwell was convinced that Gollancz and his allies were taking all steps to prevent the book's success, such as pressuring their friends in the press not to review it.

The existence of something referred to as 'the establishment' is sometimes dismissed as a conspiracy theory but Orwell believed, and not without reason, in the existence of a fellow-travelling publishing establishment which found his writing unhelpful to the cause. When the USSR was obliged to join the war as an ally, his anti-Stalin views were deemed unhelpful –unpatriotic even – to a wider establishment. While the war continued, Orwell failed completely to find a publisher for his masterpiece *Animal Farm* – a book he himself described as 'murder from the Communist point of view'.[9] One originally supportive publisher, Jonathan Cape, decided against publication after receiving representations from the Ministry of Information that Cape would be 'highly ill-advised to publish [*Animal Farm*] at the present time' (98). Had the book been a generalized attack on dictatorship and not one so clearly aimed at Stalin and the USSR, there would have been no problems. Orwell failed to secure a publisher for what is arguably the greatest work of satire in the English language since *Gulliver's Travels*. It was even turned down by an American publisher, ostensibly because there was no market in the USA for animal stories. Three days after the Japanese surrender on 17 August, *Animal Farm* was finally published by Secker and Warburg.

Orwell was surely right to see himself as a victim of the 'prevailing orthodoxy' of uncritical admiration for the USSR. When he railed against the ensuing censorship, when he argued that liberty meant the 'right to tell people what they do not want to hear' (107), he was clear that the opponent of liberty in Western societies was not so much the state (except in times of crisis) or indeed the 'common people' but rather the intellectuals who seek to deny freedom 'for the other fellow', as he paraphrased Rosa Luxemburg in the 'Freedom of the Press' essay (103). Perhaps he was wrong here: though prior to 1941 it was indeed the pro-Soviet intelligentsia that tried to silence him, the state clearly colluded with them between 1941 and 1945. Moreover, evidence that the working class was supportive of Orwell's notion of individual liberty is also hard to come by.

It is easy to understand why Orwell should define liberty as the right to tell people what they do not want to hear. This takes us back to the beginning: Orwell was first and last a writer and not a political thinker. Any form of political commitment that caused a writer to say, for ideological reasons, things he did not truly believe was a form of censorship. While it can be argued that all writers are politically committed – even those who make a show of detachment are the 'tacit supporters' of the prevailing political system – it clearly makes no sense at all to think of writers as equally committed.[10] Having said that, nobody surely would consider Orwell to have been engaged in anything but what Sartre called *littérature engagée*. He acknowledged as much himself in his essay 'Why I Write', in which he elucidates his motives for writing: sheer egoism and aesthetic enthusiasm need no comment, but historical impulse and political purpose are a different matter. He expresses a desire to 'see things as they are, to find out true facts and to store them up for posterity'. He wishes to push the world in a different direction, to 'alter other people's ideas of the kind of society that they should strive after'.[11] How can Orwell square his ambition to discover and store up 'true' facts with a desire to alter people's ideas by taking sides? How can he avoid the kind of censorship imposed by the 'smelly little orthodoxies' to which some writers self-subscribe and which Orwell claimed to despise? After all, as one critic pointed out, '*Homage to Catalonia* is about as unbiased a piece of history as an account of the English Civil War by one of John Lilburne's Levellers'.[12] It is clear that distinguishing self-censorship (choosing to subscribe to an ideological position) and simple bias – the habits of our eyes – is not easy, but it can be done.

What distinguishes a writer from a political thinker surely is precisely the relationship of each to reality. The political thinker tries to examine reality through an ideological prism whereas the task of the writer is to examine reality through experience. Orwell conceded that *Homage to Catalonia* gave a partisan perspective to the events he was writing about, but he resolutely claimed nevertheless to have recorded his own experiences as truthfully as possible. This was the duty of the writer. The reason that Orwell is generally regarded as a writer of integrity, a writer who did not opt for a self-denying ideological framework, is that he wrote what he thought was the truth: as Lionel Trilling pithily observed, Orwell *was* what he wrote.[13] For Orwell, this experiential truth equated to a truth beyond relativism, in fact to objective truth. Not everybody would follow him to this conclusion but it is important to bear in mind that this was what Orwell thought.

It is not surprising then to discover in Orwell's last and best-known book *Nineteen Eighty-Four* that Winston Smith's first act of rebellion was to write. And it is no coincidence that the moment that he makes his first diary entry he recognizes that he is doomed. The writer is the natural enemy of the totalitarian state and its censorship, because in creating an account of experiential reality he is taking on the whole apparatus of the Ministry of Truth, indeed its whole rationale. Even in modern liberal states the importance of creating a party line is seen to be crucial. How much more thorough is the Ministry of Truth, which not only spins the party line as Big Brother develops it but immediately amends all historical records to show that this had always been the party line. Truth is too important to be left to the individual.

Orwell's championing of the individual as guardian of the truth is only half of the story.[14] When O'Brien taunts that the 'truth' of the individual is not more than the delusion of the lunatic he is expressing crudely the fears of Dostoevsky's Inquisitor: there is one truth or there is no truth. When Winston declares that 'reality' reveals itself to the undeceived intelligence – if you know that two plus two equals four then you have a grasp on it – he is going beyond Orwell's original claim for the writer, that he faithfully records facts as he sees them, for posterity. But this implies a whole social process through which a private truth finally becomes a public one. This important social process is absent in Oceania because there is no public sphere outside of the state through which 'the truth' can be captured and sustained.

Nevertheless, O'Brien cannot allow even the individual writer of a diary freedom of expression. All modes of thought must be censored and the party apparatus is hard at work developing a means of censorship so comprehensive as to render such thought impossible: Newspeak. In purging the vocabulary relating to everyday life and inventing a language for politics the state seeks to control thinking. The express function of words in Newspeak was 'not so much to express meanings as to destroy them'.[15] Orwell provides an example. The entire world of sexual desire and activity is encompassed by two Newspeak words: *goodsex*, which is based on chastity and sex within marriage specifically for procreation (until such time as reproduction can be engineered and the orgasm abolished) and *sexcrime*, which covers all other sexual activities from normal intercourse practised for its own sake through to child molestation via rape, adultery, masturbation and so on. The Party believes that since all these illegitimate forms of sexual activity are described by only one word, each will eventually be recognized as equally reprehensible and anti-social. The immediate objective of those working on the shrinking and regulating of vocabulary is to render heresy, especially heretical writing, simply impossible. This is surely the ultimate form of censorship.

We can take some comfort from the sheer enormity and complexity of this task but we would be foolish to overlook the attempt to manipulate political behaviour through 'vocabulary censorship' that is prevalent within liberal democracies in today's world. Orwell used the term 'duckspeak' to denote words without meaning, words used actually to disguise meaning, words that act as symbols for the cognoscenti while leaving ordinary people floundering in ignorance. The best examples of duckspeak, perhaps inevitably, come from the military. We are familiar with phrases such as friendly fire, collateral damage, or ambient non-combatants (for civilians) but less familiar perhaps is the Pentagon's description of peace as permanent pre-hostility. The phrase 'extraordinary rendition' offers a perfect example of duckspeak. Who could guess that it referred to the sending of suspected terrorists overseas to be tortured? The official misappropriation of language is meant to inhibit debate; it is a form of censorship towards which writers like Orwell would be especially sensitive.[16]

Orwell's hatred of censorship was personal. We have seen how a pro-Soviet intelligentsia in liberal Britain sought to restrict his access to publication. This was not official state censorship but unofficial censorship by an intellectual and social elite, and Orwell felt it was all the more difficult to combat for that reason. We then considered Orwell's attack on state-sponsored censorship in *Nineteen Eighty-Four* and his more general concern with the destruction of vocabulary and language. Orwell saw the task of the writer as being to tell the truth, by which he meant presenting accurately one's experience and not adapting it for ideological reasons. He worried deeply about censorship, official and unofficial, and he worried about the insidious manipulation of the basic rules of language by the state, and indeed by corporate institutions. Orwell's own writing, in which aesthetic integrity is suffused with political integrity, stands as a lasting rebuttal of institutional censorship, both official and social, and censorship through lies and obfuscation. More than sixty years after his death Orwell remains a champion of individual liberty, a beacon of truth-telling, and an enemy to the death of all forms of censorship.

Sphinx with a Secret: Leo Strauss's 'Persecution and the Art of Writing'

Thomas Meyer

Persecution … gives rise to a peculiar technique of writing, and therewith to a peculiar type of literature, in which the truth about all crucial things is presented exclusively between the lines. That literature is addressed, not to all readers, but to trustworthy and intelligent readers only. …

Another axiom, but one which is meaningful only so long as persecution remains within the bounds of legal procedure, is that a careful writer of normal intelligence is more intelligent than the most intelligent censor, as such. …

[If] an able writer who has a clear mind and a perfect knowledge of the orthodox view and all its ramifications, contradicts surreptitiously and as it were in passing one of its necessary presuppositions or consequences which he explicitly recognizes and maintains everywhere else, we can reasonably suspect that he was opposed to the orthodox system as such….

Being a philosopher, that is, hating 'the lie in the soul' more than anything else, he would not deceive himself about the fact that such opinions are merely 'likely tales,' or 'noble lies,' or 'probable opinions,' and would leave it to his philosophic readers to disentangle the truth from its poetic or dialectic presentation. …

An exoteric book contains then two teachings: a popular teaching of an edifying character, which is in the foreground; and a philosophic teaching concerning the most important subject, which is indicated only between the lines.[1]

On 6 December 1939, Union College in Schenectady invited Leo Strauss, a visiting lecturer from Middlebury College, to present a paper. This provided the occasion for his lecture with the title 'Persecution and the Art of Writing'.[2]

In November 1941, Strauss published an entirely revised version of the lecture in the journal *Social Research* which in 1952 – slightly modified – became part of the monograph *Persecution and the Art of Writing*.[3] Only a few days before Strauss first gave his lecture in Schenectady, he had learned that the synagogue in his German home town had been destroyed during the 'Kristallnacht' pogrom on 9 November 1938. Although, after 1945, Strauss considered over and over again supplementing his article with new insights gained through his study of Islamic-Jewish medieval philosophy, he never accomplished the task. However, his central argument set a key problem for subsequent interpreters of past political philosophy – how to understand texts composed to evade or negotiate conditions of censorship or persecution.

The central argument in 'Persecution and the Art of Writing' can be summarized as follows. In one way or another, any form of government persecutes independent, i.e. philosophical, thinking, since politics takes authority and common sense as the markers of truth, directing philosophers towards popular, edifying arguments. But the writing of such exoteric books for the purpose of educating young men, i.e. for potential and not for fellow philosophers, opens up a space for free thought without destabilizing a wider audience. The education of 'young men … is the only answer to the always pressing question, to the political question par excellence, of how to reconcile order which is not oppression with freedom which is not license' (37). Being as old as philosophical thought itself, this knowledge leads to a specific 'art of writing' that contains both an exoteric, public message for the masses and an esoteric message 'between the lines' for the few, the philosophers. Persecution and censorship have never been and will never be able to punish this specific 'art of writing' because the esoteric message is only accessible to the uncorrupted philosopher (26, 35).

Strauss argues that true philosophers, from Anaxagoras to Kant, often lived in relatively liberal societies, while still facing sterner forms of censorship than the ostracism of public opinion (33). However, Strauss notices a significant shift in the 'art of writing'. While up to the middle of the seventeenth century, the distinction between 'the wise' and 'the vulgar' was commonly regarded as 'a basic fact of human nature' which could never be subjected to popular education, Enlightenment philosophers believed they could encode messages in between the lines that could evade overt censorship while being accessible enough to reach the masses (33–34). Philosophical thought, so Strauss argued, started to undergo a process of progressive assimilation to mainstream thought and to submit to the developments of political change.

Another, parallel process intensified the formation of the fundamental gap between the 'Ancients' and the 'Moderns'. The emergence of a new rationalism, aligned with the knowledge of the natural sciences, generated new hermeneutic approaches in philosophy. Thus, precision and coherence became the new measure of philosophy (33–34), while the traditional exoteric-esoteric divide became increasingly neglected as an optional hermeneutic procedure for interpreters. Mostly due to the rise of liberal societies, the original meaning of the 'art of writing' faded more and more into oblivion and finally led to the disentanglement of the traditional correlation between exotericism and esotericism. Strauss named this process 'historicism', exceeding hereby the common understanding of the term.

Constitutive for Strauss's concept of historicism is the shift from pre-modern censorship to modern self-censorship. He regards classical censorship as the reaction to obvious transgressions of ruling norms. Challenged by authors who developed techniques of 'hiding' the actual message 'between the lines', the classical censor took philosophers and the content of their texts seriously. In contrast, the archetypal 'historicist' takes the view that esotericism is a form of speculation that derives from an irrational weakness of the mind. The historicist takes over the role of the classic censor by choice and assumes that precision and coherence provide the only tools for falsifying or verifying any proposition. Any saying has to be stated in such a way that it can be proven. These assumptions cause a certain scholarly behaviour that seeks to explore the philosophical arguments as actual facts, to remove ambivalences in statements, to harmonize contradictions and to explain certain philosophies in history through the given political and social circumstances under which they were developed. Since these hermeneutic categories follow primarily historical and only secondarily analytical principles, philosophy itself becomes a matter of history.

Strauss interprets this procedure as an act of self-censorship. Thus, the importance of every single analysis derives from the historical narrative which it is considered to be a part of. Hereby, the construction of 'continuities' or 'fissures' helps to generate a history of philosophy that may be regarded as having lasted from Plato to Heidegger.[4] The 'importance' of one particular philosopher will be judged according to the impact he allegedly had on the history of philosophy. Categories such as 'progress or decline' (29) define the capability of specific philosophies in the present, and modern philosophers create narratives intended to verify their own positions by overcoming the philosophies of the past as 'failures'. It is obvious that radical historicism applies structures of thought we are acquainted with through Hegel. Unknowingly, those modernists keep up with Hegel's system and its immanent philosophy of history that eventually intends to justify the very possibility of the absolute.

The kind of self-censorship advanced by those thinkers follows a dangerous path. Here Strauss points to two things: they marginalize the actual hazards pre-modern philosophers had to struggle with, and thereby, against their own intention, harshly separate thought from reality. Philosophical thought becomes a matter of history and history is understood philosophically. This self-contained system of history has lost any connection to reality. Furthermore, the radical philosopher-historicists overestimate themselves and do not assume responsibility for the catastrophes they have generated. In their reckless attitude, the historicists suppose that they are able to understand the philosophers of the past better than they have understood themselves. The result of these false assumptions is that historicism with its immanent tendency towards radicalization leads to nihilism. It is here that Strauss encounters Friedrich Nietzsche and Martin Heidegger – both classified by Strauss as radical historicists.[5]

The extent to which Strauss considered his own analysis to be valid becomes more visible when we consider that he republished his text on 'Persecution and the Art of Writing' without notable modification in 1952 at the initial height of the Cold War. This highlights the fact that already, in 1941, when he published the text for the first time, he argued likewise against National Socialism and communism, which he regarded as different but consequent outcomes of the same nihilism. Obviously, the political circumstances in 1952 gave him no reason to revise the argument.

Strauss develops his major argument by stating a process that emerges in a modern sense of superiority. The process unfolds through the abandonment of classical censorship, leads to performing self-censorship and finally ends up in nihilism. Strauss's major argument holds together the various lines of arguments that structure 'Persecution and the Art of Writing'. I will give one example to illustrate. The radicalization of censorship due to the emergence of self-censorship grounds the interrelation Strauss establishes between the anonymous historian of religion who lives under conditions of tyranny in Strauss's own times (24–25) and Friedrich Schleiermacher's interpretation of Plato (28). The historian of religion who has to adhere to a 'government-sponsored interpretation of the history of religion' uses the tools of esoteric writing and leads the reader –an 'intelligent young man' – through complicated ways of understanding (24–25). Slowly and by degrees, the latter will be able to comprehend that the central passage of the studied work makes a stand against the totalitarian state in a much more radical sense than any direct attack from a liberal point of view would be able to do. The historian of religion had to be a philosopher in order to write an exoteric book with an esoteric message which as such could be understood only by a future philosopher – the 'intelligent young man' – while looking back on the historical episode. Strauss sees in Schleiermacher's interpretation of Plato the anti-thesis to the scene roughly described here. Schleiermacher paved the way for a new and integrative understanding of Plato's doctrine and prevented future philosophers from gaining access to Plato's esoteric teachings. Schleiermacher, therefore, marks the beginning of historicism.[6]

'Persecution and the Art of Writing' is – as any text of Strauss – an autobiographical text. To Strauss, authors who have practised the classical art of writing have always been writing about themselves in the most non-personal way. The philosophies of Plato and Socrates are even presented in the form of intellectual biographies which the authors stage as drama or comedy while ironically re-defining these genres. A philosopher who is not able to say 'I' or to speak out of his own experiences fails to transmit 'education' because his sayings lack orientation as well as persuasive power. Strauss does not refer here to the modern, overcharged and self-authorized concept of the 'I' but rather to the natural way to say 'I' which everybody does and nobody can avoid. But also the latter 'I' has to step back in favour of a more general idea which all philosophers in all times have been highly committed to: the idea of a good life. This form of self-censorship is a task for the philosopher who subordinates himself to a more general idea and thus exposes himself to the danger of free and independent thought. This alternative type of censorship is opposed to the concept of self-censorship promoted by radical historicism.

We are confronted here with a twofold contradiction. In the first place, we have to identify the contradiction between Strauss's fundamental diagnosis that his own times do not produce philosophers in the classic sense of the word, i.e. philosophers who master the art of exoteric-esoteric writing, and the very existence of our anonymous historian who breaks the rule Strauss himself had established. Furthermore, we have to take seriously the contradiction between the autobiographical features of true philosophy and the fact that a neo-romantic prototype of the biographical paradigm has become in modernity the key par excellence to decode past and contemporary philosophies.

Strauss developed a systematic interest in how contradictions were conceptualized and dealt with in classical and medieval philosophical texts. Maimonides' theory of contradictions in the *Guide for the Perplexed*, especially, became the object of Strauss's investigations.[7] He demonstrates very convincingly that the classical and medieval authors neither intended to overcome censorship nor discussed problems in order to find the one and only solution for a specific problem. In fact, they aimed to name and to isolate contradictions which as such would fully explain the complex nature of the problem itself. Strauss teaches that not coherence but truth is the criteria of philosophy and that truth may take various forms. To follow the truth does not mean to resolve contradictions but to comprehend them as part of the truth. In 'Persecution and the Art of Writing', Strauss justifies his doctrine of contradictions by alluding to that of Xenophon twice in different contexts (26, 30).[8] At the end of his essay, Strauss claims that 'order which is not oppression' and 'freedom which is not license' (37) is brought into being on the very basis of open questions and intrinsic contradictions. When philosophers harmonize or dissolve contradictions, they conceal systematically the intrinsic meaning of 'order' and 'freedom'. However, the esoteric task of the true philosopher is to disclose/expose such concealments.

With these insights in mind, I return to the two major contradictions in Strauss's own argument in 'Persecution and the Art of Writing'. The philosopher who practises the esoteric art of writing acts beyond, and is superior to, the general business of philosophy that unfolds from censorship to self-censorship. This philosopher type aims to establish a 'truly liberal society' (36) and applies the technique of exoteric-esoteric writing against the prevalent tendency. The parable told by Strauss through the teacher-student relationship between the historian of religion and the 'intelligent young man', as well as Strauss's analysis of Schleiermacher's interpretation of Plato, indicate the possibility of undermining the fundamental conditions of modernity within modernity itself. To establish an essential bond between the philosopher's autobiography and his very thought means to abrogate censorship and self-censorship. And taking into account that political things are natural things and vice versa, this bond emerges as a genuine political bond. Strauss's authorities for these assumptions are none other than Plato and Aristotle (22, 32–36; 28, 33).

When Strauss republished 'Persecution and the Art of Writing' in the book *Persecution and the Art of Writing* alongside texts on Maimonides, Yehuda Halevi and Spinoza, the essay was put in a new context and asks for a new reading. This reading reveals that the book *Persecution and the Art of Writing* is an answer to Harry Austryn Wolfson's research in the field of Jewish philosophy. Wolfson (1887–1974), the first chairman of a Judaic Center in the US, argues for an evolving continuity in religious philosophy from Philo to Spinoza. Like Strauss, Wolfson developed a complex theory of exoteric-esoteric writing. Wolfson had studied in a *yeshiva* in the small Lithuanian town of Slabodka and the traditional East-European Jewish learning had a lasting effect on his thought in general and on his theory of esoteric writing in particular. According to Wolfson, Jewish self-censorship began with the destruction of the second temple and is not a symptom of decline but rather the reaction to an entirely hostile environment that had forced the Jews to transfer their oral teachings into writing. Wolfson argues that transferring the Jewish teachings into scripture necessitated developing a repository of exoteric and esoteric techniques of writing.

At this point the philosophies of Strauss and Wolfson start to conflict with each other: Strauss disputes the possibility of being an orthodox Jew and a philosopher at the same time (32). He argues that Maimonides' *Guide for the Perplexed* is based on that insight and caused his preliminary decision to write the book exoterically as a Jewish book and esoterically as a philosophical book. Wolfson, on the other hand, held the view that there is no need to take a side about Maimonides' initial decision. He valued Maimonides' art of writing precisely because of the fact that traditional esotericism had allowed him to remain an orthodox Jew while philosophizing. The second point of conflict between Wolfson and Strauss arises out of two opposing notions of censorship. While Strauss thinks that a philosopher is an atheist, Wolfson argues that the philosopher could be Christian, Jewish or Muslim. *Persecution and the Art of Writing*, the book as well as the article within the book, was written to put the rule to the test that the true philosopher has to capture the chance of the good life, i.e. to live according to the natural order and not according to a particular law.

Strauss's introduction to the *Guide for the Perplexed*, edited together with Shlomo Pines, presented in the first part a plan of the *Guide* that was published there for the first time and republished as a separate article in a *festschrift* for Wolfson.[9] This plan was intended to convince Wolfson that the *Guide* could be read and understood as a text written from an atheistical point of view. Wolfson's understanding of the *Guide* as a Jewish book, in both its exoteric and esoteric reading, corresponds to Strauss's concept of self-censorship. Strauss's philosophical reading of the book demonstrates how Maimonides succeeded in overcoming self-censorship and giving esotericism a philosophical meaning. Wolfson never accepted Strauss's challenge, and none of his many publications even notes Strauss's theses.

'Persecution and the Art of Writing' is a constructive enigma. Only very randomly is it a guide to the exoteric or exoteric-esoteric character of Strauss's own writings. While *Thoughts on Machiavelli*[10] and *Socrates and Aristophanes*[11] are definite examples of the exoteric-esoteric genre, Strauss's late writings on Xenophon and Plato create some doubt about his intentions. Strauss's essay and book *Persecution and the Art of Writing* keep alive the discourse about the options and dangers of conceptualizing exotericism and esotericism in general. Can we expect more from a sphinx with a secret?

The Silencing of Women's Voices: Catharine MacKinnon's *Only Words*

Katherine Smits

Protecting pornography means protecting sexual abuse as speech, at the same time that both pornography and its protection have deprived women of speech, especially speech against sexual abuse. There is a connection between the silence enforced on women, in which we are seen to love and choose our chains because they have been sexualized, and the noise of pornography that surrounds us, passing for discourse (ours, even) and parading under constitutional protection. The operative definition of censorship accordingly shifts from government silencing what powerless people say, to powerful people violating powerless people into silence and hiding behind state power to do it.[1]

The previous chapters in this book have discussed censorship as it has been addressed by men over the course of the past twenty centuries. The absence of women from this debate is not accidental but reflects the gendered history of political thought. Women were not explicitly the subject of government censorship; rather, the social, economic and legal structures which make up the system of patriarchy meant that they were confined almost entirely to the private sphere, prevented from participating in public life and largely ignored and derided when they spoke up against their subjection. In the twenty-first century, the legal barriers to women's public speech have been eliminated, but, many feminists argue, persisting social, cultural and economic structures continue to silence and discount their voices. American legal theorist and feminist Catharine MacKinnon's *Only Words*, the focus of this chapter, identifies pornography as a key source of the continuing 'censorship' of women – although it is, ironically, defended on anti-censorship grounds.

Like John Stuart Mill (see Chapter 17), MacKinnon argues that the most dangerous agent of censorship is not the state but, rather, dominant social groups – in this case men – who exert power and influence over subjected groups, imposing their own subordinating speech upon them. When called to account, they claim freedom of speech and expression, discounting the effect that their speech has upon those they dominate. Their case draws much of its power from the crucial distinction, famously made by Mill, between expression on the one hand and action that directly harms others on the other.

In the powerful critique that MacKinnon makes in *Only Words* and elsewhere, one she addressed to courts and city councils considering the legal regulation of pornography, the focus is on photographs, films, videos and online images of sexual activity. These are defended by civil libertarians on the grounds that they are forms of expression which do not directly injure others and thus deserve the same protection as unpopular opinions shouted at a protest march or the burning of national flags. MacKinnon argues on the contrary that pornography is action in the world, against others, representing, enacting and promoting the sexual exploitation and degradation of women. It harms its victims – both the women who make it and those involved with men who use it – and reinforces social and cultural inequalities of power. Her account aims to turn the tables on relations of power between those speaking and the authorities seeking to control them. Defenders of pornography invoke freedom of speech to protect the images they make against the censorship of the state. MacKinnon counters that pornographers' 'speech' is not merely words or expression; it is itself the exercise of power over women. Moreover, pornographers claim that they are representing the expression of women. In fact, MacKinnon argues, women's speech – their resistance to exploitation and their angry and injured responses to their subordination – is drowned out by 'the noise of pornography' which is in reality the clamour of the powerful, masquerading as the voices of the women it subordinates (9–10).

Pornography is thus a political practice in a patriarchal system, which both reflects and reinforces the power of men and the powerlessness of women. It silences the voices of women who resist it, replacing them with those of men, and where women do speak, their words are reinterpreted to indicate their willing subjection. In the production and consumption of pornography, MacKinnon argues, if women's voices are heard, their words are distorted so that 'no' means 'yes' and expressions of pain and refusal – and simulated pleasure – are interpreted as signs of authentic delight. In response to their inability to express themselves and make themselves heard, women learn to separate themselves from their sexual experience, and to create inauthentic selves: 'you develop a self who is ingratiating and obsequious and imitative and aggressively passive and silent – you learn, in a word, femininity' (7). In the essay from which this extract is taken, MacKinnon describes graphically the experiences of women who have been subjected to sexual exploitation and torture, which they are powerless to speak against:

> You cannot tell anyone. When you try to speak of these things, you are told it did not happen, you imagined it, you wanted it, you enjoyed it. Books say this. No books say what happened to you. Law says this. No law imagines what happened to you, the way it happened. You live your whole life surrounded by this cultural echo of nothing where your screams and your words should be. (3)

The feminist anti-pornography case that MacKinnon articulates is often interpreted as supporting censorship, but her aim is to protect the right of women to speak in a system that silences them.

MacKinnon's case for suppressing pornography has attracted opposition from civil libertarians who argue against state control of sexual expression, as well as from feminists who see the state as historically an unreliable ally in the struggle for women's rights, liable to use censorship as a means of controlling women's sexual freedom. Nadine Strossen and other feminist civil libertarians point to the unlikely alliance between anti-pornography feminists and conservatives who support censorship on the grounds of obscenity.[2] More fundamentally, some feminists reject MacKinnon's claim that pornography necessarily silences women or distorts their voices. In her view, it is only women's expressions of resistance to their exploitation and subjection which are authentically theirs, and which reflect their true experience. 'Anti-censorship' feminist critics, who reject state regulation of pornography, deny that the women depicted in it, or who watch it, are necessarily victims, incapable of authentic speech. They contend rather that pornography, particularly that made by and for women, can express female sexual agency and can subvert or displace gendered relations of power that operate elsewhere, such as in the family.[3]

We might suggest that much depends here upon what is being defined as 'pornography'. MacKinnon cites material that depicts the graphic and often violent subordination of women to men – which in her view only makes explicit women's powerlessness that is constitutive of patriarchy and indeed sexuality itself. Anti-censorship feminists counter that these images are an extreme minority, and much pornographic material depicts sexual play rather than domination. In their view, pornography constitutes at least potentially a space that can be seized by women to act in and express themselves freely; for MacKinnon, however, sexuality is already fatally compromised by its inextricable ties to the patriarchal order that defines it. It cannot, in that context, be a 'free space'.

Pornography, according to MacKinnon, is the graphic representation of a silencing of women that extends more broadly in society. It embodies – in a metaphorical as well as a literal sense – the relationship between the private and public spheres which has been essential to the subordination of women. Pornography brings into public space, by selling and circulating, relations of sexual domination that have been enforced in the private sphere. As we have noted, it is not only in relation to pornography that women's voices have been suppressed. For most of the history of Western thought, until roughly the last hundred years, political philosophy has been the preserve of men, with very few exceptions, and was until the nineteenth century singularly unconcerned with women's ability to participate in politics. Where women were even acknowledged in political discourse, it was assumed that their interests were encompassed by the men to whom they were legally subject, and who, when their concerns were invoked, were assumed to speak for them.

Not surprisingly in this context, those few women who wrote about politics concentrated on defending the rights of their sex to speak about and participate in it: in the fourteenth century, the Italian-French noblewoman Christine de Pizan argued against misogyny and in defence of women's contributions to public life, in particular their ability to argue for peace.[4] In the late eighteenth century, a powerful and sustained argument against women's exclusion from public life was made by English feminist Mary Wollstonecraft. Wollstonecraft argued that women should be educated to develop their capacity to reason, not only for their own good, but also because women educated in the civic virtues would contribute to, rather than corrupt, society and the public good.[5]

With these and a few other exceptions, the canon of political philosophy historically is a succession of male voices, from which women have been absent not for the most part because they were explicitly censored by the state, but because they and the concerns to which they were limited – the family, sexuality and reproduction – were excluded from political discourse. From Plato's dark and womb-like cave, out of which wise men struggle towards the light of truth, on through the Western tradition, the stories of origin of political societies are rebirths enacted by men, from which women are absent. For the early modern social contract theorists, as Carole Pateman has shown, the formation of civil society assumes a prior, private and unarticulated sexual contract enforced by men upon women.[6] For Marx, the labour of production substitutes for the labour of reproduction. When women have asserted their rights to speak in public, their private, sexual behaviour has been used to denigrate their arguments about public virtue. Mary Wollstonecraft, for example, was roundly condemned for living with a man outside marriage and bearing his child. A half-century later, Mill attracted gossip about his close friendship with the married Harriet Taylor, but this did not diminish his public reputation. Women who struggled into the public sphere found themselves dogged by their association with the private.

It is remarkable that although the distinction between the private and the public spheres has been differently articulated in different historical periods, women have consistently been confined to the private and excluded from the public. Some feminists have ascribed this to women's consistently primary role in reproduction and child-raising. In MacKinnon's argument, the fundamental lever of exclusion is sexuality, which has been consistently defined in terms of domination and subordination across historical periods. This is not to say that it is biologically essential and inescapable, but rather, according to MacKinnon, it is a persistent and fundamental feature of the exercise of power and the construction of human identities.[7]

In response to women's exclusion from the public, feminists have followed a three-tracked approach. Much argument from Wollstonecraft and the first-wave feminists of the nineteenth century onwards has been directed at bringing women into the public sphere, allowing them the right to vote and participate in politics and giving them a voice on traditionally 'male' political subjects. These essentially liberal arguments preserve the distinction between public and private but insist that women are as capable of being public actors and citizens, and deliberating upon public and non-gendered issues, as are men.

Feminists following the second track have argued that it is not enough to simply bring women into a world already defined and distinguished as public and political. In addition, the private sphere concerns associated with women must be recognized as part of the public conversation. As the second-wave feminist slogan from the 1970s put it: 'the personal is political' – meaning that issues to do with domestic life, sexuality, social and familial reproduction become the concerns of politics. Mill was the first to publicly articulate this concern in his 1869 *Subjection of Women*, where he described the family as a 'school of despotism'.[8] Mill argued that the social behaviour learned in the family has a political effect and thus must be regulated by principles of justice that recognize and take into account the views of women. More recently, Susan

Moller Okin developed the argument that the full equality of women depends upon recognizing the political status of gender-structured marriage and the family.[9]

Both strands of argument examined so far have focused on ensuring women have a voice in public life rather than the nature of what they say. Feminists taking a third approach contend that women have a distinctive voice: that the socially and culturally constructed behaviour they learn in the private sphere should be recognized as publicly valuable and as changing our way of thinking about moral and political concerns. Historically, this argument was made by some second-wave feminists who argued that as a result of their child-raising practices, women were innately more pacifist and cooperative than men. Today, it is associated with the views of feminist moral psychologist Carol Gilligan, who argues that women's socialization leads them to reason morally in a different way, rather than, as male psychologists had previously concluded, as only partially developed moral thinkers.[10] Gilligan suggests that women's moral thinking is more likely to be relational and contextual rather than abstract and impersonal. They possess a 'different voice', which is authentically theirs, not simply an expression of their powerlessness, and should be brought into the public sphere. An 'ethics of care' has been proposed as an alternative to the ways of thinking about justice that have dominated political philosophy.

All of the feminist claims we have considered acknowledge the relationship between expression and the material circumstances and power structures from which it comes. For MacKinnon, as we saw, the subordination of women means that their authentic speech cannot be heard. For Gilligan, by contrast, the speech that women learn and practise as they negotiate their lives under patriarchy emerges as theirs and should be recognized in public discourse. Both the arguments assume that women have authentic voices and can be empowered by instating these in the public sphere. Where they differ is in the relationship they assume between subordination and authentic speech. Can women express their own morally valuable but different voices under patriarchy? For MacKinnon, the answer must be no. In her view, theories such as Gilligan's simply try to attach a positive value to that

> which has accurately distinguished women from men, by making it seem as though those attributes, with their consequences, really are somehow ours, rather than what male supremacy has attributed to us for its own use. For women to affirm difference, when difference means dominance, as it does with gender, means to affirm the qualities and characteristics of powerlessness.[11]

When you are powerless, MacKinnon concludes, you do not speak with a different voice; rather, you do not speak much at all. Not being heard is not a function of lack of recognition: 'it is also silence of the deep kind, the silence of being prevented from having anything to say'.[12]

The argument among feminists over the potential for women to express their sexuality freely in public mirrors the broader debate over women's authentic voice, as we have seen. But it also prompts us to consider why freedom of speech and expression is defended as a fundamental human right. When it emerged as a modern idea in the wake of the religious pluralism of the Reformation, it was defended chiefly on the grounds that minority opinions and conceptions of truth should not be prohibited. Individual conscience was protected by freedom of speech at this point, but in later formulations, the grounding of this freedom shifted increasingly to its necessary relation to individual expression and development in spheres beyond religion. Since Mill, liberals have held that people exercise their autonomy – they direct and carry out their life projects – in part through their free expression. When he defends the liberty of thought and discussion in *On Liberty*, Mill invokes the argument that it will lead to people examining and changing their views and opinions and reaching the truth. But he also argues that being able to question, examine and express oneself freely is an essential attribute of individuality.[13]

MacKinnon's critique of pornography invites us to consider cases where the free speech of some inherently infringes the autonomy and individuality of others. Despite its associations with both a radical feminist critique of patriarchy and conservative opposition to obscenity, it is, in its opposition to patriarchal censorship, a liberal argument. The opposing feminist case also depends upon seeing the relation between free expression – sexual, in this case – and the full development of human individuality. The real disagreement between them lies in whether or not free action and expression is in fact possible within the confines of inequality.

Notes

Introduction

1 Jonathan Kaiman, 'China anti-censorship protest attracts support across country', *Guardian*, 7 January 2013, www.guardian.co.uk/world/2013/jan/07/china-anti-censorship-protest-support [accessed 15 January 2014]; S.G. Tallentyre, *The Friends of Voltaire* (London: John Murray, 1906), p. 199. The attribution of this quotation to Voltaire has been part of the myth, being instead a summary of his presumed viewpoint by Tallentyre, the version used here. The Chinese protester's variant is reported as beginning, 'I may not agree with everything you say...'

2 Robert B. Downs, 'Foreword' to Ralph E. McCoy, *Freedom of the Press: An Annotated Bibliography* (Carbondale, Ill.: Southern Illinois University Press, 1968), p. vii.

3 Lord Justice Brian Leveson, *An Inquiry into the Culture, Practices and Ethics of the Press: Report* (4 vols, London: The Stationery Office, 2012) 'Executive Summary', p. 4; vol. 1, pp. 56, 58–59, 61, 67.

4 Dan Hodges, 'Regulating press is not in public interest ... 300 years of freedom under threat this week', *The Sun*, 27 October 2013, www.thesun.co.uk/sol/homepage/features/5226721/Regulating-Press-is-not-in-public-interest.html [accessed 20 January 2014]; Mick Hume, 'CENSORED: The Mail on Sunday stories Leveson's law would have barred', *Mail on Sunday*, 2 December 2012, www.dailymail.co.uk/news/article-2241699/CENSORED-The-Mail-On-Sunday-stories-Levesons-Law-barred.html [accessed 20 January 2014].

5 Geoff Kemp and Jason McElligott, 'The Constitution of Early Modern Censorship', in Kemp and McElligott, general eds, *Censorship and the Press*, 1580–1720 (4 vols, London: Pickering & Chatto, 2009), 1: xxvi (this volume edited by Cyndia Susan Clegg).

Chapter 1

1 Plutarch, *Lives*. 'Cato', 22.1–23.1. Loeb Classical Library 47, vol. II (Cambridge: Harvard University Press, 1912). Section numbers to this edition will be given in parentheses throughout the text of this essay.

2 Plutarch, *Lives*. 'Alexander', 1.2–1.3. Loeb Classical Library 99, vol. VII (Cambridge: Harvard University Press, 1919).

3   See also Alan E. Astin, *Cato the Censor* (Oxford: Clarendon Press, 1978), p. 78: 'The censorship was the most senior, the most select, and the most prestige-laden of the Roman magistracies. To be elected to it was in itself an outstanding achievement and a coveted prize'.

4   Plato, *Phaedo*, Loeb Classical Library 36, vol. I (Cambridge: Harvard University Press, 1914), p. 118a. All subsequent references to Plato's works will be noted by Stephanus pagination in parentheses in the text.

5   Xenophon, *Memorabilia*, 1.2.3. Loeb Classical Library 168. vol. IV (Cambridge: Harvard University Press, 2013).

6   John Stuart Mill, *On Liberty*, edited with an Introduction by Gertrude Himmelfarb (Harmondsworth: Penguin Books, [1859] 1974), pp. 84–85.

7   See further Arlene W. Saxonhouse, *Free Speech and Athenian Democracy* (Cambridge: Cambridge University Press, 2006) Chapter 5; and R. Waterfield, *Why Socrates Died: Dispelling the Myths* (New York: W.W. Norton, 2009).

8   Aristophanes, *The Clouds* in *Four Texts on Socrates*, translated Thomas G. West and Grace Starry West (Ithaca and London: Cornell University Press, 1984) lines 1073–1074.

9   I take the language of 'corrosive' citizenship from Dana Villa, *Socratic Citizenship* (Princeton: Princeton University Press, 2001).

Chapter 2

1   Tacitus, *Annals*, trans. A.J. Woodman (Indianapolis: Hackett Publishing Company, 2004), pp. 138–139, 4.34–4.35. References to Tacitus' book and chapter, the standard citation form, will be given in parentheses throughout the text of this essay. In addition to Tacitus' *Annals*, I cite Tacitus' *Histories* and *Dialogue on Oratory*; references are to the following editions: Tacitus, *Histories*, trans. Clifford H. Moore (Cambridge: Harvard University Press, 2006); Tacitus, *A Dialogue on Oratory*, trans. W. Peterson, in Tacitus *Agricola, Germania, Dialogus* (Cambridge: Harvard University Press, 1970). References to those editions will also be given in parentheses.

2   R. Rogers, 'The Case of Cremutius Cordus', *Transactions of the American Philological Association*, 96 (1965), pp. 351–359, at p. 351.

3   Ronald Syme, *Tacitus* (Oxford: Oxford University Press, 1958), vol. 2, p. 520.

4   Tacitus, *Annals Book IV*, edited by R.H. Martin and A.J. Woodman (Cambridge: Cambridge University Press, 1989), p. 177.

5   Rosalind Thomas, *Literacy and Orality in Ancient Greece* (Cambridge: Cambridge University Press, 1992), p. 169.

6   P.A. Brunt, '*Libertas* in the Republic', in P.A. Brunt, *The Fall of the Roman Republic and Related Essays* (Oxford: Oxford University Press, 1988), pp. 281–350, at p. 314.

7   Brunt, 'Libertas in the Republic', p. 316. For further detail on the meaning of 'song' in the Twelve Tables, see Thomas Habinek, *The World of Roman Song: From Ritualized Speech to Social Order* (Baltimore: Johns Hopkins University Press, 2005).

8   Brunt, '*Libertas* in the Republic', p. 317.

9   For a helpful chart listing these examples and others of speech being punished under Augustus and Tiberius, and an excellent discussion, see Mary R. McHugh, 'Historiography and Freedom of Speech: The Case of Cremutius Cordus', in Ineke Sluiter and Ralph M. Rosen (eds), *Free Speech in Classical Antiquity* (Leiden: Brill, 2004), pp. 392–408, at pp. 406–407.

10 Nicola Mackie, 'Ovid and the Birth of *Maiestas*', in Anton Powell (ed.), *Roman Poetry and Propaganda in the Age of Augustus* (London: Bristol Classical Press, 1992), pp. 83–97, at p. 88.

11 Mackie, 'Ovid and the Birth of *Maiestas*', p. 90.

12 Suetonius, *Domitian*, trans. J.C. Rolfe, in *Suetonius*, vol. II (Cambridge: Harvard University Press, 1992) XXI, p. 383.

13 Tacitus, *Annals Book IV*, ed. Martin and Woodman, p. 179.

14 Frederick Ahl, 'The Art of Safe Criticism in Greece and Rome', *The American Journal of Philology*, 15:2 (1984), pp. 174–208, at pp. 174, 187.

15 J. Moles, 'Cry Freedom: Tacitus *Annals* 4.32–35', *Histos*, 2 (1998), pp. 95–184, at p. 145. research.ncl.ac.uk/histos/documents/1998.06MolesCryFreedom95184.pdf [accessed 19 December 2013].

Chapter 3

1   Augustine, *The City of God Against the Pagans*, ed. and trans. R.W. Dyson (Cambridge: Cambridge University Press, 1998), Book XIX, 7, p. 928. Augustine's works will be cited in the standard way throughout this chapter. All subsequent translations are by the author. Augustine's works are available in Latin and Italian in the online version of the *Nuova Biblioteca Agostiniana* (Roma: Città Nuova Editrice, 1986) www.augustinus.it [accessed 5 January 2014]. There are English translations of a good proportion of Augustine's works at the website of the *New Advent Catholic Encyclopedia*, http://www.newadvent.org/fathers [accessed 5 January 2014].

2   Peter Brown, *The Rise of Western Christendom: Triumph and Diversity, A.D. 200–1000* (Oxford: Blackwell, 2003), p. 78.

3   *Sermons*, XXVI, 54.

4   1 Pet. 4.11.

5   *On the Predestination of the Saints*, LXIII, 23.

6   *Against the Letters of Petilian*, II, 121.

7   Hans Foerster (ed.), *Liber Diurnus Romanorum Pontificum* (Berne: Francké Verlag, 1958), p. 81.

8   I should say, modern scholarship after W.H.C. Frend and his pioneering work *The Donatist Church: A Movement of Protest in Roman North Africa* (Oxford: Oxford University Press Reprints, 1985). It was Frend who first combined the archaeological with the written evidence to open up this episode to analysis by ethnicity and identity and resistance.

9   After the wedding feast described in Scripture at Luke 14.15–24. Specifically verse 23: 'And the Lord said unto the servant, Go out into the highways and hedges, and compel *them* to come in [*conpelle intrare*], that my house may be filled.' 'Conpelle' in the Vulgate is usually rendered 'compelle' in discussion of Augustine's argument.

10   *Letters*, CLXXXV, 21.

11   Bernard Crick, *In Defence of Politics* (London: New York, Continuum, 2005), p. 114.

12   *City of God*, XIX, 23.

13   Augustine is referencing the Roman tradition of forcing newly conquered peoples to parade beneath a yoke, in the ancient ritual of sub[*iug*]ation.

Chapter 4

1   St Thomas Aquinas, *Summa theologica*, 2.2.72. All quotations from the *Summa* are my own translation from the on-line *Opera omnia* of St Thomas, edited by Enrique Alarcón http://www.corpusthomisticum.org/iopera.html [last accessed 18 May 2014]. Further references to this edition will be given parenthetically hereafter. For further discussion of issues raised in this chapter, see Debora Shuger, *Censorship and Cultural Sensibility: The Regulation of Language in Tudor-Stuart England* (Philadelphia: University of Pennsylvania Press, 2006).

2   *De iniuriis et famosis libellis* is title 47.10 of the *Digest*, the second of the three volumes that comprise the *Corpus iuris civilis*; the *Digest* title treats verbal *iniuria* as a civil offence, with a corresponding title, *De famosis libellis*, treating the criminal aspect, in the *Codex*, the third volume (book 9, title 36). Both titles can be found in S. P. Scott's seventeen-volume 1932 English translation of the *Corpus iuris civilis* and related texts, online at http://www.constitution.org/sps/sps.htm [accessed 30 May 2014].

3   *Corpus iuris canonici … Gregorii XIII. Pont. Max. iussu editum* (Lyon, 1616), C. 5, q. 1, c.1 (translation mine); the wording here is very close to that of the *Codex* (see note 2).

4   Sir Francis Bacon, *The Use of the Law* in *The Works of Francis Bacon,* 10 vols (London: C. and J. Rivington, 1826), vol. 4, p. 81. There is some question regarding

the attribution to Bacon; see *The Works of Francis Bacon*, James Spedding, Robert Leslie Ellis and Douglas Heath (eds), 15 vols (Boston: Houghton, Mifflin, [1900?]), vol. 14, pp. 364–368.

5   The thirteenth-century statutory offence of *scandalum magnatum* only protected, as its name implies, the upper nobility.

6   Sir Edward Coke, 'The Case *De Libellis Famosis*, or of Scandalous Libels', in John Henry Thomas and John Fraser (eds), *The Reports of Sir Edward Coke*, 6 vols (London, 1626; rprt. Union, NJ: The Lawbook Exchange, 2002), vol. 3, pp. 254–256. This had been originally published (in law French) in the *Quinta pars relationum Edwardi Coke* in 1607.

7   These remarks apply principally to the Indices issued between 1559 and 1610. See Franz Heinrich Reusch, *Der Index der verbotenen Bücher: ein Beitrag zur Kirchen- und Literaturgeschichte*, 2 vols (Bonn, 1883; rprt. Aalen: Scientia Verlag, 1967).

8   These are handled in 2.2.72–2.2.75. A final *quaestio* (2.2.76) deals with a fifth species of verbal *iniuria, maledictio*, which has no English counterpart, but involves hostile wishing or commands, such as 'I hope you drown', or 'go to hell'. Thomas views such expressions of ill-will as less damaging, and therefore less significant, than the other four.

9   Samuel D. Warren and Louis D. Brandeis, 'The Right to Privacy', *Harvard Law Review*, 4:5 (1890), pp. 193–220.

10 Martin Luther, *Sermo contra vitium detractionis*, in *D. Martini Lutheri opera latina varii argumenti ad Reformationis historiam imprimis pertinentia*, 7 vols, ed. Henricus Schmidt (Frankfurt: C. Heyderus and H. Zimmerus, 1865–1873), vol. 1, pp. 76–77, 82.

11 William Ames, *Conscience with the power and cases thereof* (n.p., 1639), p. 150.

Chapter 5

1   William of Ockham, *Dialogus*, I, iv, 20, which refers to Part I, Book 4, chapter 20 (references to the *Dialogus* in the text follow this conventional referencing method). This work is available at the British Academy's website: http://www.britac.ac.uk/pubs/dialogus/ [accessed 18 May 2014]

2   See for instance Thomas Aquinas, *Summa Theologiae*, 2a2ae, q. 11, a. 3, vol. 32, *Consequences of Faith*, ed. and trans. Thomas Gilby (London: Blackfriars, 1974), pp. 88–89.

3   See Takashi Shogimen, *Ockham and Political Discourse in the Late Middle Ages* (Cambridge: Cambridge University Press, 2007), pp. 88–101.

4   Brian Tierney, *Origins of Papal Infallibility, 1150–1350*, second impression (Leiden: Brill, 1988), pp. 235–236.

5   William of Ockham, 'Contra Ioannem', in H.S. Offler (ed.), *Opera Politica* (Manchester: Manchester University Press, 1956), c. 7, pp. 49–50.

6   Ockham, *Contra Ioannem*, c. 33, p. 128.

7   Cicero, *On Duties*, edited by M.T. Griffin and E.M. Atkins (Cambridge: Cambridge University Press, 1996), p. 10.

8   William of Ockham, *A Short Discourse on Tyrannical Government*, edited by A.S. McGrade, trans. John Kilcullen (Cambridge: Cambridge University Press, 1992), p. 3 (emphasis mine).

Chapter 6

1   Johannes Reuchlin, 'Augenspiegel (1511)', in Widu-Wolfgang Ehlers, Hans-Gert Roloff, and Peter Schäfer (eds), Reuchlin, *Sämtliche Werke* (Stuttgart and Bad Cannstadt: Frommann-Holzboog, 1999), vol. 4/1, pp. 48–49. Page numbers to this edition will be given in parentheses throughout the text of this essay, and all translations are mine. The best published translation is Johannes Reuchlin, *Recommendation Whether to Confiscate, Destroy and Burn All Jewish Books*, trans. Peter Wortsman (New York: Paulist Press, 2000).

2   For all details, see David H. Price, *Johannes Reuchlin and the Campaign to Destroy Jewish Books* (Oxford: Oxford University Press, 2012).

3   Reuchlin, *Defensio* (1513), in *Sämtliche Werke*, vol. 4/1, p. 344.

4   John Friedman, Jean Connell Hoff, and Robert Chazan, *The Trial of the Talmud* (Toronto: Pontifical Institute of Mediaeval Studies, 2012).

5   Ruth Langer, *Cursing the Christians?: A History of the Birkat HaMinim* (Oxford: Oxford University Press, 2011).

6   See 'Who Saved the Jewish Books?', in Price, *Johannes Reuchlin and the Campaign to Destroy Jewish Books*, pp. 113–137.

7   Ibid., p. 161.

8   Johannes Reuchlin, *Briefwechsel*, edited by Matthias Dall'Asta and Gerald Dörner, 4 vols (Stuttgart: Frommann Holzboog, 2000–2013), vol. 3, pp. 448–449.

9   Johannes Pfefferkorn, *Ajn mitleydliche claeg* (Cologne: Servas Krufter, 1521), fol. H2r.

10   Kenneth R. Stow, *Catholic Thought and Papal Jewry Policy, 1555–1593* (New York: Jewish Theological Seminary of America, 1977).

11   Amnon Raz-Krakotzkin, *The Censor, the Editor and the Text: The Catholic Church and the Shaping of the Jewish Canon in the Sixteenth Century* (Philadelphia: University of Pennsylvania Press, 2007).

12   Reinhold Lewin, *Luthers Stellung zu den Juden* (Berlin: Trowitzsch und Sohn, 1911), p. 98.

Chapter 7

1   Sebastian Castellio, *Contra Libellum Calvini* (Against Calvin's Book, 1562), sig
    E16r; the translated passage appears in excerpts under the title 'Reply to Calvin',
    in Sebastian Castellio, *Concerning Heretics*, trans. Roland H. Bainton. *Records of
    Civilization: Sources and Studies 22* (New York: Columbia University Press, 1935),
    pp. 265–287, at pp. 268, 271.
2   The best biography of Castellio remains, Hans R. Guggisberg, *Sebastian Castellio,
    1515–1563. Humanist and Defender of Religious Toleration in a Confessional Age*,
    trans. and ed. Bruce Gordon (Aldershot: Ashgate, 2003).
3   Castellio, *Concerning Heretics*, trans. Bainton, p. 126.
4   Castellio, *Concerning Heretics*, trans. Bainton, passim.
5   R. White, 'Castellio against Calvin: The Turk in the Toleration Controversy of the
    Sixteenth Century', *Bibliotheque d'humanisme et renaissance*, 46 (1984), pp. 573–586.
6   Perez Zagorin, *How the Idea of Religious Toleration Came to the West* (Princeton:
    Princeton University Press, 2003), pp. 127f.
7   *Contra libellum*, sig A2r. Quoted in Guggisberg, *Sebastian Castellio*, p. 106.
8   On Castellio's circle in Basel, see Peter G. Bietenholz, *Encounters with a Radical
    Erasmus. Erasmus' Work as a Source of Radical Thought in Early Modern Europe*
    (Toronto: University of Toronto Press, 2009), esp. pp. 95–108.
9   Quoted from Guggisberg, *Sebastian Castellio*, p. 107.
10 Guggisberg, *Sebastian Castellio*, pp. 129–130.
11 Gary Remer, 'Rhetoric and the Erasmian Defence of Religious Toleration', *History of
    Political Thought*, 10 (1989), pp. 377–403.
12 Guggisberg, *Sebastian Castellio*, p. 109.

Chapter 8

1   Paolo Sarpi, *The Historie of the Councel of Trent Conteining eight Bookes. In which
    (besides the ordinarie Actes of the Councell) are declared many notable occurrences,
    which happened in Christendome, during the space of fourtie yeeres and more. And,
    particularly, the practises of the Court of Rome, to hinder the reformation of their
    errors, and to maintaine their greatnesse. Written in Italian by Pietro Soave Polano,
    and faithfully translated into English by Nathanael Brent* (London: Robert Barker,
    John Bill, 1620), Book 6, pp. 474–475, referring to debates in 1562. Page references
    to this edition will be given in parentheses in the text of this chapter.
2   On Sarpi, see 'Suggestions for Further Reading', particularly the essays in Corrado
    Pin (ed.), *Ripensando Paolo Sarpi* (Venice: Ateneo Veneto, 2006); also Gaetano
    Cozzi, *Paolo Sarpi tra Venezia e l'Europa* (Turin: Einaudi, 1979).

3   Frances A. Yates, 'Paolo Sarpi's *History of the Council of Trent*', *Journal of the Warburg and Courtauld Institutes*, 7 (1944), pp. 123–143; Graham Rees and Maria Wakely, 'Folios Fit for a King: James I, John Bill, and the King's Printers, 1616–20', *Huntington Library Quarterly*, 68:3 (2005), pp. 467–495.

4   *Concilii Tridentini Eviscerator*, inscribed on a contemporary portrait, apparently by Wotton: Yates, 'Paolo Sarpi's *History of the Council of Trent*', pp. 137–139.

5   Paolo Sarpi, *The History of the Inquisition*, trans. Robert Gentilis (London: Humphrey Mosley, 1639). See Nigel Smith, 'Milton and the Index', in Donald R. Dickson and Holly Faith Nelson (eds), *Of Paradise and Light. Essays on Henry Vaughan and John Milton in Honor of Alan Rudrum* (Cranbury: Associated University Presses, 2004), pp. 101–122; also Mario Infelise, 'Ricerche sulla fortuna editoriale di Paolo Sarpi (1619–1799)', in Pin (ed.), *Ripensando Paolo Sarpi*. pp. 519–546.

6   See Corrado Pin (ed), *Paolo Sarpi: Consulti* (Pisa: Istituti editoriali e poligrafici internazionali, 2001), 2 vols. For the role of Sarpi as a 'consultore' during the Interdict of 1606 see Filippo De Vivo, *Information and Communication in Venice: Rethinking Early Modern Politics* (Oxford: Oxford University Press, 2007).

7   *Acta Ecclesiae Mediolanensis a Carolo Cardinali S. Praxedis Archiepiscopo condita Federici Card. Borromaei archiepiscopi Mediolani iussu* (Milan: Ponti, 1609), p. 431.

8   *Index Librorum Prohibitorum* (Rome: Paulum Manutium [Paolo Manuzio], 1564), p. 27; reprinted in Jesùs-Martinez de Bujanda (ed.), *Index de Rome, 1557, 1559, 1564: les premiers index romains et l'index du Concile de Trente* (Sherbrooke, Québec: Centre d'études de la Renaissance, 1990, p. 817). An English translation of the rules is available online at www.fordham.edu/halsall/mod/trent-booksrules.asp [accessed 18 May 2014].

9   On the Papal censorship system: Mario Infelise, *I libri proibiti da Gutenberg all'Encyclopedie* (Bari: Laterza 1999); Gigliola Fragnito (ed.), *Church, Censorship and Culture in Early Modern Italy* (Cambridge: Cambridge University Press, 2001); Gigliola Fragnito, *Proibito capire. La Chiesa e il volgare nella prima età moderna* (Bologna: il Mulino, 2005). For the Venetian case: Paul F. Grendler, *The Roman Inquisition and the Venetian Press, 1540–1605* (Princeton: Princeton University Press, 1977); Federico Barbierato, *The Inquisitor in the Hat Shop. Inquisition, Forbidden Books and Unbelief in Early Modern Venice* (Farnham: Ashgate, 2012).

10   Antonio Possevino, *La colture de gl'ingegni* (Vicenza: Antonio Greco, 1598), p. 97.

11   Paolo Sarpi, 'Del vietare la stampa di libri perniciosi al buon governo (17 agosto 1615)', in Giovanni Gambarin (ed.), *Paolo Sarpi: Scritti giurisdizionalistici* (Bari: Laterza, 1958), p. 218

12   Sarpi, *The History of the Inquisition*, p. 69.

13   See De Vivo, *Information and Communication in Venice*.

14 See, for example, the case of Bellarmine and his role in Galileo's trial: Thomas F. Mayer, *The Roman Inquisition. Papal Bureaucracy and its Laws in the Age of Galileo* (Philadelphia: University of Pennsylvania Press, 2013).

15 Sarpi, *The History of the Inquisition*, p. 71.

16 Paolo Sarpi, 'Del vietare la stampa di libri perniciosi al buon governo', pp. 213–214.

17 Marco Cavarzere, *La prassi della censura nell'Italia del Seicento* (Rome: Edizioni di Storia e Letteratura, 2012).

Chapter 9

1 Henry Parker, *To the High Court of Parliament: The Humble Remonstrance of the Company of Stationers* (1643), reprinted in Geoff Kemp and Jason McElligott (eds), *Censorship and the Press, 1580–1720*, 4 vols. (London: Pickering & Chatto, 2009), vol. 2, 1640–1660 (this volume edited by Jason McElligott), pp. 65–71, at p. 71. Page references to this volume will be given in parentheses throughout the text of this essay. The *Remonstrance* as originally printed does not indicate author, publisher, date, or place of printing (London); it lacks page numbers; and the title as printed does not capitalize 'humble'.

2 John Milton, *Areopagitica; A Speech of Mr. John Milton for the Liberty of Unlicenc'd Printing, to the Parlament of England* (London, 1644), reprinted in Kemp and McElligott, *Censorship and the Press*, vol. 2, pp. 93–125, at p. 125. Given the frequent comparison between the *Remonstrance* and *Areopagitica*, page references to this volume will be given for both works in parentheses in the text.

3 British Library, Thomason Collection, E.247.(23.). Thomason was a Stationer and in a position to know the author's identity. The petition was one of 'a number of commissioned tracts that Parker wrote for private interests in the 1640s': Michael Mendle, *Henry Parker and the English Civil War* (Cambridge: Cambridge University Press, 2003), pp. 144–148, pp. 180–181; Michael Mendle, 'Henry Parker, 1604–1652', *Oxford Dictionary of National Biography*.

4 'An Order of the Lords and Commons Assembled in Parliament. For the Regulating of Printing', in Kemp and McElligott (eds), *Censorship and the Press*, 2, pp. 72–79.

5 Quentin Skinner, *Hobbes and Republican Liberty* (Cambridge: Cambridge University Press, 2008); Quentin Skinner, *Liberty Before Liberalism* (Cambridge: Cambridge University Press, 1998); Quentin Skinner, 'John Milton and the Politics of Slavery', in Skinner, *Visions of Politics*, vol. 2 (Cambridge: Cambridge University Press, 2002), pp. 286–307, at pp. 302–303; Martin Dzelzainis, 'Republicanism', in Thomas N. Corns (ed.), *A Companion to Milton* (London: Blackwell, 2003), pp. 294–308; Eric Nelson, '"True Liberty": Isocrates and Milton's *Areopagitica*', *Milton Studies*, 40 (2001), pp. 201–221.

6   Roger L'Estrange, *Considerations and Proposals in Order to the Regulation of the Press* (1663), reprinted in Kemp and McElligott, *Censorship and the Press*, vol. 3, pp. 23–49.

7   Charles I, 'His Majesty's Declaration to All His Loving Subjects, of the 12 of Aug. 1642', in *Basilika* (London: Richard Chiswell, 1687), pp. 286–314, at pp. 286, 312; Henry Parker, *A Political Catechism* (London: Samuel Gellibrand, 1643), pp. 1, 10.

8   Henry Parker, *A Discourse Concerning Puritans* (London: Robert Bostock, 1641), pp. 21–23, pp. 41–42; John Milton, *Animadversions Upon The Remonstrants Defence* (London: Thomas Underhill, 1641), pp. 7–8; John Milton, *An Apology Against a Pamphlet* (London: Thomas Rothwell, 1642), p. 28.

9   Henry Parker, *Jus Populi* (London: Robert Bostock, 1644), p. 1; Henry Parker, *The Contra-Replicant* (London: Robert Bostock, 1643), p. 20. Milton refers to the 'country's liberty' in *Areopagitica* (94).

10 Thomas Hobbes, *Leviathan*, ch. 21, quoted in Skinner, *Hobbes and Republican Liberty*, p. 162. The present paragraph follows *Leviathan* ch. 21 and Skinner's account.

11 Skinner, *Liberty Before Liberalism*, pp. 52–53.

12 Henry Parker, *The Case of Ship-Mony* (London: s.n., 1640); John Milton, *Eikonoklastes* (1649), quoted in Skinner, *Hobbes and Republican Liberty*, p. 146.

13 Quentin Skinner, 'A Third Concept of Liberty', *Proceedings of the British Academy*, 117 (2003), pp. 237–268, partic. p. 257.

14 Henry Parker, *Observations upon Some of his Majesties Late Answers and Expresses* (London: s.n., 1642), pp. 3, 18.

15 Parker, *Observations*, pp. 9, 13–15; Parker, *Case of Ship-mony*, p. 35; Mendle, *Henry Parker*, p. 147.

16 Skinner, 'John Milton and the Politics of Slavery', p. 302; Dzelzainis, 'Republicanism', pp. 302–303.

17 Parker, *Observations*, pp. 23–24.

Chapter 10

1   Matthew Henry Lee, *Diaries and Letters of Philip Henry, 1631–1696* (London, Kegan Paul, Trench & Co., 1882), p. 12.

2   One of three 1649 editions acquired by George Thomason was inscribed with the date 'Feb. 9th': British Library, Thomason Tracts E.1096[1].

3   Charles I, *Eikon Basilike. The Pourtraicture of His Sacred Majesty in His Solitudes and Sufferings* (London, 1649). William Marshall's frontispiece appeared with the initial editions published by Richard Royston. The image

used here is from a William Dugard edition, also 1649, at the British Museum Reg. No. 1867,0309.1712; Image 00140478001. © The Trustees of the British Museum.

4   F.P. Verney, *Memoirs of the Verney Family*, 4 vols (London, Longmans, Green, and Co., 1892–1899), vol. 2, p. 402.

5   The publication history of the *Eikon Basilike* is given in Francis F. Madan, *A New Bibliography of the Eikon Basilike of King Charles I* (London: Bernard Quaritch, Ltd, 1950), Appendix II.

6   *An Act Against Unlicensed and Scandalous Books and Pamphlets, and for Better Regulating of Printing* (London, 1649); see C.H. Firth and R.S. Rait (eds), *Acts and Ordinances of the Interregnum*, 3 vols (London, 1911), ii, pp. 245–254.

7   See, for example, 'A Memorial Picture of Charles I', Royal Collection (RCIN 405715); 'Embroidery with Charles I', Victoria and Albert Museum, London (V&A T.117-1936).

8   John Milton, *Eikonoklastes in Answer to a Book Intitl'd Eikon Basilike* (1649), sig. B3r.

9   Milton, *Eikonoklastes*, sig. B3r-v, p. 230; Joseph Jane, *Eikon Aklastos* (London, 1651), p. 30.

10 *Basilika: The Workes of King Charles the Martyr, with a Collection of Declarations, Treaties and Other Papers Concerning the Difference Betwixt His said Majesty and His Two Houses of Parliament* (1662); the expurgated copy was donated to Lambeth Palace Library in 1678 and is catalogued as MS322.

11 On the authorship of the *Eikon Basilike*, see Madan, *A New Bibliography*, Appendix I; Robert Wilcher, '*Eikon Basilike*: the printing, composition, strategy and impact of "The King's Book"', in Laura Lunger Knoppers (ed.), *The Oxford Handbook of Literature and the English Revolution* (Oxford: Oxford University Press, 2012), pp. 290–292.

12 *Journal of the House of Common* (London: 1802) vol. II, p. 617 (10 June 1642).

13 Stent's advertisement is reproduced in Alexander Globe, *Peter Stent, London Printseller circa 1642–1665* (Vancouver: University of British Columbia Press, 1985).

14 Helen Pierce, 'Artful Ambivalence? Picturing Charles I during the Interregnum' in Jason McElligott and David L. Smith (eds), *Royalists and Royalism During the Interregnum* (Manchester: Manchester University Press, 2010), pp. 67–87.

15 Elizabeth Staffell, 'The Horrible Tail-Man and the Anglo-Dutch Wars', *Journal of the Warburg and Courtauld Institutes*, 63 (2000), pp. 169–186; Sheila O'Connell, *The Popular Print in England, 1550–1850* (London: British Museum Press, 1999), p. 168, n. 2.

16 Lois Potter, *Secret Rites and Secret Writing: Royalist Literature, 1641–1660* (Cambridge: Cambridge University Press, 1989), pp. 161–162.

Chapter 11

1 Benedict de Spinoza, *Tractatus Theologico-Politicus* (1670) (henceforth, the *TTP*), in Carl Gebhardt (ed.), Spinoza, *Opera* (Heidelberg: Carl Winter, 1925), vol. III, pp. 3–247, at p. 7 (my translation). The quotation is from Spinoza's preface. Page references to this volume of Gebhardt's edition will be given in parentheses in this essay. My edition of the *TTP*, forthcoming from Princeton University Press, will give the Gebhardt pagination in the margins.

2 Tacitus, *Histories* I, i (my translation).

3 Letter 30: vol. IV, p. 166 in Gebhardt.

4 The following account of religion in the Dutch Republic draws on William Temple, *Observations upon the United Provinces of the Netherlands* (1673), ed. George Clark (Oxford: Clarendon Press, 1932, 1972). See also Jonathan Israel, *The Dutch Republic, Its Rise, Greatness and Fall, 1477–1806* (Oxford: Clarendon Press, 1995), particularly chapters 16 and 27.

5 Temple, *Observations*, p. 103.

6 Peter van Rooden, 'Jews and Religious Toleration in the Dutch Republic', in R. Po-Chia Hsia and Henk van Nierop (eds), *Calvinism and Religious Toleration in the Dutch Golden Age* (Cambridge: Cambridge University Press, 2002) pp. 132–147.

7 Here Spinoza anticipates a view common in modern critical scholarship. See, for example, James Kugel, *How to Read the Bible* (New York: Free Press, 2007) p. 243.

8 Compare the teaching of Matthew 5:31–32 with the teaching of Mark 10:2–12.

9 Cf. Romans 3:21–28.

10 Most notably in John 3:16–18, though there are other, less clear, passages in John to a similar effect.

11 See Jaroslav Pelikan and Valerie Hotchkiss, *Creeds and Confessions of Faith in the Christian Tradition*, vol. II, Part Four: Creeds and Confessions of the Reformation Era (New Haven: Yale University Press, 2003).

12 Some Jewish scholars hold that Judaism has no credal requirements, and seem to regard obedience to the law as sufficient. See, for example, Menachem Kellner, *Must a Jew Believe Anything?* (Oxford: Littman Library of Jewish Civilization, 1999).

13 For a good account of the reaction to Spinoza's work, see Steven Nadler, *A Book Forged in Hell, Spinoza's Scandalous Treatise and the Birth of the Secular Age* (Princeton: Princeton University Press, 2011).

14 Quoted in Jonathan Israel, 'The Banning of Spinoza's Works in the Dutch Republic (1670–1678)', in Wiep van Bunge and Wim Klever (eds), *Disguised and Overt Spinozism around 1700* (Leiden: Brill, 1996) pp. 3–14.

15 See Israel, 'The Banning of Spinoza's Works in the Dutch Republic'.

16 See David Hume, *Treatise of Human Nature*, I, iv, 5.

17 See, for example, Hume's essay 'Of Superstition and Enthusiasm' (1741) in Eugene F. Miller (ed.), David Hume, *Essays, Moral, Political and Literary* (Indianapolis: Liberty Fund, 1985), pp. 73–79.

18 The common view among Hume scholars has been that Hume knew Spinoza only through Bayle's account. But recently Paul Russell has made a strong case that Hume is very likely to have known at least the *TTP* and to have been aware of the significance of the epigram from Tacitus. See his *The Riddle of Hume's Treatise* (Oxford: Oxford University Press, 2008, pp. 71–73). I would add that the penultimate paragraph of Hume's essay on miracles shows that if Hume did not know the *TTP* at first hand, he was at least aware, through secondary sources, of its central argument about the authorship of the Pentateuch.

19 See Ernest Campbell Mossner, *The Life of David Hume*, 2nd ed (Oxford: Clarendon Press, 1980) p. 112.

20 I owe these observations about Tacitus to my colleague, David Potter.

21 To James Oswald, October 1747, quoted in Mossner, *The Life of David Hume*, p. 207.

22 See the accounts of these affairs in Mossner, *The Life of David Hume*, pp. 153–162 and 246–249.

23 Mossner, *The Life of David Hume*, p. 249.

Chapter 12

1 Jean-Jacques Rousseau, 'On the Social Contract, or Principles of Political Right [1757]', in Roger D. Masters and Christopher Kelly (eds), *The Collected Writings of Rousseau*, vol. 4, trans. Judith R. Bush, Roger D. Masters, and Christopher Kelly (Hanover and London: University Press of New England, 1994), pp. 127–224, at pp. 214–215 (Book IV, Chapter 7). Page numbers to this edition will be given in parentheses throughout the text of this essay. For a standard French edition of this and other texts quoted in translation, see Jean-Jacques Rousseau, *Oeuvres Complètes*, Bernard Gagnebin and Marcel Raymond (eds.) (Paris: Gallimard, 1959–1995). For research assistance, the author is grateful to Sarah Cotterill and to the financial support offered by Princeton University.

2 James Miller, *Rousseau: Dreamer of Democracy* (New Haven: Yale University Press, 1984), p. 52.

3 There is surprisingly little on censorship in the otherwise excellent accounts by John P. McCormick, 'Rousseau's Rome and the Repudiation of Populist Republicanism', *Critical Review of International Social and Political Philosophy*, 10 (2007), pp. 3–27, and Paul Cartledge, 'The Socratics' Sparta – and Rousseau's', in Stephen Hodkinson and Anton Powell (eds), *Sparta: New Perspectives* (London: Duckworth, 1999), pp. 311–337.

4   A.E. Astin, *Cato the Censor* (Oxford: Oxford University Press, 1978), p. 98.

5   Astin, *Cato the Censor*, p. 91.

6   Astin, *Cato the Censor*, p. 96, referring to Plutarch, *Cato Maior*, 16.7.

7   Charles Louis de Secondat, Baron de Montesquieu, *The Spirit of the Laws* (Cambridge: Cambridge University Press, 1989), p. 109 (Part I, Chapter 14).

8   Rousseau, 'Political Economy [1755]', in Roger D. Masters (ed.), *On the Social Contract, with Geneva Manuscript and Political Economy*, trans. Judith R. Masters (New York: St. Martin's Press, 1978), p. 235.

9   Helena Rosenblatt, *Rousseau and Geneva: From the* First Discourse *to the* Social Contract, *1749–1762* (Cambridge: Cambridge University Press, 1997), pp. 25, 200–203.

10 See Rosenblatt, *Rousseau and Geneva*, pp. 22–29, who stresses that the concern in Geneva was a Calvinist as well as a republican one.

11 Plutarch, *Cleomenes* 9.3.

12 Rousseau, 'Political Fragments', in Masters and Kelly (eds), *The Collected Writings of Rousseau*, pp. 16–75, at p. 33 (Section IV, fragment 23).

13 Allan Bloom writes, 'One of the last voices raised in favor of censorship was Jean-Jacques Rousseau, who presented a detailed account of the effects of the arts on civil society', in his 'Introduction' to Jean-Jacques Rousseau, *Politics and the Arts: Letter to M. D'Alembert on the Theatre*, trans. and ed. Allan Bloom (Ithaca: Cornell University Press, 1960), pp. xi–xxxiv, at xiii. Similarly, Jim MacAdam asks, 'Can Rousseau's inculcation of democratic virtue to obtain self-rule justify censorship of popular arts?' in his 'Can Democratic Freedom Justify Self-Censorship?', in Melissa A. Butler (ed.), *Rousseau on Arts and Politics. Autour de la Lettre à d'Alembert* (Ottawa: North American Association for the Study of Jean-Jacques Rousseau, 1997), pp. 119–129, at p. 120.

14 Jean-Jacques Rousseau, 'Letter to D'Alembert', in Roger D. Masters and Christopher Kelly (eds) *The Collected Writings of Rousseau*, vol. 10, trans. and ed. Allan Bloom, Charles Butterworth and Christopher Kelly (Hanover: University Press of New England, 2004), pp. 251–352, at 294 and 329 for the respective quotations.

15 Rousseau, 'Letter to D'Alembert', p. 306.

16 Jean-Jacques Rousseau, 'On the Government of Poland', in Roger D. Masters and Christopher Kelly (eds) *The Collected Writings of Rousseau*, vol. 11 trans. Christopher Kelly and Judith Bush, ed. Christopher Kelly (Hanover and London: University Press of New England, 2005), pp. 167–240, at p. 227.

17 Rousseau, 'On the Government of Poland', p. 227.

18 Rousseau, 'On the Government of Poland', p. 228.

19 Rousseau, 'On the Government of Poland', p. 229.

20   Jean-Jacques Rousseau, 'Discourse on the Origins of Inequality (Second
     Discourse)', in Roger D. Masters and Christopher Kelly (eds), *The Collected Writings
     of Rousseau*, vol. 3, trans. Judith R. Bush and Terence Marshall). See Rousseau's
     Note 15 to the *Discourse on the Origins of Inequality*, pp. 94–95, with editors' note
     98, p. 188 ('This note is of particular importance').
21   Rousseau, note 15 to 'Discourse on the Origins of Inequality', p. 95.
22   Rousseau, 'On the Government of Poland', p. 230.

Chapter 13

1   Immanuel Kant, 'What is Enlightenment? (1784)', in James Schmidt (ed.), *What
     is Enlightenment? Eighteenth-Century Answers and Twentieth-Century Questions*
     (Berkeley: University of California Press, 1996), pp. 62–63. Page numbers to this
     edition will be given in parentheses throughout the text of this essay.
2   John Christian Laursen, 'Voltaire, Christian VII of Denmark, and Freedom of the
     Press', *Studies on Voltaire and the Eighteenth Century*, 6 (2002), pp. 331–348.
3   See J.C. Laursen, 'Luxdorph's Press Freedom Writings Before the Fall of Struensee
     in Early 1770's Denmark', *The European Legacy*, 7 (2002), pp. 61–77.
4   Immanuel Kant, 'The Contest of Faculties', in Hans Reiss (ed.), *Kant: Political
     Writings* (Cambridge: Cambridge University Press, 1991), pp. 187–188.
5   Bernard Schwartz (ed.), *The Roots of the Bill of Rights* (New York: Chelsea House,
     1980), vol. 2, p. 236.
6   Schwartz (ed.), *The Roots of the Bill of Rights*, vol. 5, p. 1164.
7   Kant, *On the Common Saying: 'This May be True in Theory, But it does Not Apply in
     Practice'*, in Reiss (ed.), Kant, pp. 84–85.
8   Kant, 'What is Orientation in Thinking?' in Reiss (ed.), *Kant*, p. 247.
9   Quoted in the 'Introduction' by Thomas Greene and John Silber to Immanuel
     Kant, *Religion Within the Limits of Reason Alone* (New York: Harper & Row, 1960),
     p. xxxv.
10   Elisabeth Ellis, *Kant's Politics: Provisional Theory for an Uncertain World* (New
     Haven: Yale University Press, 2005), and Elisabeth Ellis, *Provisional Politics:
     Kantian Arguments in Policy Context* (New Haven: Yale University Press, 2008).
11   Translated in J.C. Laursen and J. Van der Zande (eds), *Early French and German
     Defenses of Freedom of the Press* (Leiden: Brill, 2003), pp. 126–127.
12   See J.C. Laursen, 'Huguenot "Republicans" and "Conservatives" at the Prussian
     Academy: The Political Thought of Frédéric Ancillon', *Libertinage et philosophie au
     XVIIe siècle*, 13 (2012), pp. 163–179, at p. 172.
13   Ernst Martin Gräff, *Versuch einer einleuchtenden Darstellung des Eigenthums und
     der Eigenthumsrechte des Schriftstellers und Verlegers* (1794), reprinted in Reinhard

Wittmann (ed.), *Quellen zur Geschichte des Buchwesens* 7, *Nachdruck und geistiges Eigentum* (Munich: Kraus, 1981), vol. 1, pp. 191–588.

14 Kant, 'On the Wrongfulness of Unauthorized Publication of Books', in Mary Gregor (ed.), *Practical Philosophy* (Cambridge: Cambridge University Press, 1996), pp. 25–35; Kant, 'Metaphysics of Morals', in Gregor (ed.) *Practical Philosophy*, pp. 437–438.

Chapter 14

1 James Madison, *The Virginia Report of 1799–1800, Touching the Alien and Sedition Laws* (Richmond: JW Randolph, 1850), p. 220. All further references to this edition of the *Report* will be made parenthetically in the text.

2 Novanglus [John Adams], in *The Works of John Adams*, ed. Charles Francis Adams (Boston: Little, Brown, 1856), vol. 4, p. 79.

3 Tunis Wortman, *A Treatise Concerning Political Enquiry and the Liberty of the Press* (New-York: George Forman, 1800), p. 205.

4 Wortman, *Treatise*, p. 197.

5 Alexander Addison, *Liberty of Speech, and the Press: A Charge to the Grand Juries of the County Court* (Vergennes [Vt.]: Samuel Chipman, 1799), pp. 15–16.

6 Wortman, *Treatise*, p. 123.

7 See Elizabeth Ryland Priestley, 'On the Propriety and Expediency of Unlimited Enquiry, Part I', in Thomas Cooper (ed.), *Political Essays*, 2nd ed. (Philadelphia: Robert Campbell, 1800).

8 Thomas Cooper, 'On the Propriety and Expediency of Unlimited Enquiry, Part II', in Cooper (ed.), *Political Essays*, 2nd ed., p. 88.

9 *New York Times Co. v Sullivan*, 376 U.S. 254 (1964), by Brennan, J., for the court.

Chapter 15

1 Benjamin Constant, *Principles of Politics Applicable to All Governments* (1810), trans. Dennis O'Keeffe, ed. Etienne Hofmann (Indianapolis, Indiana: Liberty Fund, 2003), p. 106. Page numbers to this edition will be given in parentheses in the text of this essay.

2 François Guizot, *Quelques idées sur la liberté de la presse* (Paris: Le Normant, 1814), pp. 23–24 (my translation), http://gallica.bnf.fr/ark:/12148/bpt6k1129273 [accessed 19 May 2014].

3 Guizot, *Quelques idées sur la liberté de la presse*, p. 51.

4 Guizot, *Quelques idées sur la liberté de la presse*, p. 30.

5   Guizot, *Quelques idées sur la liberté de la presse*, p. 42.

6   Benjamin Constant, 'On the Liberty of the Press; or an Enquiry How Far Government May Safely Allow the Publication of Political Pamphlets, Essays, and Periodical Works', in *The Pamphleteer*, vol. 6, no. XI (London: Valpy, 1815), p. 212.

7   Constant, 'On the Liberty of the Press', p. 216.

8   Lucien Jaume, 'The Unity, Diversity and Paradoxes of French Liberalism', in Raf Geenens and Helena Rosenblatt (eds), *French Liberalism from Montesquieu to the Present Day* (Cambridge: Cambridge University Press, 2012), pp. 36–56.

9   Benjamin Constant, *Political Writings*, edited by Biancamaria Fontana (Cambridge: Cambridge University Press, 1988), pp. 121–126.

10   Bryan Garsten, 'Constant on the Religious Spirit of Liberalism', in Helena Rosenblatt (ed.) *The Cambridge Companion to Constant* (Cambridge: Cambridge University Press, 2009), pp. 286–312; Helena Rosenblatt, 'Madame de Stael, the Protestant Reformation, and the History of "Private Judgment"', *Annales Benjamin Constant*, 31–32 (2007), pp. 143–154.

11   Alexis de Tocqueville, *Democracy in America*, trans. Harvey C. Mansfield and Delba Winthrop (Chicago, IL: University of Chicago Press, 2002), 2.2.6, p. 493.

Chapter 16

1   British Museum Satires, no. 12797. Dorothy George, *Catalogue of Political and Personal Satires Preserved in the Department of Prints and Drawings in the British Museum, IX, 1811–1819* (London: Trustees of the British Museum, 1949), pp. 692–694.

2   www.britishmuseum.org/research/collection_online/collection_object_details. aspx?assetId=1437418&objectId=1646912&partId=1 [accessed 19 May 2014]. ©The Trustees of the British Museum. The description of this item online is taken from Dorothy George's magisterial catalogue. A hand-coloured version can also be viewed: www.britishmuseum.org/research/collection_online/collection_ object_details/collection_image_gallery.aspx?partid=1&assetid=174498&object id=1600630 [accessed 19 May 2014].

3   Vic Gatrell, *City of Laughter: Sex and Satire in Eighteenth-Century London* (London: Atlantic Books, 2006).

4   My description of the print is based upon that of Dorothy George but modifies it in significant ways.

5   William H. Ireland, *France for the Last Seven Years* (London: G. and W.B. Whittaker, 1822), pp. 283–284.

6   E.P. Thompson, *The Making of the English Working Class* (London: Victor Gollancz Ltd, 1963), p. 721.

7   Ben Wilson, *The Laughter of Triumph. William Hone and the Fight for the Free Press* (London: Faber, 2005).

8   William Hone, *The Three Trials of William Hone for Publishing Three Parodies* (London: William Hone, 1818), pp. 9–10, 82.

9   A copy of the pamphlet will be found on the 'William Hone Bio Text' project: http://honearchive.org [accessed 19 May 2014].

10 These epigrams may be a nod to the uprising against the Spanish monarchy which began in the weeks immediately prior to the publication of *The Man in the Moon*.

11 William Hone, *Facetiae and Miscellanies* (London: William Hone, 1827), p. iii.

Chapter 17

1   John Stuart Mill, *On Liberty* 3rd edn (London: Longman, Green, Longman, Roberts & Green, 1864), pp. 110–111. Page numbers to this edition will be given in parentheses throughout the text of this chapter.

2   Alexis de Tocqueville, *Democracy in America* 2 vols (London: Longmans, Green, 1875), vol. 1, pp. 267, 269.

3   John Stuart Mill, *Nature, The Utility of Religion, and Theism* (London: Longmans, Green, Reader, and Dyer, 1874), p. 85.

4   For exploration of this case, see Gregory Claeys, *Mill and Paternalism* (Cambridge: Cambridge University Press 2013), pp. 173–210.

5   See generally my 'Mill, Moral Suasion and Coercion', in Thom Brooks (ed.), *Ethical Citizenship: British Idealism and the Politics of Recognition* (London: Palgrave-Macmillan, 2014).

6   Maurice Cowling, *Mill and Liberalism* (Cambridge: Cambridge University Press, 1963), pp. 13, xiii. For another account emphasizing some similar features in Mill's thought, see Joseph Hamburger, *John Stuart Mill on Liberty and Control* (Princeton: Princeton University Press, 1999).

7   John Stuart Mill, *The Collected Works of John Stuart Mill* (London: Routledge and Kegan Paul, 1977), vol. 18, p. 277.

8   Hamburger, *John Stuart Mill on Liberty and Control*, p. 16.

Chapter 18

1   Oliver Wendell Holmes, Abrams v. United States, 250 US 616' (1919) in Ronald K.L. Collins (ed.), *The Fundamental Holmes* (Cambridge: Cambridge University Press, 2010), pp. 273–277. Justice Brandeis concurred. Page references to this edition will be given in parentheses throughout the text of this essay.

2   V.I. Lenin, Speech at the Opening Session of the Congress Opening Speech, First
    Congress of the Communist International, 2–6 March 1919 in *V.I. Lenin: Speeches
    at Congresses of the Communist International* (no editor or translator listed)
    (Moscow: Progress Publishers, 1972), pp. 7–29. The attribution of the term 'mass
    media' to Lenin in the 1972 translation is problematic. The earliest use of the term
    is conventionally dated to the early 1920s, when it was used in the US advertising
    industry. A literal translation of the phrase from a 1933 Russian language edition of
    the speech is 'means of the enlightenment of the masses'. I am indebted to Mohsin
    Hashim for this translation.

3   Margaret MacMillan, *Paris 1919: Six Months that Changed the World* (New York:
    Random House, 2003).

4   Walter Lippmann, *Liberty and the News* (New Brunswick, NJ: Transaction, 1995),
    pp. 26–27. Originally published in *The Atlantic Monthly*, 1919.

5   Sheldon M. Novick, *Honorable Justice: The Life of Oliver Wendell Holmes* (Boston:
    Little, Brown and Company, 1989).

6   World War I Document Archive, The Sedition Act: http:// www.gwpda.
    org/1918/usspy.html [accessed 19 May 2014]; also in United States, *The United
    States Statutes at Large*, vol. 40 (Washington, DC: Government Printing Office,
    1918), p. 553: http://www.constitution.org/uslaw/sal/040_statutes_at_large.pdf
    [accessed 19 May 2014]. The Sedition Act was repealed in 1921.

7   Full texts of the leaflets are reprinted in Collins, *The Fundamental Holmes*,
    pp. 304–307.

8   Novick, *Honorable Justice*, p. 332; Collins, *The Fundamental Holmes*; David
    M. Rabban, *Free Speech in Its Forgotten Years* (Cambridge: Cambridge University
    Press, 1997).

9   An inventory of use of the phrase by specific Supreme Court justices, compiled by
    Browne et al, shows a marked increase in its use beginning in the 1970s: M. Neil
    Browne, Justin Rex and David L. Herrera, 'The Potential Tension Between a "Free
    Marketplace of Ideas" and the Fundamental Purpose of Free Speech', *Akron Journal
    of Constitutional Law and Policy*, 3 (2012), pp. 55–82. In *The Fundamental Holmes*,
    Collins provides a masterful review of Abrams, the genealogy of the market
    metaphor and the controversies Holmes inspired. See also Thomas Healey, *The
    Great Dissent* (New York: Henry Holt and Company, 2013).

10 Douglas and Brennan's use of the phrase was metaphoric, closer to Holmes's
    meaning than that of free market fundamentalists.

11 John Dewey, 1928, quoted by Collins, *The Fundamental Holmes*, p. 300.

12 Joseph Blocher, 'Institutions in The Marketplace of Ideas', *Duke Law Journal*, 54:7
    (2008), pp. 821–889; Browne et al., 'The Potential Tension'; C. Edwin Baker, *Media,
    Markets and Democracy* (Cambridge: Cambridge University Press, 2002). Healy,
    The Great Dissent.

13 Albert Rhys Williams, 'Lenin and Experts', in Saul N. Silverman (ed.), *Lenin* (Englewood Cliffs, NJ: Prentice Hall, 1972), p. 166. The opening of the Soviet Archives has brought to light evidence that seriously challenges romanticizing of the good Lenin: Richard Pipes, *The Unknown Lenin* (New Haven: Yale University Press, 1996); Dmitri Volkogonov, *Lenin: A New Biography* (New York: The Free Press, 1994).

14 Lenin, 'Where to Begin?' *Iskra*, No. 4, May 1901, Marxists Internet Archive, http://www.marxists.org/archive/lenin/works/1901/may/04.htm [accessed 19 May 2014]; Rolf H.W. Theen, *Lenin: Genesis and Development of a Revolutionary* (Princeton: Princeton University Press, 1973).

15 Herman Ermolaev, *Censorship in Soviet Literature, 1917–1991* (Lanham, MD : Rowman & Littlefield, 1997), pp. 1, 3; Abbott Gleason, Peter Kenez and Richard Stites, *Bolshevik Culture: Experiment and Order in the Russian Revolution* (Bloomington: Indiana University Press, 1985).

16 Ermolaev, *Censorship in Soviet Literature*.

Chapter 19

1   George Orwell, 'The Freedom of the Press', Appendix I, in Orwell, *Animal Farm* (Harmondsworth: Penguin, 2007), pp. 97–107, at pp. 98–101. The edition of *Animal Farm* first published in 2000 in the Penguin Modern Classics series included the essay 'The Freedom of the Press', which was identified as Orwell's proposed preface to *Animal Farm* and dated 1945. Page references to this edition will be given in parentheses in this chapter. Orwell's essay, from which the extract here is taken, was first published in *The Times Literary Supplement*, 15 September 1972 (issue 3680), pp. 1037–1039.

2   Letter to Victor Gollancz, 8 January 1940, in Peter Davison, *Orwell: A Life in Letters* (London: Harvill Secker, 2010), pp. 196–197.

3   'Orwell's resignation letter', http://www.bbc.co.uk/archive/orwell/7430.shtml [accessed 19 May 2014].

4   George Orwell, *The Road to Wigan Pier* (Harmondsworth: Penguin, 1963), pp. 154–162.

5   George Orwell, 'Writers and Leviathan', *Collected Essays, Journalism and Letters of George Orwell (CEJL)* (London: Secker & Warburg, 1968), vol. 4, p. 408.

6   Letter to Raymond Mortimer, *CEJL*, vol. 4, pp. 99–101.

7   Letter to Rayner Heppenstall, 31 July 1937, in Peter Davison (ed), *George Orwell: A Life in Letters* (London: Harvill, Secker, 2010), pp. 228–229, p. 81.

8   Gordon Bowker, *George Orwell* (London: Little, Brown, 2003), p. 224.

9   Letter to Leonard Moore, 19 March 1944, in George Davison (ed.), *Orwell: A Life in Letters* pp. 228–229.

10 R.D. Charques, *Contemporary Literature and Social Revolution* (London: Martin Secker, N.D) p. 5.

11 George Orwell, 'Why I Write', *CEJL*, vol. 1, p. 4.

12 John Mander, *The Writer and Commitment* (London: Secker and Warburg, 1969) p. 99.

13 Lionel Trilling, 'George Orwell and the Politics of Truth', *Commentary* (March 1952), pp. 218–227, at p. 220.

14 Stephen Ingle, 'Lies, Damned Lies and Literature: George Orwell and the Truth', *British Journal of Politics and International Relations*, 4 (2007), pp. 730–746.

15 George Orwell, 'The Principles of Newspeak', *Nineteen Eighty-Four* (Harmondsworth: Penguin Books, 1960), pp. 241–251.

16 A discussion can be found in: Ben Grono, 'The Corruption of Language', *Cross Sections: The Bruce Hall Academic Journal*, IV (2008), pp. 55–68, http://eview.anu.edu.au/cross-sections/vol4/pdf/ch05.pdf [accessed 19 May 2014].

Chapter 20

1   Leo Strauss, 'Persecution and the Art of Writing', in Leo Strauss (ed.), *Persecution and the Art of Writing* (Glencoe: The Free Press, Illinois, 1952) pp. 22–37; quoted excerpts at pp. 25–36. Page references to this edition will be given in parentheses throughout the text of this essay.

2   In the Leo Strauss Archives in the Regenstein Library, Chicago, I have seen the lecture notes on which the lecture from 1940, repeated twice in the same year, are based. I am grateful to Hannes Kerber, München, for giving me access to new editions of 'Exoteric Teaching' and 'Persecution and the Art of Writing' before publication. These editions will be published as 'Appendix F' and 'Appendix G', in Martin D. Yaffe, Richard S. Ruderman (eds), *Reorientation. Leo Strauss in the 1930s* (Hampshire: Palgrave Macmillan, 2014). Without this background information I would not have been able to develop the argument presented here. On his personal copy of *Persecution and the Art of Writing*, Strauss noted that he gave his very first lecture under this title in October 1939. Unfortunately we have no way to verify this date. If Strauss ever gave this lecture in October 1939, then it would have been at Hamilton College, where Strauss taught for two months.

3   Leo Strauss, 'Persecution and the Art of Writing', in *Social Research*, 8:4 (1941), pp. 488–504.

4   See Leo Strauss, *Natural Right and History* (Chicago: University of Chicago Press,

1953), pp. 9–39. Various texts on the problem of historicism from the 1940s have not been published yet. Cf. Stephan Steiner's important and recently published study: *Weimar in Amerika. Leo Strauss' Politische Philosophie* (Tübingen: Mohr Siebeck Verlag, 2013).

5   See Leo Strauss, *What Is Political Philosophy?* (Chicago: University of Chicago Press, 1957).

6   See the excellent analysis in Hannes Kerber's 'Strauss and Schleiermacher on how to read Plato: An Introduction to "Exoteric Teaching"', in Yaffe and Ruderman (ed.), *Reorientation. Leo Strauss in the 1930s*, pp. 203–214.

7   Leo Strauss, 'How to Begin to Study *The Guide for the Perplexed*', in *Moses Maimonides: Guide for the Perplexed*. Two Volumes. Translated and with an Introduction and Notes by Shlomo Pines. Introductory Essay by Leo Strauss (Chicago: University of Chicago Press, 1963), pp. XI–LVI.

8   Both passages refer to Xenophon, *Memorabilia*, IV, 2, 20. In the 1941 version of the article, Strauss cited the reference in a footnote (p. 492), which was deleted in the 1952 version.

9   Leo Strauss, 'On the Plan of "The Guide for the Perplexed"', in Saul Lieberman et al. (eds), *Harry Austryn Wolfson; Jubilee Volume on the Occasion of His Seventy-Fifth Birthday* (Jerusalem: American Academy for Jewish Research, 1965), vol. 2, pp. 775–791. After many years of Maimonides research it has been almost forgotten that the plan was not only addressed against Wolfson but also against Strauss's former colleague Simon Rawidowicz (1897–1957), who had developed his own theory about the *Guide* in the 1930s.

10   Leo Strauss, *Thoughts on Machiavelli* (Glencoe, IL: Free Press, 1958). Cf. Heinrich Meier, *Politische Philosophie und die Herausforderung der Offenbarungsreligion* (München: C.H. Beck Verlag, 2013).

11   Leo Strauss, *Socrates and Aristophanes* (Chicago: University of Chicago Press, 1968).

Chapter 21

1   Catharine A. MacKinnon, *Only Words* (Cambridge, MA: Harvard University Press, 1993), pp. 9–10. Page numbers to this edition will be given in parentheses throughout the text of this essay.

2   Nadine Strossen, *Defending Pornography: Free Speech, Sex and the Fight for Women's Rights* (revised edn, New York: NYU Press, 2000), p. 24.

3   See for example: Gayle Rubin, 'Thinking Sex: Notes for a Radical Theory of the Politics of Sexuality', in Carole S. Vance, ed., *Pleasure and Danger: Exploring Female Sexuality* (Boston: Routledge and Kegan Paul, 1984), pp. 267–319.

4   Christine de Pizan, *The Book of the City of Ladies*, trans. Earl Jeffrey Richards (New York: Persea Books, 1998); *Treasure of the City of Ladies*, trans. Sarah Lawson (Harmondsworth: Penguin, 1985).

5   Mary Wollstonecraft, *A Vindication of the Rights of Woman*, edited by Deidre Shauna Lynch (New York: Norton, 2009).

6   Carole Pateman, *The Sexual Contract* (Stanford: Stanford University Press, 1988).

7   Catharine A. MacKinnon, 'Feminism, Marxism and the State: An Agenda for Theory', *Signs*, 7:3 (1982), pp. 515–544.

8   John Stuart Mill, *The Subjection of Women*, in Stefan Collini (ed.), *On Liberty and Other Writings* (Cambridge: Cambridge University Press, 1989), p. 160.

9   Susan Moller Okin, *Justice, Gender and the Family* (New York: Basic Books, 1989).

10   Carol Gilligan, *In a Different Voice* (Cambridge, MA: Harvard University Press, 1982).

11   Catharine A. MacKinnon, 'Difference and Dominance: On Sex Discrimination', in Catharine A. MacKinnon, *Feminism Unmodified: Discourses on Life and Law* (Cambridge, MA: Harvard University Press, 1984), pp. 38–39.

12   MacKinnon, 'Difference and Dominance', p. 39.

13   John Stuart Mill, *On Liberty*, in *On Liberty and Other Writings*, ed. Collini, pp. 1–115.

Suggestions for Further Reading

Given the substantial quantity of writing on most of the thinkers and many of the works covered in this volume, the following list is necessarily highly selective. For each work an attempt has been made to include a readily available reliable text in English (sometimes available online), in some cases a scholarly edition, and several works which help to contextualize the principal text and scholarly discussion of it.

Plutarch's *Life* of Cato

Plutarch, 'Marcus Cato', in Plutarch's *Lives*, accessible at www.perseus.tufts.edu/hopper/text?doc=Perseus%3atext%3a2008.01.0013 [accessed 18 May 2014].

Alan E. Astin, *Cato the Censor* (Oxford: At the Clarendon Press, 1978).

Arlene W. Saxonhouse, *Free Speech and Athenian Democracy* (Cambridge: Cambridge University Press, 2006).

Robin Waterfield, *Why Socrates Died: Dispelling the Myths* (New York: Norton, 2009).

Dana Villa, *Socratic Citizenship* (Princeton: Princeton University Press, 2001).

Tacitus's *Annals*

Tacitus, *The Annals*, translated by A.J. Woodman (Indianapolis: Hackett Publishing Company, 2004).

Shadi Bartsch, *Actors in the Audience: Theatricality and Doublespeak from Nero to Hadrian* (Cambridge: Harvard University Press, 1998).

Richard A. Bauman, *Impietas in Principem: A Study of Treason against the Roman Emperor with Special Reference to the First Century A.D* (Munich: Beck, 1974).

P.A. Brunt, '*Libertas* in the Republic', in P.A. Brunt, *The Fall of the Roman Republic and Related Essays* (Oxford: Oxford University Press, 1988), 281–350.

Thomas Habinek, and Alessandro Schiesaro (eds), *The Roman Cultural Revolution* (Cambridge: Cambridge University Press, 2004).

Augustine's *City of God*

Augustine (ed. R. W. Dyson), *The City of God against the Pagans* (Cambridge: Cambridge University Press, 1998).

Miles Hollingworth, *The Pilgrim City: St. Augustine of Hippo and his Innovation in Political Thought* (London: Bloomsbury, 2010).

Robert Dodaro, *Christ and the Just Society in the Thought of Augustine* (Cambridge: Cambridge University Press, 2008) especially 97–104.

W.H.C. Frend, *The Donatist Church: A Movement of Protest in Roman North Africa* (Oxford: Oxford University Press Reprints, 1985).

Gerald Bonner, *St Augustine of Hippo: Life and Controversies*, 3rd ed (Norwich: Canterbury Press, 2002), especially pp. 237–311.

Aquinas's *Summa Theologica*

The *Summa* is available in English translation at New Advent website: www.newadvent. org/summa/ [accessed 18 May 2014]. The translation is that of the Fathers of the English Dominican Province (revised edition, London, 1920); online editor, Kevin Knight.

Robert Post, 'The Social Foundations of Defamation Law: Reputation and the Constitution', *California Law Review* 74 (1986): 691–742.

——, 'The Social Foundations of Privacy: Community and Self in the Common Law Tort', *California Law Review* 77 (1989): 957–1010.

Debora Shuger, *Censorship and Cultural Sensibility: The Regulation of Language in Tudor-Stuart England* (Philadelphia: University of Pennsylvania Press, 2006).

Carla Casagrande and Silvana Vecchio, *I peccati della lingua: Disciplina ed etica della parola nella cultura medievale* (Rome: Istituto della Enciclopedia Italiana, 1987).

Ockham's *Dialogus*

William of Ockham, *Dialogus*, edited and translated by John Kilcullen, George Knysh, Volker Leppin, John Scott and Jan Ballweg: www.britac.ac.uk/pubs/dialogus/ockdial. html [accessed 18 May 2014].

Takashi Shogimen, *Ockham and Political Discourse in the Late Middle Ages* (Cambridge: Cambridge University Press, 2007).

J.M.M.H. Thijssen, *Censure and Heresy at the University of Paris 1200–1400* (Philadelphia: University of Pennsylvania Press, 1998).

Andrew E. Larsen, *The School of Heretics: Academic Condemnation at the University of Oxford, 1277–1409* (Leiden: Brill, 2011).

Reuchlin's *Recommendation*

Johannes Reuchlin, *Recommendation Whether to Confiscate, Destroy and Burn All Jewish Books*, translated by Peter Wortsman (New York: Paulist Press, 2000).

Valerie Hotchkiss and David H. Price, *Miracle within a Miracle: Johannes Reuchlin and the Jewish Book Controversy/Wunder in einem Wunder: Johannes Reuchlin und der Streit um die jüdischen Bücher* (Urbana, IL: Rare Book & Manuscript Library, University of Illinois, 2012, www.library.illinois.edu/rbx/exhibitions/Reuchlin [accessed 18 May 2014].

David H. Price, *Johannes Reuchlin and the Campaign to Destroy Jewish Books* (Oxford: Oxford University Press, 2012).

Dieter Mertens, editor, *Reuchlin und der Judenbücherstreit* (Ostfildern: Thorbecke Verlag, 2013).

Castellio's *Against Calvin's Book*

Sebastian Castellio, *Concerning Heretics*, translated by Roland H. Bainton. *Records of Civilization: Sources and Studies 22* (New York: Columbia University Press, 1935). This edition includes excerpts from *Against Calvin's Book*, under the title 'Reply to Calvin'.

Hans R. Guggisberg, *Sebastian Castellio, 1515–1563. Humanist and Defender of Religious Toleration in a Confessional Age*, translated and edited by Bruce Gordon (Aldershot: Ashgate, 2003).

Roland H. Bainton, *Hunted Heretic: The Life and Death of Michael Servetus 1511–1553* (rpt Gloucester, MA: Peter Smith, 1953, 1978).

Bruce Gordon, *Calvin* (London and New Haven: Yale University Press, 2009).

Perez Zagorin, *How the Idea of Religious Toleration Came to the West* (Princeton: Princeton University Press, 2003).

Sarpi's *History of the Council of Trent*

There is no full modern English translation of Sarpi's *History of the Council of Trent* but a 1676 edition of Brent's translation, together with that of the *History of the Inquisition* by Gentilis, is accessible at http://books.google.com/books?id=SQJZAAAAcAAJ [accessed 18 May 2014].

David Wootton, *Paolo Sarpi: Between Renaissance and Enlightenment* (Cambridge: Cambridge University Press, 1983).

Corrado Pin (ed), *Ripensando Paolo Sarpi. Atti del Convegno Internazionale di Studi. Nel 450° anniversario della nascita di Paolo Sarpi* (Venice: Ateneo Veneto, 2006).

Filippo De Vivo, *Information and Communication in Venice: Rethinking Early Modern Politics* (Oxford: Oxford University Press, 2007).

William J. Bouwsma, *Venice and the Defense of Republican Liberty: Republican Values in the Age of the Counter Reformation* (Berkeley-Los Angeles: University of California Press, 1968).

Marie Viallon (ed), *Paolo Sarpi: Politique et religion en Europe* (Paris: Editions Classiques Garnier, 2010).

Parker's *Humble Remonstrance*

Henry Parker, 'To the High Court of Parliament: The Humble Remonstrance of the Company of Stationers, London (1643)', in Geoff Kemp and Jason McElligott (general eds.), *Censorship and the Press, 1580–1720* (London: Pickering & Chatto, 2009), vol. 2, 65–71. This volume also includes John Milton's *Areopagitica*, at 93–126.

Ernest Sirluck (ed.), *Complete Prose Works of John Milton, vol. 2* (New Haven: Yale University Press, 1959).

Michael Mendle, *Henry Parker and the English Civil War* (Cambridge: Cambridge University Press, 1995).

Quentin Skinner, *Hobbes and Republican Liberty* (Cambridge: Cambridge University Press, 2008).

Richard Tuck, *Philosophy and Government, 1572–1651* (Cambridge: Cambridge University Press, 1993).

Eikon Basilike

Jim Daems and Holly Faith Nelson (eds), *Eikon Basilike with Selections from Eikonoklastes* (Peterborough, ON: Broadview Press, 2005).

Francis F. Madan, *A New Bibliography of the Eikon Basilike of King Charles I* (London: Bernard Quaritch, 1950).

Robert Wilcher, 'Eikon Basilike: The Printing, Composition, Strategy and Impact of "The King's Book"', in Laura Lunger Knoppers (ed.), *The Oxford Handbook of Literature and the English Revolution* (Oxford: Oxford University Press, 2012), pp. 289–308.

Elizabeth Skerpan Wheeler, 'The first "royal": Charles I as celebrity', *PMLA* 126, 4 (October 2011): 912–934.

Spinoza's *Theological-Political Treatise*

Benedict de Spinoza, *Theological-Political Treatise*, edited by Jonathan Israel, translated by Michael Silverthorne and Jonathan Israel (Cambridge: Cambridge University Press, 2007).

Yitzhak Melamed and Michael Rosenthal, (eds), *Spinoza's Theological-Political Treatise, A Critical Guide* (Cambridge: Cambridge University Press, 2010).

Steven Nadler, *A Book Forged in Hell: Spinoza's Scandalous Treatise and the Birth of the Secular Age* (Princeton: Princeton University Press, 2011).

Susan James, *Spinoza on Philosophy, Religion and Politics: The Theologico-Political Treatise* (Oxford: Oxford University Press, 2012).

Jonathan Israel, *Radical Enlightenment: Philosophy and the Making of Modernity, 1650–1750* (Oxford: Oxford University Press, 2001).

Rousseau's *Social Contract*

Jean-Jacques Rousseau, 'On the Social Contract, or Principles of Political Right [1757]', in Roger D. Masters and Christopher Kelly (eds), *The Collected Writings of Rousseau*, vol. 4, trans. Judith R. Bush, Roger D. Masters and Christopher Kelly (Hanover and London: University Press of New England, 1994).

——, *Oeuvres Complètes*, vol. 3, Bernard Gagnebin and Marcel Raymond (ed.) (Paris: Gallimard, 1959–1995).

Allan Bloom, 'Introduction' to Jean-Jacques Rousseau', in trans. and ed. Allan Bloom, *Politics and the Arts: Letter to M. D'Alembert on the Theatre* (Ithaca: Cornell University Press, 1960), xi–xxxiv.

John P. McCormick, 'Rousseau's Rome and the Repudiation of Populist Republicanism', *Critical Review of International Social and Political Philosophy* 10 (2007): 3–27.

Helena Rosenblatt, *Rousseau and Geneva: From the* First Discourse *to the* Social Contract, *1749–1762* (Cambridge and New York: Cambridge University Press, 1997).

Kant's *What Is Enlightenment?*

Immanuel Kant, 'What Is Enlightenment? (1784)', in James Schmidt (ed.), *What Is Enlightenment? Eighteenth-Century Answers and Twentieth-Century Questions* (Berkeley: University of California Press, 1996).

——, *Political Writings* ed. Hans Reiss (Cambridge: Cambridge University Press, 1991).

Adrian Johns, *Piracy: The Intellectual Property Wars from Gutenberg to Gates* (Chicago: University of Chicago Press, 2009).

J.C. Laursen, 'Kant, Freedom of the Press and Book Piracy' in Elisabeth Ellis (ed.), *Kant's Political Theory: Interpretations and Applications* (University Park: Penn State University Press, 2012), 225–237.

——, 'Hamburg/Altona as Fertile Ground for Theories About Freedom of the Press in the Mid-Eighteenth Century' in Anselm Steiger and Sandra Pott (eds), *Hamburg: Eine Metropolregion zwischen Früher Neuzeit und Aufklärung* (Berlin: Akademie Verlag, 2012), 315–327.

Elisabeth Powers, *Freedom of Speech: The History of an Idea* (Lewisburg: Bucknell University Press, 2011).

Madison's 'Virginia Report'

James Madison, 'The Virginia Report', in Marvin Meyers (ed.), *The Mind of the Founder: Sources of the Political Thought of James Madison* (Waltham, MA: Brandeis University Press, 1981), 229–273. The 1850 Randolph edition is available in an online version at www.constitution.org/rf/vr_1799.htm [accessed 18 May 2014].

Robert W.T. Martin, *The Free and Open Press: The Founding of American Democratic Press Liberty, 1640–1800* (New York: New York University Press, 2001).

——, *Government by Dissent: Protest, Resistance and Radical Democratic Thought in the Early American Republic* (New York: New York University Press, 2013).

Colleen Sheehan, *James Madison and the Spirit of Republican Self-Government* (New York: Cambridge University Press, 2009).

Constant

Benjamin Constant, *Principles of Politics Applicable to All Governments* (1810) translated by Dennis O'Keeffe, edited by Etienne Hofmann (Indianapolis, Indiana: Liberty Fund, 2003).

——, *Political Writings*, ed. Biancamaria Fontana (Cambridge: Cambridge University Press, 1988).

Stephen Holmes, *Benjamin Constant and the Making of Modern Liberalism* (New Haven, CT: Yale University Press, 1984).

Helena Rosenblatt, *Liberal Values: Benjamin Constant and the Politics of Religion* (Cambridge: Cambridge University Press, 2008).

K. Steven Vincent, *Benjamin Constant and the Birth of French Liberalism* (New York: Palgrave Macmillan, 2011).

Hone and *The Royal Shambles*

A copy of *The Royal Shambles* is available at www.britishmuseum.org/research/collection_online/collection_object_details.aspx?objectId=1646912&partId=1&searchText=royal+shambles&page=1 [accessed 18 May 2014].

Ben Wilson, *The Laughter of Triumph: William Hone and the Fight for the Free Press* (London: Faber & Faber, 2005).

An online resource for the life and career of Hone is Kyle Grimes's 'William Hone Bio Text' at http://honearchive.org/ [accessed 12 January 2014].

Jason McElligott, 'William Hone, Print Culture, and the Nature of Radicalism', in Ariel Hessayon & David Finnegan (eds), *Varieties of Seventeenth- and Early Eighteenth-Century English Radicalism in Context* (Farnham: Ashgate, 2011).

Mill's *On Liberty*

John Stuart Mill, *On Liberty and Other Writings*, ed. Stefan Collini (Cambridge: Cambridge University Press, 1989).

Gregory Claeys, *Mill and Paternalism* (Cambridge: Cambridge University Press, 2013).

Maurice Cowling, *Mill and Liberalism* (Cambridge: Cambridge University Press, 1963).

Ronald Dworkin (ed.) *Mill's On Liberty* (Totowa, N.J: Rowman & Littlefield, 1997).

Joel Feinberg, *The Moral Limits of the Criminal Law*, 4 vols (Oxford: Oxford University Press, 1984–1990).

Joseph Hamburger, *John Stuart Mill On Liberty and Control* (Princeton: Princeton University Press, 1999).

Holmes and Lenin

Ronald Collins, (ed.), *The Fundamental Holmes* (Cambridge: Cambridge University Press, 2010).

V.I. Lenin, *Speeches at Congresses of the Communist International* (Moscow: Progress Publishers, 1972).

Thomas Healey, *The Great Dissent: How Oliver Wendell Holmes Changed his Mind – and Changed the History of Free Speech in America* (New York: Henry Holt, 2013).

Helen Rappaport, *Conspirator: Lenin in Exile* (New York: Basic Books, 2010).

Saul Silverman, (ed.), *Lenin* (Englewood Cliffs, NJ: Prentice Hall, 1972).

Orwell

George Orwell, 'The Freedom of the Press', Appendix I, in George Orwell, *Animal Farm* (Harmondsworth: Penguin, 2007).

———, *Nineteen Eighty Four* (Harmondsworth: Penguin Press, 1989).

———, *The Penguin Essays of George Orwell* (Harmondsworth: Penguin Press, 1994).

Gordon Bowker, *George Orwell* (London: Abacus Books, 2003).

Peter Davison, *Orwell: A Life in Letters* (London: Harvill Secker, 2010).

Strauss's *Persecution and the Art of Writing*

Leo Strauss, *Persecution and the Art of Writing* (Glencoe: The Free Press, Illinois, 1952).

———, 'Persecution and the Art of Writing', in *Social Research* 8, 4 (1941): 488–504.

Martin D. Yaffe and Richard S. Ruderman (eds), *Reorientation. Leo Strauss in the 1930s* (Hampshire: Palgrave Macmillan, 2014).

Steven B. Smith (ed), *The Cambridge Companion to Leo Strauss* (Cambridge: Cambridge University Press, 2009).

MacKinnon's *Only Words*

Catharine A. MacKinnon, *Only Words* (Cambridge, MA: Harvard University Press, 1993).

Carol Gilligan, *In a Different Voice* (Cambridge, MA: Harvard University Press, 1982).

John Stuart Mill, 'The Subjection of Women', in Stefan Collini (ed.), *On Liberty and Other Writings* (Cambridge: Cambridge University Press, 1989).

Susan Moller Okin, *Women in Western Political Thought* (Princeton: Princeton University Press, 1979).

Nadine Strossen, *Defending Pornography: Free Speech, Sex and the Fight for Women's Rights* (revised edition, New York: NYU Press, 2000; first edition 1995).

Index